WITCHLINGS

HOUSE OF ELEPHANTS

CLARIBEL A. ORTEGA

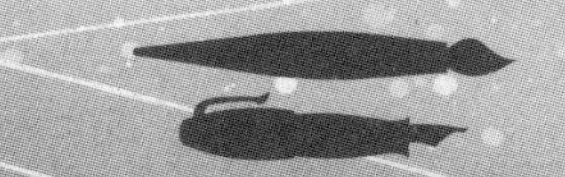

SCHOLASTIC PRESS
NEW YORK

Warmest thank-yous to my New Leaf team, especially my champion, Suzie. To everyone at Scholastic; Emily, you're the best editor anyone could ask for! To my family and friends for their constant support. And to my readers: Thank you all for showing up for Witchlings again and again. It means the world to me.

Library of Congress Cataloging-in-Publication Data

Names: Ortega, Claribel A., author.

Title: House of elephants / Claribel A. Ortega.

Description: First edition. | New York : Scholastic Press, 2024. | Series: Witchlings ; book 3 | Sequel to Golden frog games. | Audience: Ages 8 and up. | Audience: Grades 4–6. | Summary: Seven and Thorn still have not found a way to cure the hex that turned their friends into stone, magic seems to be working backwards, every new witchling at the Black Moon Ceremony is a spare—and the Hill Society blames the Spares and wants to prevent them from using magic.

Identifiers: LCCN 2024012278 (print) | LCCN 2024012279 (ebook) | ISBN 9781338853841 (hardcover) | ISBN 9781338856088 (ebook)

Subjects: LCSH: Witches—Juvenile fiction. | Magic—Juvenile fiction. | Conspiracies—Juvenile fiction. | Monsters—Juvenile fiction. | CYAC: Witches—Fiction. | Magic—Fiction. | Conspiracies—Fiction. | Monsters—Fiction. | BISAC: JUVENILE FICTION / Fantasy & Magic | JUVENILE FICTION / Social Themes / Friendship | LCGFT: Fantasy fiction.

Classification: LCC PZ7.1.O768 Ho 2024 (print) | LCC PZ7.1.O768 (ebook) | DDC 813.6 [Fic]—dc23/eng/20240328

LC record available at https://lccn.loc.gov/2024012278
LC ebook record available at https://lccn.loc.gov/2024012279

ISBN 978-93-5954-221-8

First edition, October 2024

This reprint edition February 2026

Book design by Christopher Stengel

Printed in India at Shivam Offset Press, New Delhi

FOR PETER, A TRUE FRIEND AND A STORYTELLER. I LOOK FORWARD TO THE DAY WHEN OUR BOOKS SHARE A SHELF.

This reprint edition February 2026

TABLE OF CONTENTS

CHAPTER ONE

HAPPY BIRTHDAY, VALLEY

IT HAPPENED BY CHANCE, thirteen years ago, that all three Witchlings were born in the month of All Hallows Eve. Seven was born on the final day of October, just as the final leaf fell from the final tree in the Cursed Forest. Thorn was born on the warmest day of autumn that year, the sun so bright and reluctant to set that witches forwent their warmer cloaks. The first to be born, the oldest of the three Witchlings, was Valley Pepperhorn. And today she would turn thirteen years old.

Or at least, she was supposed to. Seven Salazar wasn't sure if you still got a year older if you had been turned into stone, but she and Thorn Laroux were determined to celebrate Valley Pepperhorn's thirteenth either way.

It had been six long months since the Golden Frog Games, when the hexers upended the Twelve Towns. Four stone statues, the victims of Lotus Evenstar and an unknown accomplice, remained in Ravenskill's Bluewing Infirmary like some gruesome monument, while Lotus herself awaited sentencing in the Tombs. They were no closer to a cure, the archaic magic snaking ever closer to the hexed witches' hearts. If that happened . . . they'd be stone forever. But that couldn't be Valley's fate. Seven would die herself first.

Seven stood in front of the rows of flowers at Valley's feet. Ever since the hexings, witches from all over the Twelve Towns had come to pay tribute to the stone witches—the name they'd come up with in the *Squawking Crow*. Valley had been moved into a separate room on an elevated platform, both because of the vast number of flowers other Spares brought every day and because, more than once, witches had tried to vandalize or smash her statue.

"Here, I'll clear a path," Seven said as she flicked her wrist and the flowers parted for them. Seven's magic had continued to bloom in disquieting ways. Powerful wordless spells, magic above her level, the ability to conjure from thin air, all things no Spare had ever been able to do. Until Seven Nightshade Salazar.

Soon they were looking up at Valley: three Witchlings, three best friends, standing together as they were always meant to, but twisted by the cruel hand of destiny. Even in their most harrowing moments, they had never imagined things would turn out like this.

"I wonder if she can still hear us," Seven pondered aloud.

"She can." Thorn pushed her jet-black hair behind one ear, her brow furrowed in defiance. Her hair had gotten longer, almost to her shoulders, and she'd added a pink streak the same color as Valley's hair in tribute to her friend.

"Yeah, you're right." Seven smiled softly. "She can definitely hear us."

She knew better than to push back when it came to Valley and Thorn. Thorn had been having a hard time ever since the games. She wasn't sleeping well, she was forgetting to eat, and she had become more than a bit obsessed with Valley. One summer night as they sat on the roof outside Seven's bedroom window, looking at the stars, Thorn had told her that the pain in her heart brought her back to the most wretched moment of her life—losing Valley had reminded her of losing her twin brother, Petal.

"Maybe for now, you can just take it one day at a time," Seven had said. "You can focus on that accelerated costura program, right?"

"I don't deserve it. I shouldn't be happy. Not when Valley is like that," Thorn had said.

Dr. Blackwood had called it "survivor's guilt" when Seven spoke to him about it. Thorn kept losing the people she loved most, and she thought it was somehow her fault. Seven didn't know what to say or do, so she just stayed by her side. She really hoped that was enough.

"It's too cold in here," Thorn said, unwrapping a carefully tied bundle of fabric.

She got up slowly, as if her bones ached. Without a word, Seven flicked her wrist and sent Thorn levitating a few toadstools off the ground until she was level with Valley. More magic she shouldn't be able to do. Thorn draped Valley's shoulders in a beautiful glittering scarf she'd made for her.

"This will help if you're cold," Thorn said softly, before reaching out to touch Valley's cheek and then pulling back. Seven helped her float back down gently. They sat side by side, looking up at Valley's stone form. Her face was frozen in the same expression of determination she'd had when she'd thrown herself in front of Seven, saving her and becoming a statue in her place. The only difference from that night was the scarf and a small bracelet clasped around her wrist—from Valley's girlfriend, Graves Shadowmend.

A pang of white-hot pain rushed over Seven as she remembered the horrible night. Some days the guilt was so strong, she felt it might consume her. They had stopped Lotus, but her accomplice was still on the loose and it had left Seven uneasy. Finding a cure for Valley and the other victims was their top priority, sure, but finding the other hexer was too—before something like this happened again.

"We're trying hard to bring you back, Val," Thorn said, her eyes filling with tears.

Seven nodded and slid her hand over Thorn's.

"Happy birthday, Valley," Seven said.

"Happy birthday," Thorn said, her voice hitching on a sob. She turned her head and buried it in Seven's shoulder, and Seven just let her cry, patting her head with her free hand, her own face wet with tears. Turning thirteen in the Twelve Towns was supposed to be special, important. Like the quinces of the humdrum world. It wasn't supposed to be like *this*. In the distance, Seven heard the unmistakable sound of Nightbeast cubs growling cutely, and it calmed her erratic breathing a bit.

Seven reached into her cloak pocket and pulled out a small parcel containing mini bizcochos—cream-filled sponge cakes with light pink frosting that fizzled when you ate them, which she knew were Thorn's favorite. They were still warm from the oven, and she had spent hours and caused a disastrous mess in the kitchen making them, but they had turned out . . . sort of okay.

"Do you want some?" Seven asked hopefully.

Thorn looked up, her eyes red and her face puffy. "Are those bizcochos?"

"Erm . . . they're supposed to be?" Seven smirked and Thorn gave the smallest of smiles. It felt like breathing fresh air again to see her friend smile.

Thorn took one of the misshapen cakes and ate it in three bites.

"When's the last time you ate?" Seven asked.

Thorn shrugged. "I don't know. I think yesterday."

Seven handed her another cake, and Thorn ate this one as well. Good. Now, if Seven could only find a way to make her sleep a full night, they'd be getting somewhere.

"We're gonna be late," Seven said once all the cakes were gone. Thorn wiped her tears and nodded.

"Let's go." Thorn got up and held her hand out for her friend. As they walked away, Seven turned to look at Valley one more time. Perhaps it was a trick of the light, but she could've sworn her friend's expression had changed—that it was just as sad and hopeless as theirs.

Seven and Thorn walked out of the Bluewing Infirmary and into the crisp fall evening. Seven could see the eyes of her raccoons glowing in the dark, and then slipping away into the shadows as she entered the busy part of town. Ravenskill was filled with the buzz of energy that always came on this night, the night of the Black Moon Ceremony. Normally, it was much later in the month, but for whatever reason it had come early this year, leaving Sybell the Oracle perplexed.

"The magic in this town is topsy-turvy, I swear," they had said as they recounted their discovery to Seven over tea one evening. The Stars had told them when the ceremony was to take place, and despite Sybell demanding an explanation from their celestial ancestors, the Stars did not explain themselves to anyone. They just did as they saw fit.

Seven was just grateful for the heads-up about the ceremony, because the two Witchlings had made a vow that when the new Spares were sorted, they would be there to welcome them.

Every year, Spares hung their heads in shame as they walked away from downtown Ravenskill. As their friends and fellow witches celebrated by taking their very first broom flights, they spent the night alone and afraid for their future. Seven remembered it well: looking up into the skylights of her attic bedroom on the night of her own Black Moon Ceremony, as witches flew overhead among the stars, her face tear streaked and red. She could not change the unfairness, the cruelty, of being cast away as a Spare, but she could do something else—prove to Spares that there was *hope*.

After all, hadn't she and Thorn done great things? Hadn't Valley shown bravery and friendship deserving of honor and celebration? Hadn't Thorn overcome her greatest fear and fought alongside the Nightbeast? Hadn't Seven shown that a Spare could be powerful, an *Uncle* only second to the Gran, even if that power was secretly monstrous? If the adults in this town wouldn't recognize that Spares were worthy of love too, then Seven and Thorn would be the ones to show the Spares they were just as important and capable, just as much a part of Ravenskill, as any other witch.

"I've never seen so many witches at the Black Moon Ceremony," said Thorn as they made their way to the gathering. The streets were decorated in twinkling lights and enormous floral arrangements in vases so fancy Seven felt they looked a bit out of place in their town. Ravenskill was a beautiful place—a friendly town, as their official motto suggested—but it had never been extravagant.

As part of her costura training, Thorn had been assigned to help design the decorations around town, and particularly in the Ravenskill Theater. Gold ribbons were threaded through the weeping willows like plaits of long, flowing hair. Twelve soapstone columns erected along the path to the ceremony were embellished with intricate carvings of Ravenskillian history. Enchanted orbs above each column lit up the pathway, washing the town in a warm amber glow. Witches sat on ancient-looking benches made of twirling, twisted ore, and birdhouses adorned with gems hung from the trees. The birds fluttered in and out, singing friendly songs about Seven as they did.

"It's not the normal style, but it *is* beautiful," Seven said, waving at a cooing pigeon.

Thorn shrugged. "They gave us the strict direction to stick to olden days decor; it's all this kind of Hill style. They're making a fuss this year because the town is famous."

Not the town. Us, Seven thought. Their Black Moon Ceremony had become infamous. Books about them were sold in stores and a special documentary, *Stupendous Spares: Heroes? Or Menaces?*, had even been made for the telecast. Guides on how to avoid your coven circle not closing and on avoiding the impossible task—all inspired by Seven, Valley, and Thorn's dilemma last year—were also particularly popular, with advice like "Smile through it all, no matter what!" and "Better a Spare than a humdrum, after all!" There were even Stupendous Spares pins and posters in the gift shops around town. Embarrassing.

"My my, the town is quite busy tonight, isn't it?" observed Edgar Allan Toad from her pocket.

"If it gets too loud, let me know. I'll put a quieting spell on your habitat," Seven said.

"Pfft. I'm not that old yet. I can handle a little ruckus," Edgar said.

"Hmm, you're *pretty* old . . ."

"Did you know toads have performed hexes before? Deadly ones. Quite interesting."

Seven put her hands up in surrender. She wondered if that was true.

"What's he saying?" Thorn asked.

"You don't wanna know," Seven said with a scared little laugh.

As they approached the theater, eyes followed their every move, something Seven had become *somewhat* accustomed to. In the year since their own ceremony, the one constant had been witches staring and gossiping about them.

"Spares this way! This way, all Spares!" A Gran's Guard dressed head to toe in golden armor ushered Spares through a separate line, leading them toward the far end of the square.

"Come on, we're on the balcony," Thorn said, grabbing Seven's hand and walking up to the outside seating overlooking the town square. Seven looked back at the line of Spares—they'd barely be able to see from their designated area, while she and Thorn sat overlooking the whole event. It stirred something in her, an uneasy feeling taking hold of her heart.

They fought their way through the throngs of witches and emerged on the airy balcony, where Seven's parents, Fox and Talis, along with her ever-growing baby brother, Beefy, were already sitting with Thorn's family. Valley's mother, Quill, would normally be with them, but she hadn't been out much lately. Not because she was ashamed . . . but because she was *busy*. And Seven and Thorn knew all too well what she was busy with. Pixel Gibbons, a Spare—and a Laroux family friend who worked at Mrs. Laroux's boutique as an assistant—also sat with them, happily fussing over a cooing Beefy. She still wore her hair in her signature cropped cut, but now, unlike when she was employed by the butt-toad Dimblewit family, her clothing was beautiful and she had the healthy glow provided by good meals and rest.

As Seven looked around, she noticed that in one shrouded corner of the square, a cluster of witches stood motionless. They wore head-to-toe black and gray, veils covering their faces. They had begun appearing around town a few weeks after the Golden Frog Games in the spring, some sort of cult, everyone said. Seven wasn't sure who they were or what they wanted aside from the anti-Spare pamphlets they were always scattering around town, but she did know one thing: They frightened her.

"I was starting to worry," Fox said as Seven slid into her seat.

"We were just visiting Val," Seven said. Fox kissed the top of her head and took her hand as they waited. Normally, Fox didn't worry so much. Ever since Valley's stonification though, the girls' parents had been on edge. Understandably so.

"Pictures!" A witch on a broom glided through the night air toward them. A long green cape floated behind her, a small witch's reporter hat, embroidered with little felt cameras and stars, tipped on her head. She was holding a completely see-through camera as she hovered right in front of the balcony. They all smiled, Seven throwing her arm around Thorn's shoulder as the witch snapped a few pictures, then nodded.

"You can buy copies at the *Squawking Crow* offices!" she called out as she flew toward the night's Witchlings to take pictures. Seven wondered suddenly, her heart giving the smallest flutter of excitement, if Tiordan Whisperbrew was in the crowd. If they were . . . maybe Seven could finally meet her lifelong idol.

"Beefy, no!" Fox said as the giant toddler picked up one of the crystal candelabras at the far end of the balcony.

"I hope these are, oof, insured," Talis said as he wrested the crystal candelabra from Beefy's grip.

"Aw, butt-toad," Beefy said, pouting. It was his new favorite word.

Fox shot him a look and Beefy blushed. "Sowy, Mommy."

"Come, Beef," Seven said, and her baby brother toddled over and sat down beside her. Beefy was only two, but he was already the size of a five-year-old Witchling. At this rate, he'd be taller than their parents soon.

Just as Talis wiped the sweat from his forehead, the Gran emerged and the crowd below them went silent. It was time to begin.

"Welcome to the Black Moon Ceremony!" said the Gran, to cheers and applause. A petrifying crash of thunder erupted in the sky, and everyone jumped and yelled out in collective surprise. Seven Salazar should've known then that everything was about to go very, very wrong.

CHAPTER TWO

A BLACK MOON CEREMONY WHERE ABSOLUTELY EVERYTHING GOES WRONG

THE GRAN RAISED her arms into the air, the gilded bell sleeves of her star-studded black cloak billowing in the wind, and the crowd settled down. She was, as she always was during the Black Moon Ceremony, standing on a floating platform at the center of the Ravenskill fountain, making her look like a beautiful, regal statue instead of just a witch. Seven shivered, thinking of Valley, then willed the thought from her mind.

"I know you are all anxious to get to this evening's sorting, but before we begin, I would like to say a few words," said the Gran.

Seven and Thorn exchanged looks. The Gran was usually straight to business with big ceremonies like this, the magic weaved into the ceremony being fragile and time sensitive. From the ground beside the fountain, Seven could see Sybell worrying the hems of their sleeves.

"We have a much larger crowd than usual here

tonight, so to our visitors, I'd like to extend the warmest of welcomes to Ravenskill."

The crowd cheered. One witch screeched "YEAH, RAVENSKILL!" at the top of his lungs to scattered laughter in the audience.

"There is something that has always helped our towns in the direst of times: togetherness. We have seen some terrible happenings in the past year, and I want to remind you all to rely on, support, and love your neighbors. Many times, it seems we forget the lessons taught to us as young Witchlings—that the only wish of the Stars is that we should remain as one, and treat one another with the kindness we would hope to be treated with. If we remember these small but important lessons, I believe that any obstacle can be overcome." The Gran nodded and there was polite but slightly confused applause and chattering.

"Wonder what that was for," Thorn said softly.

Seven was staring at the Gran intently and wondering the very same thing.

"And now, finally, it is time for the forming of the covens!" the Gran announced. Trumpets, a new addition, resounded all around them and the crowd cheered loudly.

"Witchlings, prepare your amulets!"

The Witchlings below shifted, pulling crystal amulets from their cloaks and holding them in front of their faces. They looked so young to Seven and she wondered if she had looked that small and scared last year.

"This is when we met," whispered Thorn.

"Yeah," said Seven, trying to focus on the ceremony.

"I was so scared that night!" Thorn said.

"Mm-hmm," Seven said, hoping Thorn would take the hint.

"It feels like it all happened so long ago," Thorn said wistfully.

"And yet, some things are *exactly* the same. Like you not being able to keep quiet," Seven said, and Thorn covered her mouth, eyes wide. She and Seven laughed.

"At least you didn't threaten to hex me this time," Thorn said.

"The night is still young."

The Gran continued. "Now intone the spell with me!"

The young Witchlings below began to sing, their voices high and sweet, as they recited the Black Moon Song for the first and only time in their lives.

A coven is five
In death and in life
To believe
To protect
Never doubt
Or neglect.
Bound with our magic
Before the Black Moon
Bound by a circle
For no circle
Spells doom.

The moment they finished, a purple smoke left all their lips and swirled in the center of the circle right above the Gran's head like a small tornado. The Gran gracefully flicked her crystal wand and sent the smoke hurtling back into the amulets. Seven remembered how her own amulet had vibrated so much she thought it would fall right out of her hands, but now, watching it happen, they didn't seem to be moving at all.

She knew how the Witchlings below were feeling: scared, nervous, hopeful. After all, this was the moment that would decide their fates as full-fledged witches. And for three of them, their uphill climb as Spares would begin, but that's what Seven and Thorn were there for.

"You brought the stuff, right?" Seven whispered.

"Yup, my dad carried it all over," Thorn said.

"Perfect." Seven smiled.

They had gotten all sorts of supplies tonight: fresh baked goods courtesy of Seven's mom and Grandma Lilou, special Spare pins with their seal, a pamphlet written by Seven herself entitled "So, You've Just Been Named a Spare (Don't Despair!)" filled with tips and tricks, and most importantly of all: coven cloaks. Three beautiful gold-trimmed red cloaks for whoever was deemed a Spare. You didn't get your own house cloaks as a Spare, but Seven didn't think that was very fair. She and Thorn—well, okay, mostly Thorn—had made custom magic-infused garments for whoever was deemed a Spare tonight. So they'd feel less left out, so they'd feel a bit special. It wasn't much, but Seven really hoped it helped.

“Why aren’t the amulets changing?” asked Talis. Seven was pulled out of her thoughts and stood up, noticing for the first time the weird uneasiness all around her. Normally, the pendants lit up and then the Gran announced the house name and motto, but something was clearly off this year.

“Perhaps the magic needs a bit of coaxing,” said the Gran, raising her wand into the air.

“House of Stars, brilliant, beautiful, generous to all!” The Gran waved her wand in the air but . . . nothing happened. Seven was beginning to worry.

The crowd’s whispers rose to a gentle roar and Seven saw the Gran exchange a panicked glance with Sybell. If something didn’t happen soon, Seven was afraid there’d be a full-blown riot.

“Maybe the Oracle was wrong after all?” Thorn asked.

“I doubt it,” Seven said, before looking at her parents, who were whispering anxiously. “What the hex is going on?”

“It’s probably nothing. Let’s just wait and see,” said Talis.

“Probably nothing my foot. I smell trouble,” said Fox.

“Magic has been acting strangely for months,” said Thimble, Thorn’s mom. The other adult witches nodded in agreement.

Seven looked back down. The crowd was getting louder and louder as the pendants failed to change color. The new Witchlings below looked like they were about to be sick.

The Gran cleared her throat. "We shall try another coven: Moth House! Mysterious, morbid, dependable friends!"

Once again, nothing happened.

The magic smoke whirled and whirled in an endless loop inside the amulets, but nobody's changed color.

"This is a disaster," Thorn said.

"I wonder what Sybell is saying," Seven said as she watched the Oracle whisper something to the Gran. After a few moments, the Gran raised her arms for silence and most witches stopped talking.

The Oracle stood beside the Gran on her platform and spoke.

"There has been some unfortunate unbalance present in our magic as of late and I think perhaps this is part of it. I apologize; I must've gotten something wrong with the Stars . . ."

Parents in the crowd began to shout.

"How can you get THIS wrong?!" one yelled.

"This is completely unacceptable!" screamed others.

"Please," the Gran said, the crowd immediately silenced at her booming voice. "I am sure we'll be able to—"

But before she could get the words out, a Witchling in the crowd shouted: "My amulet is changing!"

Everyone watched as a small red-haired witch held her amulet up. Indeed, the smoke inside was changing colors rapidly: purple, to green, to pink, to blue, to gray, and then it settled . . . on red.

“A Spare?!” she shrieked. But Spares were never sorted first. They were the leftovers, after all.

“Another one!” said a witch, and the amulet of another Witchling, a brown-haired boy this time, began to turn colors.

“No!” he screamed as his amulet turned red.

“Maybe it’s . . . just going in backward order?” Thorn’s father, Leaf, tried.

But nobody responded because this was not only unusual, it had never, ever happened before. They were all leaning against the balcony now, looking down in awe.

A third Witchling was sorted as a Spare and the crowd calmed down. Perhaps this was the end of the whole terrible dilemma. The magic did seem to be working in reverse for some reason. Seven and Thorn began to ready their supplies, but as they did, a scream ripped through the night.

“A fourth Spare!” yelled a witch, and now the crowd was absolutely thrown into chaos. The Gran’s Guard surrounded the Gran to ward off approaching witches. Other witches argued; young Witchlings sobbed uncontrollably, but things were only about to get worse.

“I’m a Spare too!” yelled one Witchling, looking up gleefully at the balcony. Seven was surprised to see the twelve-year-old wave at her enthusiastically.

Five Spares. Somehow, this was even weirder than their own ceremony.

“What in the warlock is going on?” Thorn asked.

“We should get down there, try to help Sybell. They look upset,” Seven said.

“We’d probably make it worse . . .” Thorn gestured subtly to a group of witches trying to get past a row of Gran’s Guard who had lined up in front of the theater. The witches were gesturing wildly toward Seven and Thorn.

“Look!” someone yelled, and everyone in the crowd stopped cold. A red cast had fallen over the sky, menacing and cryptic. When Seven looked at the Witchlings again, she realized the sky hadn’t turned red—it was reflecting the amulets below. A sea of Spares stood bewildered, looking at their amulets and then one another. The smoke inside their necklaces had stopped swirling, the magic above the Gran’s head was gone, and the Black Moon Ceremony had ended. Every last Witchling had been sorted as a Spare.

“We’re gonna need more cloaks,” said Seven.

CHAPTER THREE

BETTER TO BE A SPARE . . .

IN ANY OTHER CIRCUMSTANCE, the Ravenskill Uncle would be beside the Gran and the Oracle, helping them out of this precarious situation. But when Seven stood up, prepared to go down into the fray, the Gran shook her head no with a look that meant *no frogging way*. And by the venomous looks of the other witches below the balcony, the Gran was right—they might just try to toadify Seven after all if she went down there now.

But Seven was afraid they had much bigger problems than the angry parents of the new Witchlings class.

"The Oracle said the magic was being topsy-turvy, and now look," Seven whispered.

Thorn nodded. "Do you think the Stars were wrong?"

Another clap of thunder resounded overhead and Seven and Thorn jumped.

"I mean . . . of course they weren't!" Thorn said. "But . . . something is definitely going on with the magic in Ravenskill."

“There’s no froggin’ way there isn’t,” Seven said as she thought of everything that had happened since their own Black Moon Ceremony. By the end of last year she was being named the Town Uncle, something that no Spare had ever been named before. Sure, the Nightbeast that had tried to kill them could communicate with Seven, and she had magic that was inexplicably entwined with monstruos, but that was another story altogether. Thorn had become the first Spare champion and winner of the Golden Frog Games. Valley had become a hero, saving the town with her sacrifice. The so-called Stupendous Spares had broken the rules of magic over and over again, and now . . . Seven wondered if all this was part of something bigger, some broken piece of magic in their town.

“What now?” Thimble asked.

“They . . . couldn’t possibly seal the covens, could they?” muttered Talis.

“It’s either that, or chance that these Witchlings are happy with their sortings and won’t all invoke the impossible task,” Fox said. “That would be utter mayhem.”

When Seven, Valley, and Thorn invoked their own impossible task to fell the Nightbeast monstruo, it had been terrifying and had caused a ripple effect across the Twelve Towns. Spares, of course, had ended up paying the highest price. With a wolf the size of an elephant circling the town, blame quickly fell on the Witchlings and all Spares for . . . well, just about anything that went wrong. New laws to take even more rights away from the already poor and mistreated Spare population were passed, keeping Spares out of certain parts of town, and in some cases out of school and workplaces, as if that would somehow help anything. Spares' wages were slashed in half, businesses could legally turn them away if they wished, and they were no longer allowed to vote in their towns' elections. It was all terrible, and it made Seven equal parts furious and sad, not to mention helpless. But Seven supposed people just needed someone to blame, someone to punish for their anger, and judging by the glares currently being cast their way, the Witchlings would be blamed for this too.

"If the new Witchlings don't seal in their covens, they'll remain Forever Witchlings and lose their magic," Thorn said.

Seven wasn't so sure the incoming Witchlings weren't prepared to accept their fate as Spares though. Some Witchlings even looked genuinely happy to be Spares. *Better a Spare than a humdrum, after all!* The words from the guide to avoid the impossible task came back to Seven then. They had studied it well. All the while, Seven did not take her eyes off the Gran and the Oracle, who would ultimately decide what was to be done.

At long last, the Gran raised her arms, and everyone leaned in at once.

"The only solution is to seal the covens," she said, her voice so loud, so commanding, that no one uttered a single word. "If we let the covens go unsealed, these witches will lose their magic, and there will be no way to undo that."

The crowd looked anguished at the truth of it. "But if we seal the covens," the Gran continued, "we might somehow be able to reroute the magic so that they are later placed in their proper covens. It is the only way."

There were glances between witches: of shock, anger, sadness, and . . . contempt. The Hill witches—some of whom had children among the incoming Witchlings—bristled, but it seemed true that there was no other choice.

The Gran raised her wand and cast the spell to seal the Witchlings' covens, binding them for life. The veiled witches shifted in unison, like a shadowy organism. They shook their heads in disapproval and then disappeared into the woods behind the square. Seven narrowed her eyes. What did these strange witches want? Where had they come from and, most worryingly of all, who exactly were they?

CHAPTER FOUR
THE VEILED WITCHES

THAT NIGHT, all across the Twelve Towns, the sky glowed scarlet. Ravenskill wasn't the only place to be afflicted with what was coined the Red Moon Ceremony by Tiordan Whisperbrew. A somber air had fallen on Ravenskill, a quiet unlike any Seven had ever experienced. The Gran had ordered everyone to designated magical emergency safety zones, while the Gran's Guard did security sweeps of the town to ensure nothing nefarious was afoot. They were being extra cautious because of the hexings in the spring and had strongly advised witches to remain in their safety zones until they were cleared to go home.

Of course, not everyone heeded this warning, and some witches from the Hill had retreated to their mansions instead. Seven wondered what would happen at nine, the curfew for unaccompanied Spares according to the new heinous laws. Seven and Thorn were assigned to the library. There were quite a few Spares here, and

Seven could only hope their employers hadn't left them to fend for themselves against the Gran's Guard.

She hated herself for it, but Seven couldn't help but glance around and see if anyone was looking at their table. Seven knew they hadn't done anything wrong, but it was hard not to let the torrent of awful theories about them get to her sometimes. This was just one more thing to add to the list of mishaps they'd be blamed for, and Seven was tired, and scared, and most of all, *she was angry.* When did she get to just focus on being the best witch she could be? On growing up? Everything else kept getting in her way, and she was ready to explode.

Don't feed the fire. Dr. Blackwood's voice came to her.

He had been trying to help her get her anger under control, but so far, it hadn't been working. Instead, her anger was a quiet spark, low and steady in the background. She was afraid of what would happen when that spark turned into a flame.

Just as the thunder promised, it had begun to rain and the crowds were funneled into the theater, the Spegg, and the Ravenskill Library, while the council, including Seven's and Thorn's parents, met with the Gran to discuss the ceremony disaster.

"A phenomenon never before seen in the Twelve Towns!" said Ambert Lophiifor, a witch from Crones Cliff Manor who also happened to be Miss Dewey's brand-new fiancé.

"Don't get too excited about the news, my pumpkin,

you'll get heartburn again." Miss Dewey was passing out lavender fae tea to the anxious witches in the library, her familiar, Almanac, fluttering around her hair. Seven had never seen Miss Dewey as happy as she'd been since Ambert moved to Ravenskill along with his twin sons. She was always cheerful, sure, but now her eyes were bright and filled with a warm, glowing light.

"I'll try." Ambert smiled shyly.

Miss Dewey winked at Seven.

"Are you two okay?" she asked in a whisper as she crouched beside them.

"We're as okay as we can be. But what the hex do you think just happened?" Seven asked.

Miss Dewey bit her lip. "I don't know. But I do know we must be there for those Spares. The town . . . won't be kind about it."

The Witchlings nodded. Seven had no doubt the Spares would be all right; being a Spare wasn't the end of the world. But to the rest of Ravenskill it was.

Miss Dewey cleared her throat. "How's our little project going?" She gestured subtly toward Ambert's twins, Helio and Dusk, who were sitting at a nearby table.

"It's been good. Well . . . Helio's been good. He made friends with the spaceball team, and the wand duelers . . ." Thorn said.

"*And* the toad racers. I wouldn't worry about Helio; he's got more friends than I do," added Seven.

When the Lophiifors had moved to Ravenskill, Miss Dewey had asked Thorn and Seven to help the twins make friends, and they had, of course, agreed. The Witchlings would do anything for Miss Dewey, but this wasn't a hard ask.

Seven liked the brothers. Helio was pure sunshine, with blond hair and freckled skin, and a smile that seemed to light up any room he went in. Of the two, he had definitely inherited his father's charm, and he shared Thorn's love for talking. He was always busy with friends and activities, but he did occasionally stop by to study, or for a movie night or to play some games, including one that Dusk had invented where they tried to guess what Edgar said before Seven revealed the answer. (He was usually insulting her.)

Meanwhile, Dusk was a typical mysterious Moth House witch, down to his dark hair, doe-like eyes, and quiet nature, with an affinity for history to rival his father's. Despite their opposite personalities, they were identical in all but their hair color and a small sunburst birthmark on Dusk's cheek—as if he carried a bit of his brother's sunshine everywhere with him.

"We're working on Dusk. He's a tough nut to crack." Seven shook her head.

"Don't let his brooding fool you; he won't stop talking about you two when we're alone. Your kindness is working, and I appreciate it." Miss Dewey smiled.

"Oh, Miss Dewey, I'm putting the finishing touches on your wedding dress. The beading took longer than usual, I'm sorry," Thorn said. "But I think you're going to love it."

"Thank you, Thorn!"

"It should be ready by this weekend," Thorn said.

"I can't wait. It's the prettiest wedding dress I've ever seen. Just you wait till you see it, Seven." Miss Dewey winked, then got up to keep passing out beverages.

Ambert read aloud from an emergency news alert from the *Squawking Crow* on his portaphone, his squirrel familiar, Tidbit, soundly asleep on his shoulder.

"I've never read about anything like this in any of my history books . . . and I have *two hundred* of them," Dusk said softly, hunched over his book.

"This is quite the mess," Helio said, looking at his father.

"Indeed," Ambert said.

"What will happen to them?" Dusk asked Seven. "The Spares?"

"Erm." Seven loosened her collar. "Not sure, but the Gran and the Oracle will come up with something."

"They'll be fine!" Helio said. "Look at Thorn and Seven. They're the most famous witches in school."

"Fame is not an indication of their quality of life," Dusk said.

"Brother! Don't be such a bore!" Helio smacked Dusk's back, making him cough.

"Do that again," Dusk said, his eyes narrowed, "and I'll hex you so everything you eat tastes like worms."

"Not again!" Helio cried. "Dad, he's threatening me! And he's reading that book you told him not to!"

"Dusk . . ." Ambert started.

Seven looked closer at the book. *Cuentista Spellwork* by Basil Birdwish.

"Father, I was just reading . . ."

"About a dangerous magic. Too dangerous for a witch your age." Ambert held his hand out and Dusk didn't budge. So Helio snatched it.

Dusk put one hand up toward his brother, preparing to hex him, no doubt, but Helio was too quick. He scrambled out of the way and handed the book to Ambert before hiding behind him. Dusk shook his head and ruffled his dark hair angrily.

Ambert smiled apologetically at the rest of the table. "Please, boys, settle down. Everyone is already upset enough as it is."

Dusk stood up, his chair scraping the floor. "Don't worry about me. I'll make myself invisible, like I always do."

"Dusk, please—" Ambert tried, but it was too late. The brooding twin was already halfway across the library.

"He's always throwing tantrums like that," Helio said.

"You were being a butt-toad though," Seven said.

Helio shrugged. "I know. But it was for his own good. I don't want my brother getting hurt, and you heard our dad; that magic is too dangerous."

"I guess," Seven said. "What kind of magic was it? The book said something about memories . . ."

But before Helio could answer, two shadows stretched, dark and unnatural, across the table, so they all looked up.

There were two large witches directly in front of Seven and Thorn. They stood so close, the girls had to move their chairs back. Their faces were hidden behind enchanted veils.

"Can we help you?" Ambert asked.

"We need these two to come with us," said one of the witches, pointing at Seven and Thorn.

"Us?" Thorn squeaked.

"What for?" Seven asked angrily. She inspected the weird witches, noticing a seal on their cloaks: the letters *B*, *A*, and *T* stitched over a crest with a strange symbol on it.

"You will see once we arrive," one of them said.

"Uh, I don't think so," Seven said.

"Now, Spare scum!" yelled the other witch, stretching his hand out menacingly.

Seven, Thorn, and even Ambert stood up, startling the slumbering Tidbit. The creepy witches took a step forward. Seven clenched her fists and Thorn held on to Seven's arm.

"Don't make us ask again, or it won't be as kind," said the veiled witch.

"*That* was kind?" grumbled Thorn.

"Is this language and toadally unwarranted aggression part of your . . . your group's procedures?" Ambert's voice was kind but held a threat. His magical skills were legendary in the Twelve Towns. He had won his own Golden Frog Games years before, after all.

"Our brothers as well as some witches from the Hill Society have some questions," one of the veiled witches said, her mask contorting into an uncanny smile.

The other witch plastered on a smile. "Yes, some

questions, nothing more. There is nothing to fear."

"Then you won't mind if I accompany them," Ambert said. "To make sure it's 'questions and nothing more,' of course?" On Ambert's shoulder, Tidbit yawned.

The two veiled witches nodded rapidly. They all swept out of the library, Seven's stomach in knots. The strange witches had been silently stalking around Ravenskill all fall; at least now maybe she'd be able to see for herself what they were up to. The first chance she got, she'd tell the Gran.

As they walked out into the night, a blur of black-and-gray fur materialized in the dark, little glowing eyes blinking rapidly in Seven's direction.

"Please, stay back," she whispered, hoping they'd hear. But her ten raccoon friends weren't fond of listening if it meant they had to stay away from Seven.

"What is this?!" cried one of the veiled witches. She gathered her robe and nearly jumped on top of a planter.

"Raccoons; you've heard of them?" Seven asked.

"Seven, Seven, Seven," chanted the raccoons, and Seven had to hold back a smirk.

"Monstruos," hissed the veiled witch.

"Half, technically," Seven countered.

"You little—" The beady-eyed witch leaned in close.

"Enough of this," Ambert said. "Lest you forget, this witch is a future Uncle."

The veiled witch straightened up slowly, a smile made of contorted fabric on her face. She nodded at Ambert, the reminder of who Seven was enough to stop her. For now.

Thorn grabbed Seven's arm. "What's gonna happen?" she asked.

Seven was trying to burn a hole in the veiled witches' capes with her eyes. "I don't know, but don't worry. We won't let them hurt you."

"We?" Thorn asked.

"Look up," Seven said.

Thorn looked up and very likely saw what Seven already knew to be there: skeleton birds. Hundreds of them. They flew high above them in formation, a secret security detail made of bones.

"What . . . what's going on, Seven? What are those? Birds?"

"Of sorts," Seven said. "The Cursed Forest owes me something. They're just trying to repay it." Seven looked up and somehow knew that among the skeleton birds was the baby bird she'd helped heal in the spring. It was alive because of her, and the skeleton birds had been loyal companions ever since. They seemed to sense when Seven needed them, and she too could sense when they were near.

"Seven . . ." Thorn began, but Seven shook her head.

"We can talk about it later. Don't want to take any chances," Seven said. Thorn nodded and Seven was relieved. She knew that her friend wouldn't let it go for much longer though; she would want an explanation as to why Seven could speak to the Nightbeast, to all monstruos; why she seemed to have command over the Cursed Forest. All things Seven had desperately tried to keep a secret the last few months. But lately her anger was becoming greater than her fear, and the Twelve Towns' fear of her and Thorn and all the Spares felt more like . . . kindling.

"I am here if you need me," the Nightbeast reminded her, an answer to her rage. The Nightbeast always knew when Seven might need to fight.

They walked past the Hall of Elders, deeper into the residential area of town and to a heavily wooded path.

"This way," one witch said, ushering them into a home with very tall roofs, dark gray planks, and a door fit for a fortress.

The raccoons sat in a neat row along the side of the home, and Seven knew that they would be there waiting for her when she emerged, just like the skeleton birds would be in the sky watching, and somewhere far in its glade, the Nightbeast and its cubs would be there for her too. The witches of her world might not always want her there, or believe in her, but she could count on the monstruos. The one inside her most of all.

Seven and Thorn followed the two witches, Ambert beside them as they ascended the stairs and emerged in a great room.

The veiled witches stood in a row on either side of an imposing throne, where a tall witch wearing a necklace made of bones sat looking down, almost as if he were sleeping. They all wore black-and-gray robes, witch's hats with twisted rims, and gloves. The witch's hats had veils that covered their faces so none of their skin was exposed and only a shadow of who they were was visible. Seven wondered if some sort of magic was infused in those veils, since their features seemed to swirl and blur as she tried to figure out who they were. If she looked at any one witch for too long, she began to feel sick. Yep, it was definitely magic.

The two witches who had escorted them bowed before the witch who sat on a throne that looked to be made of . . . slithering creatures. It moved but kept its form, making Seven shiver with fear.

"Master Beetle, the witches you requested," one of them said, and the throned witch came to life suddenly.

"Seven Salazar, Thorn Laroux, step forward," said the witch on the throne, or . . . erm, Master Beetle.

"Seven . . ." Ambert whispered, and stopped her, one hand on her shoulder. "These witches are dangerous, a newly formed group made up of Hill Society witches and some other powerful Twelve Townians who are against Spare rights. We do not know what they're capable of and it is better to err on the side of caution and cooperation. For now, of course." Ambert winked.

Seven nodded, and tempered the beast within her. Ambert was right: These witches seemed dangerous, and they were *painfully* outnumbered. She couldn't just unleash her fury on anyone who tried to cross them. It would mean a never-ending battle. Beside her, Thorn stepped forward, and Seven did the same. As they stood before Master Beetle, the Witchlings held hands, like they had done so many times before when met with the icy-cold sting of fear. The warmth of Thorn's palm infused power and calm into Seven. Their friendship was always its own special kind of magic, and Seven had never been more grateful for it.

"The time has finally arrived for Ravenskill to recognize the authority of our movement," Master Beetle said. "And we have decided to begin with *you*. You are here today to answer for the crimes that so many are willing to overlook and let you get away with."

"On what authority?" Seven asked, unable to hold her tongue.

She could not see the witch's face, but somehow, Seven could tell that Master Beetle had broken into a demented smile. She could . . . *feel* this witch's emotions so strongly, almost as if they were her own, and wondered if Thorn could too or if this was yet another symptom of her monstruo magic.

"On the authority of our ancestors. What greater inheritance than the power and magic of the prosperous? Every witch is afforded power from those who came before, their bodies becoming dirt after their death day, that dirt being the soil where nature grows, and that nature becoming the *little* magic you have in your veins. They are the reason you have any power at all. You understand, don't you? How much you are indebted to real witches? To *our* ancestors?" His voice was lilting and musical, but every word, every syllable was laced in venom.

As Master Beetle spoke, something happened. A putrid smell filled the air, foul and hot and sick-making. Seven felt ill and yet she could not seem to look away. There was something about this room, or this witch, or maybe they had been hexed already without her realizing it, but she felt oddly *drawn* to this Master Beetle. It reminded her of something her muddled mind couldn't put its finger on just yet, but it was certainly familiar.

"Our ancestors have just as much stock in Ravenskill as yours," Thorn said. "They weren't all Spares. And even if they were . . ."

"Why should that matter?" Seven finished.

"Ravenskill, you say?" Master Beetle tilted his head to the side. "Why, I seem to recall you being from another little town. Boggs Ferry, was it not? Where your cursed brother was killed by the Nightbeast that has now mysteriously vanished somewhere."

Seven tried not to twitch and prayed that the Nightbeast wouldn't speak to her. What did these witches know about it? Did they know about the cubs? Seven wouldn't be able to hold back if they were threatened.

"Thorn Laroux, age twelve, almost thirteen, one of two Laroux children. Brother Petal . . . deceased." Master Beetle tilted his head and once again, Seven could feel the smile emanating from the witch, the putrid smell around them growing. Thorn squeezed Seven's hand, and Seven squeezed back. *I'm here. I'm right here and I'm not going anywhere.*

"Thorn, you are the youngest and only Spare winner of the Golden Frog Games, brava! However . . . your final entry was an abomination, to put it mildly. It went against every tenet of our magical system." Master Beetle shook his head rapidly. "That . . . simply . . . cannot . . . stand.

"And as for you, Seven Salazar." Master Beetle turned to face Seven and her stomach dropped. What if he knew about her monstruo magic? What if they tried to kill her just like Delphinium?

"You are a Spare Uncle. Quite the coincidence, that two witches from the same Spare coven should be so extraordinary. It's almost as if it's not a coincidence at all."

Get to the point, Seven wanted to say, and her heart broke a bit more when she thought that Valley would've just gone and said it.

"What's your point?" Thorn asked, tucking her pink-streaked hair behind her ear and shocking Seven just a little bit. She couldn't help but smile.

Master Beetle twitched almost imperceptibly. Beside them, Ambert shifted his weight from one foot to the other, as if he was preparing for a fight. Or to run. *Say something,* thought Seven. Ambert might be powerful, but he could be timid, and right now, they needed someone who'd stick up for them. Like her mother.

"Since both of you have clearly broken the laws of magic and the laws of balance in our world, you should be punished. It is what's customary, correct, polite."

"Customary, correct, polite," said the other witches in unison.

"In accordance with our traditions, it is only fair that regrettably you should be treated just as any other witch who broke our most serious of laws." Master Beetle leaned in. "You shall be stripped of power and exiled."

Seven clenched her fists and began to step forward when the putrid stench overtook her and pushed her back.

"It would be easier if you did not cross us," Master Beetle said, and this time, both the Witchlings stepped forward. They would see how well this cult fared against the Witchlings and their army of monstruos.

"Now, now," said Ambert, finally speaking up, but before he could say anything else, the door behind them crashed open.

They all turned to look in unison, and stalking toward them, holographic cape floating behind them, an angry scowl on their perfect, glittering features, was the Oracle. Relief washed over Seven.

"What in the hex do you think you're doing?" Sybell walked right up to Master Beetle and spat.

"Why, Sybell! Welcome to our little enclave. Finally, you accept our invitation to appear before the cult. Now, if you don't mind, we're just sentencing these wretched little Witchlings and you shall be next!" Master Beetle said as if he were delivering good news.

"You have no power here. None. You can't sentence anyone to anything," Sybell said.

"It is very evident that these two are responsible for the break in our magical balance," one of the veiled escorts said. "It is only customary that . . ."

"Excuse me very much, but this does not concern you. We're leaving. Now," the Oracle said.

"And will you take responsibility for anything else that goes wrong with our magic? I will make a record of it, if so. Just please, give us the formal confirmation that any other mishaps will be on your head," Master Beetle said. The pungent smell intensified, and Seven could swear a green mist pulsed through the air.

One of the veiled witches walked eagerly to the Oracle's side, a quill and scroll in hand, but Sybell just sneered and swatted the scroll and quill to the floor.

The veiled witches gasped in unison.

"I shall do no such thing, and if you know something we have not been able to uncover, please, I'm all ears. What evidence, what proof do you have against our Witchlings?" Sybell asked.

Master Beetle sat up a bit taller, and Seven thought maybe Sybell had taken him by surprise. The warmth in their voice as they said *"our Witchlings"* made Seven forget for a moment that they were being put on trial just for existing. Just for being what they could not help being, according to rules they hadn't created. Even so, being a Spare . . . it was something Seven would not change even if she could. Better a Spare than one of the witches who looked down on them.

"It is evident!" said Master Beetle. "The moment these Witchlings corrupted our magic to gain power for themselves, the magical balance broke!"

"We never did that!" Thorn said angrily.

"Have you ever considered that whatever is affecting their powers is responsible for the magic being unbalanced and not the other way around? What if they are victims of a problem, not the problem itself?" the Oracle said.

"Now, now, do you have proof of your claim?" Master Beetle asked, sweeter than purple spring honey.

"No more than you do. Which is why we cannot rush to condemn our own *children*. You may not understand them, you may hate them for your own selfish reasons, but that makes them no less worthy of compassion, of understanding." Sybell reached out then and grabbed Seven's hand. Now the three of them were linked, almost as if the Oracle was making their puzzle of three temporarily complete. Ambert stood beside them, eyes focused on Master Beetle.

Master Beetle was silent then as he looked at the four of them. Finally, he nodded and clapped his long, gloved fingers together. "We shall meet again, yes? Delighted to have you visit. Please, please be sure you come again or, what am I saying, silly me! We shall *make sure of it*."

Seven's eyes glazed over with something thick and milky. She blinked, but it did not dissolve like tears. Instead, it became thicker. She struggled to look away from Master Beetle, but as the witch looked at her, head cocked, Seven felt a smile being forced onto her face. Maybe Master Beetle wasn't that bad. Maybe he just had their best interests at heart. She heard a hum of noise in her ear, something ringing, struggling to break through the haze of her pleasant thoughts about the very kind Master Beetle.

"Seven!" Thorn screamed, and they both careened toward the ground. Ambert tumbled and caught them as they fell, and when Seven blinked this time, she could see clearly. The Oracle had their hands up, pushing back whatever unseen magic had made Seven lose her wits. *What was that?*

"Until next time!" Master Beetle chirped as Seven, Thorn, Ambert, and the Oracle retreated. Before they left altogether, Seven chanced one look back, and saw Master Beetle still on his throne, slumped over, perhaps from the exertion of whatever hexed magic he had cast around them. Seven shivered as they escaped the house.

Outside, the raccoons were waiting for Seven and it was all she could do to not bend down and let them gather her in a hug. She felt drained and confused. What had just happened?

"Are you okay?" she asked Thorn as they walked briskly toward the center of town.

Thorn nodded. "I think so. I feel weird though."

"Same," Seven said.

"Ambert, we'll leave you here," the Oracle said as they passed the library. "Helio and Dusk are waiting for you. I shall be escorting the Witchlings home."

"You sure you don't need my help?" he asked.

"No need. Come, children," Sybell said, and Seven and Thorn followed them.

As they made their way to Seven's house, Seven still felt muddled and confused, but after a few minutes in the night air, her mind began to clear.

"Sybell, do you know what kind of magic that was? Who those witches were?" she asked.

Sybell turned, their cape billowing, their sharp features more severe than usual. They bent down closer and whispered, "Those witches are using a very powerful archaic magic I have never seen before. Not in this century. And they would not be concealing their faces if they did not have something to hide. You must never, ever go back to that house." The Oracle's voice trembled with a fear that felt unnatural coming from them. It made Seven search the darkness, new horrors blooming in the shadows around them.

"No matter what they do or say, you must never, ever go there again."

That night, as Ravenskill slept, a storm unlike any Seven had ever seen swept through the town. Her house shook, waking the whole family. When Seven looked out her window, the rain wasn't normal; it was . . . purple. When she checked the telecast, she discovered the rain hadn't been confined to Ravenskill; it had swept across the Twelve Towns and the reporters on her screen looked worried. It was another phenomenon on the heels of the already infamous Red Moon Ceremony, and Seven wondered if something was truly wrong with the magic in the Twelve Towns.

CHAPTER FIVE

A STAND-UP ROUTINE FOR DUENDES

ONE EYE OF SLITHERSONG, three dead man's fingers, a loaf of bunnybeaver fluff, and the bane of Seven's existence: three vials of duende laughter. She was straddling a bough atop a bloodwood oak in the Cursed Forest, waiting for the elusive creatures to appear.

"I know this is where they live; why won't they come out?" Thorn asked, looking up at Seven from the base of the tree.

"Because they're doing it as a personal insult to me, specifically." Seven wiped the sweat from her forehead and repositioned herself on the bough.

She'd been up there for two hours now, waiting for a duende to emerge from the tree hollow below. Every muscle in her body ached from the effort of being up there, and the glass vials, ready for Seven to collect their laughter, clinked in her cloak pocket. It was the last ingredient they needed for the latest stonification cure they'd come up with—a concoction that would hopefully crack the stone with sound, and free Valley and the other stone witches. In order to get the duende laughter though, they needed to see one, and that had proven to be more difficult than either of them had imagined. Though so many things were going wrong in the Twelve Towns, every day the stone hex snaked closer to Valley's heart, to Tia's, to Alaric's and Mayhem's, so they had no choice but to be out here, waiting.

Though Seven was comfortable here, she could see Thorn jump at the slightest sound. The Cursed Forest was not supposed to be safe for witches; Thorn's reaction to this place was normal and expected, but for Seven it was quite different. For Seven, this place where monstruos dwelled felt safer than anywhere else in Ravenskill. Especially now. But she worried for her friend.

"You okay down there?" Seven asked.

Thorn nodded. "Got my jokes ready and everything."

Duendes loved a bad joke. It *had* to be bad. And Thorn and Seven had come up with a few to tell them and hopefully get the laughter they needed for the spell. Seven shifted, her legs burning, sweat blurring her vision as she listened for any signs of the trickster monstruos.

"Anything?" Thorn asked.

Seven leaned so her body was against the bough, her ear toward the hollow, when she heard the distinct sound of arguing.

"Yes," she whispered frantically. "Get ready, get ready!"

Thorn nodded, and running in a little circle to ward

off her nervous excitement, she got in position and pulled a sparkling microphone from her cloak. "Ready," Thorn said.

Seven opened the glass vials and positioned them in the small waist pouch Thorn had fashioned for her.

"Here they come," Seven said.

From the hollow emerged a string of small creatures. They looked like very old men—all duendes did even if they were girls. They had pointy long ears, round button noses, and wore oversized overalls made of thistle of all colors. On their heads, they wore mushroom tops as hats, tied beneath their tiny faces with ribbon.

"They look delicious."

"They're not food, Nightbeast," Seven whispered as Thorn cleared her throat.

"Hey, everyone, I am Thorn Laroux, and I have some jokes for you!" Thorn said.

Seven held her breath. If the tricksters ran back into their tree, they'd burrow underground or use some spell to disappear to another part of the forest, and this cure would be toast. This was the moment of truth. Every bone in Seven's body ached as she tried not to move. After what felt like ages, the duendes conferring in their indecipherable language, they sat in a neat row and waited for Thorn to begin the show.

"Yes," Seven whispered. One step closer to curing the stonified witches. One step closer to getting their Valley back.

"Thanks for being here with me tonight!"

The duendes clapped and yelled wildly, waving their little pointed mushroom top hats in the air.

"What do you call a bear with no teeth?" Thorn asked.

The duendes looked at one another and shrugged. They hadn't heard this one before; good.

Thorn waited a beat . . . "A gummy bear!"

Seven readied the vials, waiting for their laughter to fill them up. But no laughter came; there was only silence.

The duendes did not laugh. Like at all. Not even so much as a giggle.

"The joke is too good!" said Seven desperately. "You're bombing!"

"Okay, okay, I've got more, don't you worry!" Thorn said, drying one hand on her cloak nervously. "You're really gonna like this one, I think. Why did the man return his new pair of spider silk trousers?"

Again, the duendes looked at one another in confusion, just before Thorn landed the punch line. "They looked great, but the fly kept getting stuck!"

A roar of laughter exploded through the forest. It was so loud that skeleton birds flew away angrily from their treetops, their bones click-clacking as they flapped their wings. The duendes' laugh was high-pitched and trilling, and it was so funny, Seven couldn't help but laugh herself. The duendes cried and wiped their eyes, one of them almost falling from the tree.

"Sorry!" Seven called out as she filled one, two, three vials!

"Keep going! Six more to go!" Seven said.

Thorn brightened up, buoyed by her successful stinker.

"What does a witch ask for in a hotel?" she asked.

The duendes leaned forward, excited.

"Broom service!"

Seven cringed, and the duendes howled with laughter. This time the laughter was so loud, the rest of the vials filled immediately.

"We did it!" Seven said. She secured the vials in their pouches, then shimmied quickly down the tall tree, leaving the laughing duendes behind. This time one of them really did fall off the tree, which only made the other duendes laugh harder. The echo of their chortles followed them as they ran through the forest and out into downtown Ravenskill, on their way to try to save their friend.

CHAPTER SIX

A LITTLE HELP FROM QUILL

VALLEY'S APARTMENT on Division Street had become the Witchlings' HQ. There was a full witch's kitchen in the basement, with a fireplace and a giant olla, the traditional cauldron of Ravenskill. There were potions and plants, including a flowering chismosa plant Seven was trying to grow—for spying purposes, of course. On the wall, there was a list, describing the vision the Golden Frog had given her and Thorn:

A group of witches meeting in secret.

The three witches holding the foxes.

Ravenskill, engulfed in flames.

A bright, enchanting light underwater.

And then there was the peculiar-looking house. Seven had seen a sort of symbol on its front door; at first she had thought it was a large animal, but now it looked more like . . . a blob. And Thorn had seen something completely different.

"It's just a shadow; there's nothing in the middle," she insisted.

No matter how many times they talked it over, or drew their own versions of what they saw, they couldn't agree on that one vision, and worse yet, they couldn't figure out what any of it meant. The only connection Seven could find so far was the three foxes and the three Nightbeast cubs. But that could just be a coincidence. Thorn was sure the vision had to do with curing Valley and the stone witches, so they kept it up, but every time Seven looked at the list, all she felt was frustration. How was she ever supposed to figure it out? There was also the message the brown squirrel passed on to Seven after the games: *Look for the lost one.* Seven didn't even know where to begin with that one, but she had asked every squirrel she could find about it with no luck.

Beside the list, Seven had pinned up all the information they knew about the hex, connected with red yarn crisscrossed along the wall like an enormous, complicated spiderweb. It had all their failed potion and cure attempts: They were at fifty-eight so far, but she wouldn't give up. She was grateful that Quill had let them use this space for their cure attempts and investigations. It was perfect for mixing potions, not to mention, Quill was a great help. Plus, Seven's mother, Fox, had told her if she saw just one more red string hung up on her bedroom wall, she would collect it in a giant ball and roll Seven down Oso Mountain inside it.

Valley's mother had been having the hardest time of

all of them, of course: With Valley stonified, and a nasty divorce with the terrible Mr. Pepperhorn playing out in public, her heartbreak was gargantuan. Somehow, the newspapers and telecast journalists had decided *she* was the villain in all this, breaking up a "happy" family for her own nefarious reasons, and were painting Mr. Pepperhorn as the faultless father. Pathetic. But instead of letting the beast of grief consume her or hexing Mr. Pepperhorn with forever fart breath, which Seven would've understood completely, Quill had jumped headfirst into trying to find a cure. She had proved a tremendous help, both for her knowledge of potions and for her delicious four-cheese grilled cheese sandwiches.

"What have we got?" Quill asked, wiping her hands on her apron. She had already begun mixing the other ingredients in a smaller cauldron, trying to get the consistency just right.

"Bull's-eye." Seven held up the vials.

"Wonderful!" said Quill.

More than once, Seven's magic had made an elixir too powerful, and Quill's whole basement had been covered in soot from the small explosion that ensued. She was determined to control her power this time though.

"Okay, how do we do this? We can't afford to lose even one drop of laughter," Seven said.

"Leave it to me," said the older witch.

Seven and Thorn watched as Quill placed each vial carefully in old, rusted holders made just for spell making. The laughter swirled a happy, bright blue inside the glass vessels, a muffled cackle emanating from them every few seconds.

"Now watch." Quill winked; then, after putting her long black hair up with a pencil, she opened each vial carefully. Swiftly and ever so softly, she coaxed the sound out and weaved the laughter into long, connected braids. Just as the duendes did to your hair in your sleep. Froggin' genius.

After a few minutes, all the laughter had been weaved into beautiful plaits and placed inside the large cast-iron olla. Quill lit the fire with a small fuego spell, then sat.

"It'll take at least an hour for the laughter to simmer before we can add the rest of the ingredients. Are you hungry? I made sandwiches," Quill said.

"So hungry," Thorn said. "I can run up and get them."

"No need," Seven said without thinking. "Convocar." She waved her hand in the direction of the stairs, imagining the tray Quill always served sandwiches on, and after one or two slightly concerning bangs, the tray came flying toward them. Two cups Seven had not intended to conjure came with it and crashed against the brick wall behind them. The three witches screamed and ducked just as the tray screeched to a halt and hovered serenely in front of them. *Ugh!* Seven knew she shouldn't really be conjuring indiscriminately, but it was almost as if she couldn't help it. Like her magic was in charge of her and not the other way around.

Quill straightened up and quirked an eyebrow, giving Seven an amused look. "I won't ask how you can already summon things, Little Uncle."

Seven loved that Quill had a nickname for her. Little Uncle would've felt weird coming from someone else, but from Valley's mom, it felt like a Stars' blessing.

"Good, because I have no idea," Seven said, already three bites into her first sandwich. Quill laughed and it was a loud, hearty sound, just like Valley's laugh. It made Seven's heart ache the tiniest bit.

"Thank you," said Thorn politely before eating her own gooey grilled cheese. The crust was perfectly toasted, it never got soggy or too hard to chew, there was the lightest layer of mayonnaise, and the most delicious four cheeses were melted to perfection. Seven closed her eyes: Grilled cheese was the *perfect* food.

"You should probably make sure not to conjure in front of other witches," Quill said. "And maybe talk to your parents about it?"

"Sure, sure," Seven said, trying to seem cool about it, when she was one hundred percent the opposite of cool about it. There was also no froggin' way she would be telling her parents a thing and she hoped Quill didn't tell them either.

"Ms. Nightingale, have you ever heard of any Black Moon Ceremony sorting every Witchling into the same coven?" Thorn asked.

No matter how many times Quill told Thorn it was okay to call her by her first name, Thorn refused.

"She is famous. *I could never"* was Thorn's explanation to Seven every single time.

Quill took a bite of her sandwich and considered the

question. "You know, I can't say that I remember anything like this ever happening. It's strange."

"Do you have any theories?" Seven asked carefully. Even though Sybell had scoffed at the weird cult witches' accusations, Seven wasn't so sure. What if they were right? What if her monstruo powers really had caused magic to break?

"I've done quite a lot of research into our history in order to write my books, and while this hasn't happened before, the laws of magic *have* been broken. Many times."

"Like the Hat of Deceit," Thorn said.

"Precisely, but I can't say if there's a connection to our magic being broken. What I do know is, there've been many instances of our balance laws being disregarded, almost always by influential Hill witches who don't adhere to rules. Balance magic is almost all theory, nothing that has been proven or tested to my knowledge. If it works how we've been told, however, it could be that breaking the balance laws somehow affects magic overall. It would have to be a big, big hex or spell or something to make a crack as big as what happened at the Black Moon Ceremony though. So, I have my doubts it's anything more than a fluke.

"My soon-to-be ex-husband went on about magic going wrong like this sometimes. He was obsessed with balance this, balance that." Quill shook her head. "He worried if Spares didn't know their place, something terrible might happen to our magic."

Mr. Pepperhorn, aside from being abusive to Valley and even keeping food from her as punishment, had also been in cahoots with the Cursed Toads, who had caused so much trouble for the Witchlings and the whole town last year. How could one witch be so terrible?

"I could eat him, if you like." Seven opened her eyes wide as the Nightbeast chuckled in the distance.

Thorn subtly squeezed Seven's arm, shooting her a meaningful look, and Seven was sure her friend was thinking the same thing she was—Mr. Pepperhorn was a menace.

"Hmm, what are you two scheming?"

"Nothing," Seven said.

"We just want to help," Thorn said.

Quill smiled. "So long as you promise to take good care of yourselves and not do anything reckless."

"We won't do anything Valley wouldn't do," Seven said.

"That . . . doesn't inspire me with much confidence," Quill said, and they all laughed together, their eyes distant and thinking of their friend, Quill's daughter, the fighter that Valley was. Valley's stone form was like a giant wedge in all their hearts, propelling them forward but snagging them on unimaginable pain at every turn.

Seven missed Valley so much, she thought her heart just might break.

"You two have been through enough. Let the adults handle this one for once. We've been known to solve an issue or two in our day." Quill winked.

"We should focus on Valley's cure anyway," Seven said.

Quill smiled and nodded. "Good. I need some hot cocoa, whaddaya say?"

"Yes, please!" both Witchlings said.

"Keep an eye on the potion." Quill went upstairs and left Thorn and Seven alone.

"All right, time to fold some more ingredients into the potion," Seven said. She closed her eyes and held her hands over the olla as Thorn added a sprinkle of rat fur into it. Seven had to focus, get this just right. Not too much magic or it would explode; not too little or it would fizzle out.

"It's working," Thorn said.

Seven opened her eyes, excited that she'd finally gotten it right, when all of a sudden . . .

BOOM!

She and Thorn were blown back in the basement, a small explosion mushrooming inside the cauldron.

They both ran to look into the cauldron and deflated. Instead of the giggles of the duendes, angry unintelligible scolding emitted from what was left of the elixir. The laughter that had been nicely simmering just moments ago had turned a deep, dark gray. They were back to square one.

Seven had fudged it again. And time for Valley and the other stone witches was running out.

CHAPTER SEVEN

SERPHENT AND BITTERBOB ANTIQUERS

AFTER SCHOOL THE NEXT DAY, Seven, Graves, and Dusk made their way through downtown Ravenskill.

"That shape-shifting exam was brutal." Graves shook her head.

"I told you to come to extra study sessions with Professor Darkpond, but noooo," Dusk grumbled. "We practiced transformacion on the rats for *hours*. It helped a lot."

Seven giggled at Dusk's signature deadpan tone. "Don't be too hard on yourself, Graves. I'm sure you did better than you think," she said.

"Easy for you to say; you could hear the rats talking." Graves smirked at Seven and her cheeks went hot.

"Some good that did me. They were practicing their harmonies for some song called 'Cheesy Does It' the whole time," Seven said.

The three witches laughed, cloaks wrapped tightly around their shoulders, rucksacks slung over their backs as they weaved through the afternoon crowds. Downtown Ravenskill was bright with the red and gold of autumn leaves. Soon snow would begin blanketing the cobblestone streets and they'd need to trade their fall uniforms for their thicker winter ones.

"You know, the rats in Professor Darkpond's class could probably just give us the answers to the test if we asked them next time . . ." Dusk looked at Seven.

"If *we* asked them or if *I* asked them?" Seven said.

Dusk had opened his mouth to answer when a putrid smell swept through Wolfberry Street and stopped them in their tracks. The little bell outside the antique shop tinkled, and out from the wooden door with its forest-green curtained window swept the weird, veiled cult.

"What are they doing here?" hissed Graves as the cult walked out, single file, in the direction of their home. "My parents said they were nothing but trouble. Some witches on the council are trying to get them to disband."

"They give me an uneasy feeling," said Dusk. "But according to my father they have powerful magic. Making them disband won't be easy."

Seven nodded in agreement. "Come on, let's go see what they were doing in there."

The three witches waited for the ten or so witches from the veiled cult to be far enough along the road before entering the shop.

Serphent and Bitterbob Antiquers was a cozy, dark shop filled floor to ceiling with everything from books to used socks, and endless clear buckets of stones and crystals. It smelled like grandparent witches and strawberry candies.

"Yes? May we help you?" one of the antiquer witches, Serphent Eferhild, asked.

Serphent was tall and moved with elegance. He had topaz-brown skin, and blond hair that was pressed and curled into an unfortunate bowl cut.

"Uh . . ." Graves began.

"What were those freaky witches doing here?" Dusk asked without hesitation.

"Dusk," Graves admonished under her breath.

Serphent cleared his throat. "Well, I believe they were hoping to take advantage of our two-for-one crystal and stone sale, though I'm afraid if you're looking for any of them . . ."

"Sale's over!" said Bitterbob Eferhild, the other owner of the shop. He was, as his name suggested, always in a bitter mood. Like his brother, he was pretty old, probably as old as some of the knickknacks in his store, but unlike his brother, Bitterbob was very short. He had blond hair and brown skin to match his brother's, but instead of a bowl cut, his hair was styled in long braids tied back with a giant blue ribbon.

"The veiled witches purchased quite a few stones and we've hit our sales target, although"—Serphent shivered—"they *do* frog me out."

"Bah! How many of those things can one creepy mansion need anyway?!" Bitterbob said.

Dusk gave a satisfied nod.

"Did they ask anything or do anything freaky and strange while they were here?" Seven tried.

"Their mere presence is freaky and strange," grumbled Bitterbob.

"Good point," Seven said.

"They mostly whispered to one another about my inventory. Impressed by our selection, no doubt," Serphent said smugly.

"Bah!" Bitterbob added.

"Thanks." Graves shrugged.

As Dusk and Graves inspected a bejeweled egg, Seven looked at the old books in their rare reading section. She ran her fingers along the impeccable spines and stopped when one particular title caught her interest.

The Lore of the Archaic: A Magical Guide to the Dark Side. Seven's eyes opened wide. A whole book on archaic magic?! She grabbed the book and sat on the carpeted floor, opening the enormous tome. The index showed that this book outlined all the levels of archaic magic.

"'The archaic magic path is a difficult but rewarding one,'" she read in the heavy pages of the book. "'There are five main levels of the archaic discipline of magic: incendiary magic, having to do with volatile fire magic; conjuration, any magic having to do with conjuring of objects and at incredibly high levels, living beings'—whoa," Seven said. She wondered if she could conjure Valley into her room. She turned to the section that interested her the most: conjuration.

"'With all levels of the occult discipline, rigorous

training is a necessity. Any witch with a propensity for the occult who does not train could risk losing control of their magic, which could lead to terrible unintended consequences such as random acts of conjuring.'"

Seven wiped her forehead. Rats. That was definitely happening to her.

"'Untamed archaic magic can lead to a tilting of the balance in that witch's skills, leading to a random but likely devastating loss of magic within the witch. In rare instances, magical power can increase to dangerous levels, which may lead to madness, uncontrollable magic, or, in extreme cases, death.' It's always death!" Seven shouted.

Graves and Dusk turned to look at her.

Seven chuckled nervously. "It's an . . . um, interesting read."

When they turned away, she went on. "'To avoid such a fate, be sure to secure a teacher who is an expert in one's discipline of choice. To forgo training is to gamble with one's life.'"

Easy for this author to say. If monstruo magic really was archaic magic, then where was Seven going to find a witch to train her? There was only Delphinium, and she was gone. So now what?

"Bitterbob?" Seven asked as the old witch enchanted spiderwebs onto a bookcase.

"What is it? What?"

"Is it possible to buy this book?"

Bitterbob had the book out of Seven's hand and

climbed a small ladder to shove it on the very top shelf of the bookcase before she knew what was happening.

"Humph. Everyone suddenly wants to buy this old book, but look there, can't ya read?" Bitterbob pointed at a sign above the books. "*Not fer sale.*"

Seven stood up, hands on her hips. "Then what are they here for, hmm? Is this a store or isn't it?"

"Listen here!" Bitterbob began as his much more reasonable brother stepped between the young Uncle and the old antiquer.

Serphent chuckled uneasily. "Now, now, no need to hex each other. What Bitterbob means is this particular book is not for sale. It's much too dangerous for a young witch like you."

"Third time this week," Bitterbob grumbled.

"Indeed, even the veiled witches asked about it and we did not allow them to take it," Serphent added.

Graves and Dusk were suddenly by Seven's side.

"They asked about the archaic magic book?" Seven asked.

"Course they did! Persistent butt-toads too. But I told them to scram, same as I'm telling you. This book can't just go to any old witch," Bitterbob said.

"Seven is the Ravenskill Uncle, you know," Dusk said, his eyes narrowed.

"In training, dear boy, in training," Serphent said. "But my brother is right: We could not in good conscience sell you something like this. I will see to it that this book is properly locked away so there are no more misunderstandings. We pride ourselves in stocking books on rare magic, but this one seems to be nothing but trouble. In fact, I was sure I had put this in the back room. Puzzling that it's out here among the books for sale." Serphent scratched his head.

Seven, Dusk, and Graves exchanged looks. *Yes, puzzling indeed.*

"Wait, do you have any books . . . for sale, that is . . . about the cuentista spell?" Dusk asked.

Serphent lit up. "Now *that* I can help you with!"

He began to scan the shelf, then walked his plump, wrinkled fingers across the spines of a few books.

"You're *obsessed* with that spell." Graves shook her head.

"What is it?" Seven asked.

"Some memory spell, I think," Graves said.

"More like history," Dusk said.

Seven groaned. "Don't remind me. History lessons have been a nightmare lately. No, thanks."

"You should take that class more seriously. The truth of history might save us one day."

"Where is it, where is it, ah yes! Here!" Serphent pulled out a book with a royal-blue cover and a golden watch etched onto it beneath the title—*The Time and Memory Compendium*.

"Now, this one is just for borrowing. Understood? It has all types of time-bending and memory spells, all wonderfully challenging magic. I'll need it back in three to seven years," Serphent said. "Of course, if you master any of the enchantments, you can simply go back in time and return it to make sure it's not late or . . . something."

"That's not how it works, you butt-toad!" Bitterbob said.

Seven and Graves giggled.

Dusk's eyes were wide, and focused on the book; his expression was unfamiliar to Seven since he normally looked uninterested or annoyed. But right now, he looked almost excited.

"I'll have it back before then, promise," Dusk said, and stuck one hand out.

Serphent passed him the book with a smile and Seven cleared her throat.

"About the archaic magic book . . ."

"Now, now, young Seven. I have already told you we cannot let that book leave this store—"

"No, I know." Seven held her hands up. "I know I can't borrow it, but, Bitterbob"—Seven turned to the cranky antiquer—"you said it's the third time this week someone asked about that book. Us, the veiled witches." She counted off on her fingers. "Who was the third?"

Lotus was behind bars, but whoever she was working with, whoever had taught the teen witch the magic that had turned Valley and their other friends into stone, was still at large somewhere. Maybe that witch had tried to take this book or maybe they had a new apprentice, a new Lotus trying to learn the archaic magic ropes. Seven wasn't even sure if it was just one witch, or many. It could be anyone in the Twelve Towns, and that knowledge made Seven uneasy.

Bitterbob and Serphent exchanged looks. Serphent's eyes were opened so wide, Seven thought his eyeballs might pop out of his head. He shook it ever so slightly, so his shiny bowl cut swayed and shimmied, but Bitterbob did not heed whatever silent warning his brother was trying to send him, and turned to Seven with a smug smile on his face.

But just as he opened his mouth to say something, the small bell chimed from the entrance.

"Seven! I've been looking for you everywhere," Thorn said, rushing into the store.

"Hey!" Seven began, and then she saw Thorn's face. It was splotchy and red, her eyes filled with tears. "What is it? Are you okay? Is it Valley?!" Seven asked, grabbing Thorn's arms.

Thorn shook her head. "No, no, Valley is . . . unchanged. But a terrible thing happened last night. Pixel has gone missing."

CHAPTER EIGHT

MISSING

"**WE LAST SAW** her after the Black Moon Ceremony. She went to get her gloves on the balcony and was supposed to go home after that," Thimble explained.

Thorn and Seven had run to Thorn's house, where their parents and Quill had gathered, while Dusk and Graves had gone home to be with their own families. Now the Witchlings and their families sat in the Larouxs' living room, sipping calming tea and trying to retrace their steps on the night of the ceremony. In the background, the *Squawking Crow* telecast played softly, mostly focusing on the Black Moon Ceremony and the sea of new Spares.

"She had a few days off after the ceremony but was supposed to come in today and didn't, which is unlike her. I called, I went to her apartment . . ." Thimble said, wiping her eyes. "And she wasn't there. I tried her portaphone many times, but no answer. It's not like Pixel to just disappear without a word."

“Is there anywhere else you could look? With her family, maybe?” Quill asked softly.

Leaf shook his head no. He had one arm over Thimble’s shoulders, trying to calm her as best he could. “Her family hasn’t had contact with her since she was sorted as a Spare.”

Like many Spare families lately, Pixel’s had moved to the town of Castle Point up in the mountains. It had become a snowy refuge for anti-Spare witches, it seemed.

“Still, we did reach out to them, and they said they hadn’t heard from her. That they wouldn’t allow her to stay with them even if she had tried. Absolute geese, all of them,” Leaf said.

Thorn’s face was bright red with anger. Pixel had become like another member of the Laroux family. She had once worked for Rafflesia Dimblewit, a Hill Society member and butt-toad in her own right. Mrs. Dimblewit was awful to Pixel, abusive even. Thimble had offered her a fair job, with good pay: as an assistant in her boutique, Oh La La, Laroux, with the possibility of promotion. Pixel had quickly become Thimble’s right hand and even more than that, a friend. She was kind and funny and capable, and all the things awful witches said Spares like Pixel couldn’t be. Thimble even helped Pixel get a nice apartment in town, which many Ravenskillians, mostly from the Hill, had been loudly against. It would set a bad precedent, they said; Spares should know their place, they complained. And now that Pixel had seemingly vanished,

Seven wondered if one of the Hill witches had been so angry that they'd hurt her.

"This is my fault. I only wanted to help, but if me offering her a job somehow put her in danger . . ." Thimble covered her face.

It seemed Seven wasn't the only one thinking this was some sort of retaliation.

"All you did was try and make right what so many in our town ignored until it hit us directly. Me included," Talis said.

"I have a bad feeling," sniffed Thimble. "A very bad feeling."

And then a breaking bulletin flashed across the screen. *Missing Spares,* the ticker said, and Seven dove for the remote, turning up the volume.

"All across the Twelve Towns, Spares are going missing . . ."

Tiordan Whisperbrew sat at their large wooden news desk, a fire roaring behind them, their witch's hat on and a somber expression on their face. Tiordan always brought a sense of calm to any reporting they did, but it was clear something was wrong.

"Over twenty-eight separate instances of missing Spares have now been reported across the Towns. From Ravenskill to Blonkers to the northern town of Castle Point, Spares have disappeared into thin air."

"What?!" they all shouted. It was bad enough Pixel had gone missing, but twenty-seven others as well? This was a disaster.

"Quiet, quiet, let's hear what else they say!" Fox said.

Now everyone was focused on the telecast, moving closer to watch. Scenes of the Twelve Towns played as Tiordan continued speaking over shots of houses, the Boggy Crone River, and local businesses. "Many employers were the first to sound the alarm, not finding their Spares in their rooms or anywhere in their expansive mansions."

The scene cut to a distraught witch on the Hill, standing in front of her home. "Normally, Oleander has our breakfast ready and on the table as soon as we wake. When I saw the table empty, well . . . I knew something was wrong."

Mage Pearsprout, the head of the Gran's Guard, appeared then. "This is an ongoing investigation, so we aren't at liberty to share everything at this time, but we ask that any Twelve Townians with information on the missing Spares please come forward."

Tiordan was on the screen again. "With the new passage of anti-Spare legislation, and increased discrimination against Spares, Mage Pearsprout advised the Squawking Crow Network that the Gran's Guard is moving swiftly and taking this very seriously. Every resident of Ravenskill, and of the Twelve Towns at large, deserves the same rights, the same protections. Hateful language and laws always end in more harm, and it could be that this is proof of that. This has been an SCN special report. We will keep you up to date on any breaking news throughout the night."

Seven turned down the volume, but scenes from the ceremony and interviews with town residents played on as they continued to cover the disappearances. She turned back to the others. "Do you think . . . someone is hurting Spares?"

Her thoughts returned to Lotus once again, and whoever taught her archaic magic. Could that same witch be behind the missing Spares?

"Oh, Seven . . ." Thimble came closer and took her hand. "I wish I could say no. I wish I was sure of it."

"We know it's possible," Thorn said. "We know everyone hates us."

Thimble's and Leaf's faces fell. "Everyone does not hate you, my rose. There are awful witches in the world, but there are good people too," Leaf said.

Seven knew Mr. Laroux was right, but it seemed that lately the evil, awful witches were always getting their way.

CHAPTER NINE

FOLLOWING MR. PEPPERHORN

SEVEN WAS SITTING on the stoop of Ambert's house with the twins and Thorn, bracing herself to go do something she *really* did not want to do.

On Seven's portaphone screen, propped up against an ornate flowerpot, was Figgs Moonchild. He looked skinnier than last time Seven had seen him, dark circles under his eyes and a sullen expression that had become normal for him.

River Moonfall, the teenage daughter of the family he had worked for, had been killed by her supposed best friend, Lotus, and River's family had left the Twelve Towns altogether—something witches rarely did, but Seven couldn't blame them. Word among the animals was, the Moonfalls had moved all the way to troll country, which was across the Atlantis and to the east of the Twelve Towns. And that meant that Figgs was out of work. With how superstitious Twelve Townians could be, it had been impossible for him to find a new employer.

"I get wanting to help the Spares, but . . . won't the towns be searching for them?" Helio asked.

Thorn and Seven shifted. Even Figgs looked uncomfortable from the screen.

"Was that a butt-toad thing to ask?" Helio asked.

"No, no, it's what anyone would expect. Don't feel bad; it's just we've got a lot of experience with this," Seven said.

"It *is* a butt-toad thing to ask, but that's normal for you," Dusk said, and he ducked out of the way as Helio tried to punch him.

"Any news from the Spares in your town, Figgs?" Thorn asked.

Figgs shook his head. "Not yet. I've asked around, but nobody seems to know what happened to the missing Spares here either. It's like they vanished into thin air."

"So strange." Seven bit her lip. It seemed that without anything else to go on, her plan was unavoidable.

"I'll keep trying though." Figgs smiled kindly, and Seven's heart swelled. She wished she could hug him. She wished she could give him some food, or a warm place to stay, but as it was, she wasn't even sure where Figgs was living. And he refused to tell her anything, which only made her worry more.

"Dusk, Helio, can you still let us know if you find anything out from Moth or Hyacinth witches? I'm sure at least some of your friends have Spare workers," Seven said. "If they've seen or noticed anything suspicious at all, it might help."

Dusk nodded. "I've already started asking around, but nothing so far."

"Oh, oh, I have been asking too!" Helio said excitedly, nearly falling over.

Seven and Thorn perked up. "Did you find something?" Thorn asked.

"No." Helio cringed, and Dusk rolled his eyes.

Thorn gently nudged Seven. "It's getting late," she mouthed, and Seven nodded. She had almost forgotten, or perhaps she was so unhappy with what they had to do next, she was avoiding it.

"We've gotta go work on our latest cure attempt," Seven said.

"That's okay, we have to finish helping Miss Dewey with the wedding centerpieces anyway, but let us know if you find anything out," Helio said.

"Be safe," Dusk said softly, before the twins went inside and Seven and Thorn made their way to a small grove where they wouldn't be easily seen.

"Glad we have the twins and Figgs to help, now that we're on double duty with Valley's cure and the missing Spares," Seven whispered as they shuffled past a row of bird-themed mailboxes.

"You mean *triple* duty. We've also got school," Thorn reminded her.

Seven groaned. She had a big paper on the history of

gnome hats due in a few weeks, not to mention her advanced arachnid final.

"If this cuts into your costura program—" Seven began, but Thorn put both hands up.

"It won't. I'm already ahead of the rest of the class and I don't need much sleep." Thorn smiled.

Seven shot her a skeptical look. Thorn's acceptance into the accelerated costura program after her win at the Golden Frog Games was a big deal that could lead to huge opportunities in the future. But Seven had noticed that Thorn was reluctant to even join the program, and she wasn't sure why.

They reached the grove and just like Thorn had instructed, she put the hood of her newly made cloak up and gasped. A magic cold as ice enveloped her body; her limbs stretched; her hair felt as if someone was pulling it; then she felt like a balloon and someone had taken all the air out of her. When she looked at Thorn, Seven had to cover her mouth to keep from screaming. Her body contorted, shifted, grew, and shrunk rapidly until finally Thorn looked . . . she looked . . .

"You look like one of the Witches of Heartbreak Cove!" Seven whispered.

Thorn chuckled. "So do you. I used some of my old fan art sketches to fashion these illusions."

Thorn's hair had grown well past her shoulders, in cascading raven waves. Her eyes had gone from their deep blue to pitch-black, her lips the shape of a heart. Seven couldn't tell what she looked like, but her hair felt short and straight, her body long like she was a grown-up. It was toadally weird.

"Don't worry, it's not archaic magic like the Hat of Deceit. I can't, like, make myself into another real witch or steal someone's identity or anything. But made-up witches . . . those aren't off-limits. Learned all about it in costura training."

"Froggin'," Seven said in awe.

"Come on." Thorn grabbed Seven's hand and the two Witchlings stood up, strolling toward Pavoroso Passage with their newfound long legs.

Seven wobbled slightly, unused to the height, but Thorn moved with the ease and grace of a practiced grown-up, so Seven held on to her friend as they walked and it kept her steady.

Finally, they approached the stone building nestled in the leafless trees at the end of Pavoroso Passage. It used to be an empty, spooky lot, but now it held something much more sinister.

In the history of the Twelve Towns, only one prison had ever existed—the Tombs on Pollepel Island. It was reserved for the most gruesome of criminals, the ones who had proven they did not wish to be better, that they, in fact, would do anything to be worse. But things in the Twelve Towns were changing. Seven had read about dungeons being built in Castle Point, even in Crones Cliff Manor, and now, thanks to the anti-Spare laws, there was one in Ravenskill.

Spares were thrown in there for anything from trying

to go into a business where they weren't welcome, to staying out past the new Spare curfew, to being in public spaces without an employer within a ten-toadstool vicinity, or simply for laughing too loudly and being reported for disturbing the peace-and-quiet laws embedded into the anti-Spare legislation. It seemed even being joyful, even *existing* as a Spare, was breaking the law.

But there was one prisoner in the dungeon who most definitely was not a Spare. That the prison existed in Ravenskill at all made Seven feel sick, but the fact that the witch who had hexed Valley was being held in there . . . well, it made her want to set fire to the enchanted stone that kept the prisoners inside. And now, Seven would have to temper her anger because they were going to speak to the very witch who had turned her friend into stone: Lotus Evenstar.

But as they prepared to head into the dungeon—

"He couldn't be visiting her . . . There's . . . no way, right?" Thorn asked.

Mr. Pepperhorn, Valley's father and a major butt-toad, was exiting, looking all around as he did, and then slipping into the shadows. He kept looking back, paranoid about something. Seven had done enough sneaking around of her own to know when someone else was sneaking.

Lotus had hexed his *daughter*. Had he gone there to berate her? Or to . . .

It was one thing for Mr. Pepperhorn to be terrible, and he was—no-good, rotten, and terrible. Seven wished she could say for sure he would never go see the witch who had turned Valley into stone, but . . .

Could *he* be working with Lotus?

If he was really visiting her, Seven might just explode with rage.

They wouldn't be sure what he had been up to in there unless Lotus gave him up, but one thing was clear: Mr. Pepperhorn was acting suspicious. And who better to know a cure for the hex, who more likely to know who was disappearing Spares, than Lotus Evenstar. This plan might have been a good one after all.

"Let's go," Seven said, and they made their way into the prison.

For the first time since the night Valley had been stonified, they were going to be face-to-face with her hexer.

CHAPTER TEN
THE EVENSTAR LEGACY

SEVEN AND THORN SWEPT into the Ravenskill dungeon in their disguises. It was a dark stone building, skinny and so tall that when you looked up, the tippy top of the structure got lost in the clouds. Jonafren had told them all about this place; it was as deep as it was skyscraping, unlike a typical Twelve Towns dungeon that was only ever underground. There had been many protests from Ravenskillians and a bitter fight between council members about its construction, but then it just seemed to . . . appear overnight. After months of fighting, and with the Hill Society providing guards and arguing that it would be more work to take it down than let it stand, the witches who had been against the dungeon were worn into submission. What the Hill Society and their allies hadn't expected, though, was for Lotus Evenstar to be thrown in among the Spares they wished to cast out of their town.

They had argued for her freedom, called her a true

Twelve Townian, whatever that meant. Some of them—Mrs. Dimblewit and her awful niece Aphra, to be precise—had the nerve to call Lotus a *hero*. Seven supposed that most anyone who stood for something could be seen as a hero. What *was* a hero but someone who fought for the things you also believed in? Even if those things were evil. To the Hill Society, the Witchlings were far from heroes, but to many in the towns, especially to Spares, they were champions. Lotus Evenstar, the witch who had turned the fierce Valley Pepperhorn into stone, was theirs.

"Visiting hours are over in fifteen minutes," said a witch guard dressed in a stiff brown uniform.

"We will only be a moment," Seven said, trying to sound older.

The guard looked them over, eyes narrowed. "You two look familiar . . ."

Of course this guard would be a Witches of Heartbreak Cove reader. Seven held in a groan.

"We get that a lot. Heartbreak Cove fans." Thorn shrugged.

The guard smiled, disarmed by Thorn. "I cannot wait for the next book, but I figured it would be a while because of, well, you know." The guard gave them a conspiratorial wink and suddenly, Seven wondered if there was a way to make sure this witch specifically didn't get to read the fourth installment of Quill's series. Her issues with Mr. Pepperhorn were treated like fun gossip, but Seven knew firsthand just how painful it had been.

Thorn cleared her throat. "Since we only have fifteen minutes . . ."

"Right, right!" the guard said, coming out from behind the desk. "Who did you want to see?"

"Lotus Evenstar," Seven said.

"Hm, popular today, isn't she?" the guard grumbled.

"Have there been many other visitors to see her today?" Thorn asked, flashing a knowing look at Seven as they followed the guard down a shadowy stone walkway.

"A few." The guard coughed. "All of 'em rotten."

"Like Mr. Pepperhorn?" Seven asked, pushing through her nerves.

The guard chuckled nervously but said no more. They went deeper into the dungeon, passing door after heavy door, the guard conjuring a different key for each and then disappearing it with a twirl of his wrist right after. This witch didn't look like he could stop anyone trying to get in or out of a prison, but Seven realized why he'd been given the job—it took strong magic and skill to open and close these dungeon doors.

"Right through there. You've only got ten minutes left; don't go over or you'll get locked in here overnight," the guard said.

"What?!" Seven and Thorn asked in tandem.

The guard shrugged. "Not up to me. Walls are enchanted."

"We'll make sure to leave before that happens," Thorn said, her voice squeaky with fear.

Seven and Thorn walked toward a solitary cell at the

end of a long, narrow passageway. There, on the other side of iron bars, stood Lotus Evenstar. She was painting, her back to the Witchlings. Her long powder-blue hair fell in loose curls over a scratchy-looking gray tunic that reached her ankles. She was nothing like the elegant, well-dressed witch they had met during the Golden Frog Games, on the team that nearly beat Thorn's, but she still stood with an air of authority and power.

With Lotus's back still to them, it was time for the riskiest part of their plan. Seven subtly waved her hand and whispered the tricky, not always reliable spell for truth—verdad—in Lotus's direction. Seven wiped her hands on her cloak and took a deep breath as they walked on. She could only implore the Stars that their spell had worked.

Lotus turned around at the sound of their footsteps, revealing *what* she was painting: the Nightbeast.

Seven tried her best not to react, but inside, everything roared with terror and the urge to protect her monstruo friend.

"Hello," Lotus said, hitching an eyebrow.

"Lotus Evenstar?" Seven said, trying to keep her voice level. She didn't know how she would feel seeing the witch again after all these months, but the Nightbeast's low, ominous growl in her mind summed it up pretty froggin' well.

"That's my name, yes. What can I help you with?"

"We're from the Hill Society," Seven said.

"Oh?" Lotus asked, her face amused. "You work as quickly as they promised, then. Good."

Who were "they"? Seven thought, nervous shivers threatening to take over.

"Well, for starters I'd like to be moved to Crones Cliff Manor. The cells there are in better condition and my parents know the guards. Are you writing this down?" Lotus held a paintbrush in one hand and a palette floated beside her easel.

How hadn't they seen her for who she was before? A spoiled, mean-spirited witch. A killer witch.

"Yes, of course," Thorn said before giving Seven a panicked look. They weren't in their normal robes, didn't have their schoolbooks or pens.

"I'll remember," Seven said, tapping her temple. "Good memory."

Lotus narrowed her eyes. "Very well, then. Better accommodations, of course. Better clothing; this is making my skin break out in hives. Oh, and *organic* honey for my morning toast. The kind from Liliprune's Shoppe is the only one that will do."

"Accommodations, clothing, organic honey, got it," Seven said.

"We ran into Mr. Pepperhorn on his way out," Thorn said. "I trust he's been helpful?"

Bold move, Thorn.

"Somewhat. I've gotten a fair amount of support. Not as much as I deserve, but Mr. Pepperhorn has been useful."

He *had* come to see her, then. How could he? After what she'd done to Valley? It seemed there was no dungeon he wouldn't sink to. Mr. Pepperhorn was lower than low.

Lotus dropped her paintbrush and came up against the bars, wrapping her hands around the metal as she did. Seven nearly stepped back, but held steady, with Thorn doing the same by her side.

"You know . . . they haven't trusted me with the full plan." Lotus looked incensed now. "For some reason I'm not worthy of knowing. I'm too much of a risk, they said," Lotus whispered as if she were gossiping with old friends. "Mr. Pepperhorn assured me they're doing all they can to get me out of this Stars-forsaken place, but if they do not trust me, how can I trust them?"

Seven tried to push past the haze of her own rage to remember this particular part. There was a plan, and someone was keeping it from Lotus. This was the second time she'd mentioned a group, a they, but who were they?

"Surely, you don't mean the Hill Society," Seven tried, and Lotus rolled her eyes.

"Of course not, *you*! Did the Hill send their biggest fools to check on me?"

Seven's stomach dropped; had she just pushed Lotus too far?

"Our apologies," Thorn choked out, and Seven could feel how much effort it took for her to say it.

"Do you at least have an update on my sentencing?" Lotus sneered.

Seven and Thorn shook their heads in unison.

Lotus dropped her hands and let out an exasperated

breath. “Does *anyone* in this Stars-forsaken town know what they’re doing? I’ve been assured you all would be doing everything you could to stop the Committee on Magical Misdeeds from going forward with their plans, but . . .” Lotus leaned in close and whispered the next part. “Do not dare repeat this, and I know I am not one to speak, but what are our Five Families even *good* for if they cannot get me out, you know?”

Our Five Families? Seven had never heard that phrase used before.

“Absolutely,” Thorn said, agreeing with Lotus though Seven was sure she had no clue what she was agreeing to.

“They’re planning on sentencing me to evaporation with no chance of reversal during my high court appearance.” Lotus shook her head. “At least, that’s what they’re saying in the council,” she said, smiling deviously. “*We* know they do not always get their way. Especially if Mr. Pepperhorn has anything to say about it. He’s quite the powerful man, you know. Despite recent unfortunate troubles.”

“Indeed,” Seven said, trying to match her evil energy, but feeling sick to her stomach.

Evaporation was a death sentence. You would turn into millions of tiny, shimmering lights known as Stardust. Then you’d float up to *meet* the Stars, who would decide your fate in the afterworlds. Seven did not think anything good was waiting for Lotus there.

“Perhaps if you show more remorse? I know the council are . . . suckers for tears?” Thorn tried.

Lotus laughed. "You're right about that. And trust me, I've tried, but it's hard to pretend, you know? I'm glad I killed River. She was a rotten witch, too good at everything. Valley, well, I made an example of *her*, didn't I?" Lotus laughed. "I showed the Twelve Towns what happens to Spare brats who cross *true* witches. Her father deserves a better daughter than her."

Seven felt Thorn shift, and she had to do everything in her power not to lunge at Lotus.

"You're getting enough to eat?" Seven asked, changing the subject because the alternative might just be striking Lotus down where she stood.

Lotus shrugged. "I suppose. If you count the common food they give me. But I insist on the organic honey; truly, it is the very least you could do for me."

Because the Hill Society owed her. They were happy with what she had done. They might as well be her accomplices.

"And no one has badgered you about the cure—for the stonified witches, I mean," Seven tried.

It was a tricky thing to ask, but perhaps if they framed it as trying to protect Lotus from harassment, she wouldn't get too suspicious.

Lotus shook her head and picked at her tunic, looking bored.

"Do you know the cure? Just out of curiosity, of course," Seven said.

Lotus cocked her head at them. Had the truth spell worked? Were they about to find out how to free Valley and the other stonified witches? Seven was sure that every prisoner, even in the deepest levels of this dungeon, could hear her heart pounding in her chest.

"We think it's froggin' cool. Not just any witch could do that," Thorn said.

A satisfied smile spread across Lotus's face. "That is quite true."

"Tell us the cure; we're so curious," Seven tried, praying to the Stars her spell had worked.

"No, why would . . ." Lotus inspected them closely. "You two are from the Hill Society, you said? What household, then?"

Rats. The truth spell hadn't worked.

"I'm from the Mango family and she's a Silverfinch," Thorn said quickly.

Lotus nodded slowly but was still staring at them intently. "I don't know the cure. And even if I did, I wouldn't tell anyone. You never know who could be listening."

"Of course." Seven nodded but her heart sank into her boots.

Lotus licked her lips, then smiled, and Seven noticed for the first time just how sharp her teeth were.

"I thank you, truly, for coming to see me. It's not easy to be here among so much Spare scum. My own family has been reluctant to come because of public perception, but I got word they were proud. They're commissioning a fairly large portrait of me for the notable ancestry wing of our estate, you know."

Lotus was a monstruo. Not like the ones Seven spoke

to and cared for, but a true, villainous monstruo. She was what witches should really be afraid of instead of Spares and Nightbeasts and creatures who had no power. This rich, powerful girl, who no one had judged or suspected, perhaps because of the very wealth she boasted about. Or perhaps it was her youth, her skill, or her beauty . . . maybe all these things had allowed her to go unnoticed as she hexed witches and conspired with killers.

It seemed that true monstruos were rarely the ones witches warned about—they were often the witches you least suspected.

"And you're not sorry?" Thorn asked, her voice low and filled with a pain she could no longer hold back. "You didn't know Valley, but River, wasn't she your friend?"

Lotus scoffed. "I'm quite glad Spares are finally getting what they deserve, and to know I had the *honor* of playing a role in their downfall? It makes it all that much sweeter. If I had to kill River to achieve our goals, so be it. It will be my legacy, my family's legacy, restoring *balance*," Lotus hissed. "What could be more important than that? So no, I'm not sorry at all."

Thorn was shaking now, and Seven knew they couldn't take any more of this. She grabbed her friend's hand and made to leave.

"We'll be sure to tell the Hill Society your requests, goodbye." She turned, Thorn by her side, and they were practically sprinting down the hall when Lotus called out.

"Seven Salazar?"

Her voice, cruel and chilling, made them both stop in their tracks.

"And that means you must be Thorn. I thought it might be you."

"Don't let her provoke you," Seven said.

"I relish the chance to fight you again, but rest assured next time it will be you that I drown like River. It will be you that I hex like your friend," Lotus screeched.

Before Seven could respond, Thorn had turned, one hand up, and Seven was sure she was about to strike. Their disguises fell away then, revealing them to Lotus, who only smiled her pointy-toothed smile at them.

"Don't!" Seven said, surprised at her own restraint.

"Seven, I can't do this. I can't just watch her gloat about hurting Valley." Thorn's voice was shaky, filled with the rage and pain Seven knew all too well.

"You're giving her what she wants. Let's just go. She's going to be evaporated anyway," Seven said.

Thorn nodded, and just as she lowered her hand, Lotus called out again.

"Before you go, know this—I will get my chance to make you pay for putting me in this hole. Know that every night, I pray to the Stars that Valley never returns simply because I hate her, I hate you, and I hate all Spares *so* much that I take joy in praying for your demise. The truth is though, there is no need for me to pray to the Stars at all. What is done cannot be undone."

At this, Seven turned back around. "What is that supposed to mean?"

Lotus threw her head back and laughed. "Your little friend will never be cured! Because there *is* no cure. Valley will be stone forever!"

The color red flooded Seven's vision, the Nightbeast howled in her mind, and in moments, much too quickly to be normal, Seven was face-to-face with Lotus again. Her hands were up toward the witch, and ready to do what she had to do to avenge Valley. Seven would turn Lotus into Stardust herself.

"STAND DOWN!" The guard from the entrance and two others were suddenly on her and pulling her away. Another guard was holding Thorn back as Lotus's laughter, haunting and dripping with joy, followed them all the way out of the Ravenskill dungeon.

CHAPTER ELEVEN
A CONSPIRACY OF WITCHES

AS THEY BOLTED from the dungeon, Seven's raccoons appeared, teeth bared and ready to attack. Overhead, a swarm of skeleton birds cawed, asking Seven if she needed their claws. And from the edges of the Cursed Forest, flor culebras threatened venom with every hiss. Eyes, both tiny and enormous, blinked from within the shadows of the trees—the monstruos sensed Seven's fury, and were ready to respond with their own.

Loudest of all was the Nightbeast, whose howl echoed through the cold winter sky. Hearing the thunderous roar of the beast, witches looked up and all around, and seeing the skeleton birds above, they ran for cover, ducking into shops and their homes.

"Seven, tell them to back off," Thorn urged. "And breathe, Seven, breathe."

"Sorry, ugh, I'm sorry," Seven said, and took a long, deep breath. "I am okay," she told the Nightbeast. "I don't need your help right now."

With that, the monstruos seemed to relax a bit, the skeleton birds flew off, and the hum of danger from the Cursed Forest subsided.

Seven was holding on to Thorn's arm as they hustled into Evanora's Tea Room.

"You need a lavender calming tea, and fast," Thorn said as they sat down near the window.

Snow began to fall the moment they sat down, and Thorn ordered them both large teas. "Piping hot, please, with an extra calming cube for each," she said as she undid her chunky knit scarf.

"You okay?" Thorn asked Seven as they settled in.

"I think so. Just . . . angry. I'm so angry. How could Lotus not even be sorry for what she did?"

"Not just unremorseful, but proud." Thorn shook her head.

Seven slammed a fist on the table. Witches in cozy booths glanced in their direction and Seven smiled awkwardly. "Sorry," she said.

The barista brought them their teas, and just the smell of the lavender was enough to soothe Seven's anger a little. She took long, slow sips, and bit by bit, Seven's heartbeat slowed, her skin returned to a normal temperature, and the thought of Lotus didn't make her head feel like it was going to explode.

"Thanks," she said, putting her cup down. "I really needed that."

"Me too," Thorn said. "Think you can talk about what just happened *without* conjuring the Cursed Forest?"

Seven laughed. "I'm pretty sure? But no promises the Nightbeast won't crash in through the window."

"You joke, but remember the Uncle trials last year . . ."

"Yeah, yeah," Seven said, remembering all too well how she'd accidentally summoned the Nightbeast to an enormous stadium filled with Twelve Townians and had almost gotten half of them killed.

"Lotus," Thorn said, refocusing the conversation. "Do you really think she could get out?"

"Not sure, but if Mr. Pepperhorn and the rest of the Hill Society are helping her, who knows? I've even heard rumors that the Hill Society is working on getting Mr. Dimblewit out of prison, so why not Lotus? They play and live by a different set of rules than the rest of us."

Thorn nodded. "Who else do you think is helping her? She said something about five families?"

"That was confusing. She said 'our Five Families' like it was a thing. I've never heard anyone use that phrase before though."

"Me either," Thorn said. "Lotus also kept saying 'they.' I wonder if she was talking about whoever the Five Families are or maybe . . ."

Seven leaned back in her chair, calm enough now that she could finally put together the things they'd heard. Lotus's anger and confidence had perhaps made her betray more than she'd meant to.

"It's not the Hill Society, she said, so it could be whoever these Five Families she mentioned are, or those veiled witches maybe," Seven said. "It would make the most sense, right? They're not being shy about how much they loathe Spares."

"That's true." Thorn took a sip of her tea and considered this dilemma. "If Lotus wasn't in the dungeon right now, she'd be suspect number one for all this. She hates us, that much is clear, and she's working with Mr. Pepperhorn, who detests Spares so much he's willing to betray his own daughter to work with the witch who hexed her."

"Not to mention the Hill Society; they're the very ones behind the anti-Spare laws," Seven said.

"So if Lotus is in the dungeon, and can't be behind the disappearances, that means the most likely culprit is . . . her accomplice," Thorn said.

"Flingo," Seven said. "Just like someone taught her archaic magic, I'd bet the fur on the raccoons' butts that's exactly who's behind all this."

"One thing's for sure: Mr. Pepperhorn is trying to help Lotus, which means he's involved somehow and probably knows something. We have to keep a close eye on him."

"What about the veiled witches?" Thorn asked.

"Maybe we can ask our friends to help. The twins and Graves can keep an eye on them. I think Mr. Pepperhorn might just be the witch we've been looking for, the other hexer, the one who taught Lotus archaic magic. Maybe he's been behind all this from the start."

CHAPTER TWELVE

A NOT-SO-VEILED THREAT

WHEN THE WITCHLINGS finally left Evanora's Tea Room to head home, Ravenskill was in absolute disarray. The line outside the Hall of Elders complaint window had more than doubled, with angry Hill residents demanding to know where their Spares had gone. Just as Seven had suspected, nobody *actually* cared about the missing Spares, at least not the majority of the town. The majority of the Ravenskillians she saw were upset about their own kid being made into a Spare or that their cook or cleaner or gardener Spare had gone missing and there was nobody to tend to their sprawling mansions or children. Witches were protesting the Gran, witches were protesting the Stars, witches were protesting Seven, Thorn, and Valley, which was interesting when they walked past them as quickly as they could.

"Awkward," said Thorn.

"Tell me about it," Seven said, bumping into a witch holding a sign with *her* face on it covered by an enormous red X. She couldn't get out of there fast enough.

Suddenly, witches rushed past them, nearly knocking Seven and Thorn over. They ran, some of them holding their protest signs, some of them following with looks of curiosity on their faces, all going toward a crowd of gathering witches down the road.

"What's going on?" Thorn asked.

"Let's go find out for ourselves," Seven said, and they walked toward the throng of witches.

There at the center of a group of Ravenskillians were the veiled witches. They stood in a perfectly straight row, the one they called Master Beetle at the center. It wasn't clear what they were doing, and Seven was prepared to strike them down if she needed to, but then Master Beetle stepped forward and cleared his throat.

"Good witches of Ravenskill, we thank you for gathering here with us today. On this glorious afternoon, we'd like to relay to you the findings of our investigation."

The crowd murmured in confusion.

"What investigation?" Thorn whispered, but Seven could not take her eyes off Master Beetle. She had a feeling that whatever these weird witches were up to, it was beyond bad.

"We come to you with a warning about the disappearing Spares and the so-called Red Moon Ceremony . . . and most importantly, the balance of our magic world."

More murmurs from the crowd. Seven shook her head. *What was their obsession with balance?*

"We, being *experts* of course, believe that order and

balance are the foundation of our towns; if we lose those two things, we lose everything. And after a thorough investigation we have concluded that the magical balance in the Twelve Towns and beyond is at risk of critical failure at any moment."

"How are you so sure?" called a witch from the crowd.

"It's simple, really. How else would you explain every new Witchling being deemed a Spare? Or Spares who can become *Uncles* . . ." Master Beetle's strange face swept over Seven and Thorn, and Thorn squeezed Seven's arm. "Witches being turned into stone, and purple rain, and flying capes . . . There is no other way to interpret this precarious situation but to admit . . . our magic is broken." Master Beetle held up his gloved hands to calm the growing chaos.

The witches all around Seven and Thorn seemed to consider this. Some of them nodded in agreement; some of them whispered worriedly. Seven clenched her fists angrily. These veiled witches were causing harm and confusion with their supposed investigation.

Master Beetle continued. "So, you see, it is a good thing that some excess Spares have been disappearing. Indeed, this is the way that order and balance are being upheld! Now it is our responsibility to ensure that we do not undo this small restoration of balance. We must uphold our traditions, our culture, so that our magic can continue to repair itself. In other words . . . Spares must know their place. It is the only way to ensure the preservation of our magic."

Seven could take no more of these lies. He thought it was *good* that Pixel was missing?! She pushed her way through the crowd, Thorn trailing her, and they both emerged face-to-face with the veiled witches.

"Where's your proof, then?" Seven asked.

The veil on Master Beetle's face warped and shifted, what passed for a smile on his peculiar non-face.

"Ah, young Seven Salazar! One of the *culprits* in our magical imbalance!"

"Where. Is. Your. PROOF?!" Seven screamed, and she felt the crowd behind her take a step back. Only Thorn stood steadfast at her side, and though Valley was not physically there, somewhere inside Seven, she could feel her.

Her raccoons appeared suddenly at the edge of the crowd, their little paws up, their teeth bared. And in the distance, the familiar, comforting sound of the Nightbeast's growl hummed in her ears.

"Now, now." Master Beetle held one hand up. "This is the very display of unbridled anger that landed us here in the first place! What an *abomination* a Spare Uncle is to our fair towns!"

"You haven't answered my question," Seven said, unmoved by Master Beetle's attempts to humble her. "You have no proof. Why should any of us believe you when we cannot even see your faces?"

Master Beetle twitched. All the veiled witches did. Seven turned around to see that the crowd of witches had only grown in size since she and Thorn had arrived here, and many of them looked just as angry as she was, their eyes pinned on the veiled witches. She spotted Miss Dewey and Ambert near the front, a few of their classmates and professors too, all nodding at Seven. They were on her side.

"Who are you anyway?!" someone screamed from the crowd to indignant cheers of agreement.

"Well, we, I . . ." Master Beetle stammered, and a satisfied grin spread across Seven's face.

"We shall return with your proof, Seven Salazar," Master Beetle seethed. "And when we do, you will be sorry."

CHAPTER THIRTEEN

RETURN TO RAVENSKILL THEATER

"THERE'S SOMETHING LOTUS, Mr. Pepperhorn, and those freaky veiled witches all have in common," Thorn said as they made their way to the Ravenskill Theater that night. Thankfully, the Spare curfew did not apply to Seven as an Uncle, and she could cover for Thorn should the Gran's Guard give them a hard time.

"They're all absolute geese?" Seven asked.

"Well, yes, that, but one more thing," Thorn said, a knowing look in her eyes. "Think: What did Lotus talk about that's the same thing Mr. Pepperhorn and that cult seem *so* preoccupied with?"

Seven stopped walking and went over their conversation with Lotus; then her eyes opened wide. "Balance!"

Thorn nodded. "Balance, they're all obsessed with it. So if anyone is trying to get rid of an 'excess' of Spares, it would be them."

"You're right," Seven said as they walked on. "The Black Moon Ceremony is supposed to keep balance in our world by putting us all in a proper coven or sorting us as Spares. If the Black Moon Ceremony has stopped providing that balance, then maybe they've taken it into their own hands."

"By making Spares disappear," Thorn said.

"I bet they're all working together. The veiled cult and Mr. Pepperhorn must be the witches helping Lotus," Seven said. "But that still doesn't explain who the Five Families are."

"First, let's see if any of your animal friends know something about Pixel. Maybe they saw Mr. Pepperhorn or the cult doing something weird at the theater," Thorn said.

Pixel was last seen running to the theater, going to retrieve gloves. Seven hoped there was something they could find there, or an animal that could help them trace her.

With the veiled witches and the crowd they'd gathered long gone, the Gran's Guard dispersed as well. The Witchlings found the side door actors used after shows, and Seven raised her hands toward the lock.

"You gonna break the whole door again?" Thorn whispered.

Seven smiled. "Not this time. Hopefully. You might want to duck though."

"Oh brother." Thorn pulled her cloak hood on and crouched into a ball next to Seven.

"Llave maestra," Seven intoned, and the ground rumbled around them.

"What's happening?!" Thorn asked.

"Not sure, first time trying this one."

"Oh my goats, Seven!"

Small gray sticks sprouted from the ground and flew together in a tiny tornado until they formed a key and landed in Seven's hand. Except they weren't sticks at all. They were bones.

Thorn stood up, looking at the small, elegant skeleton key lying in Seven's palm.

"Seven . . . what's going on? This is a different kind of magic . . . magic I don't recognize."

It's monstruo magic, Seven wished she could say, but she was scared of how Thorn would feel. Of scaring her. Even though this spell was made from the bones of small rodents long passed and it made them a useful part of nature again, which was the goal of any living thing in the Twelve Towns—to be a part of something, to be useful. But nobody would understand that; they would only accuse Seven of forbidden magic or cast her out of Ravenskill. They would fear her and what her magic could do, and lately, Seven wasn't so sure they'd be wrong for that fear. As much as she hated Master Beetle and all that he stood for, she couldn't promise that her magic *wasn't* dangerous.

"It's nothing," Seven said. "Nothing you have to worry about."

"Tell her." The Nightbeast spoke. "Tell her that you are just like me."

"Seven . . ." Thorn tried, a worried look in her eyes,

but Seven just took the key and opened the door quietly, stopping the conversation as they snuck inside. She couldn't handle that conversation right now. It could wait.

The theater was pitch-black, and Thorn intoned a farolito spell. She held a blue light in her hand like a lantern as she took the lead through the dark theater. They wove through the aisles and toward the stairs that led to the balcony where they had sat on the night of the ceremony. Thankfully, the entrance to the balcony was unlocked, and they walked back out into the cold night.

"It's scary up here," Thorn said, and Seven couldn't help but agree. It looked quite different from how it had the night of the ceremony, dark and ominous instead of bright and glittering. Could something have happened to Pixel up here?

They searched the area for signs of anything—a struggle, gloves, anything the Guards might have missed, however unlikely. There didn't seem to be anything broken or out of place, but still Seven noted everything on the balcony, the chairs, the scuff marks on the ground, the leaves that had accumulated from the trees—she wrote everything down in her notebook as Thorn took pictures. This might, after all, be a crime scene. She really hoped not, but they had to be prepared for anything.

A pigeon landed on the stone railing and hopped over to them.

"Hello," Seven said.

"Are you not the Uncle?" the pigeon asked.

"I am. Seven Salazar, nice to meet you."

"Very nice to meet you, coooo, my name is Blueberry. Have you seen my eggs? They're right up there, you might like to see them." She gestured toward the corner of the theater, above the balcony.

"Oh, congratulations," Seven said, and Blueberry cooed again. Birds, and especially pigeons, were very proud of their eggs. It was in her Uncle training module on avian friends.

"May I ask you a few questions?" Seven asked.

Blueberry got into roosting position, her little legs tucked under her fluffy feathers, and nodded. "Most certainly, Uncle. Especially if it is about my eggs."

"Were you here the night of the Black Moon Ceremony?" Seven asked.

"Yes, of course. With my eggs. This is a wonderful spot to lay eggs. Do Uncles lay eggs? Might you want to use this spot someday?"

"Oh, um, no, I don't think I'll need to, but I appreciate the offer." Seven held in a smirk.

Blueberry rustled her feathers and scrunched her little eyes happily. "Happy to, happy to offer."

"Did you see this witch?" Seven asked, holding up a picture of Pixel on her portaphone.

"Oh, yes, I do believe so. She was running up here looking for something."

"Gloves," said Seven.

"What are gloves?" the pigeon asked.

"I'll . . . show you later. Did you see what happened to her?"

Blueberry cooed, then shook her feathers again. "She ran up here after everyone had gone and I thought I would get peace and quiet. She was wearing a red sweater. Oh, I liked it a lot. I'd like some of the thread for my nest."

"Then what?" Seven asked the pigeon eagerly.

"It was cloudy and there was a storm on the winds, so I expected rain. Then there was a loud boom, like many, many eggs dropping at once, oh dear! The earth quaked ever so quickly. *My* eggs almost fell! But they did not. They are safe. My baby birds will be hatching soon; maybe you can meet them."

"I would love to meet them." Seven smiled at the sweet pigeon. "Do you know what else happened with the witch in the red sweater?"

The pigeon cooed again. "I'm afraid I did not see. I was fretting over my eggs. I am sorry."

"No, it's okay, this was helpful," Seven said, relaying what she'd found out to Thorn.

"Anything else she noticed?" Thorn asked.

Seven translated.

"Just the strange rain. It glowed purple, did you see?" Blueberry said.

"I did." Seven nodded.

"Come, come." Blueberry was suddenly up, flying beside Seven and nudging her toward the door.

"I . . . Blueberry . . ." Seven said, when Blueberry stopped and Seven was face-to-face with a neat little nest perched in a corner of a stained glass window.

"I present to you . . . my eggs," Blueberry said proudly.

From beside her, Thorn shot Seven a confused look.

"Blueberry wants us to look at her eggs." Seven smiled sheepishly.

The two Witchlings looked at the eggs carefully; they were lovingly surrounded by pieces of fluff, sticks, and one shimmering rainbow stone.

"Ooh," Thorn said, going to pick up the stone, but before she could, Blueberry was on top of her eggs, wings flapping.

"Please, young miss, do not disturb my babies," Blueberry said.

"What did I do?" Thorn asked, horrified.

"She's just being protective, don't worry," Seven said. "Thanks for helping, Blueberry. Your eggs are very lovely."

The pigeon preened. "Will you come visit me again?"

"We will, I promise. Good luck with your eggs, they're very beautiful."

Blueberry cooed and Seven and Thorn made their way out of the theater and into the night.

CHAPTER FOURTEEN

A FAMILIAR STRANGER

NESTLED IN THE DEEP DARK of the Cursed Forest, Seven felt her safest. Here there were no threats against her. There were no malicious words or cutting glances. Here she was far from the reminder that so many in their world hated her. And most importantly, here she was one step closer to a cure for the stone hex. Hopefully.

She wore a dark cloak, witch's hat, and rucksack. A giant walking stick helped her navigate the terrain as she mapped out all the corners of the Cursed Forest. Because so few witches dared to venture deep into the forest, there were no maps of all its landmarks. Not even Uncles of the past had done it, which made something inside Seven bubble with anger. They were missing out on the luminescent pond filled with jelly bean fish on the south end of the forest, and the elaborately carved and ancient birdhouses high up in the twisted oaks.

But most of all, it vexed Seven that they didn't know of all the monstruos who never left these folds of darkness.

There were dragon birds with silk-tipped wings who used their fire to light long-forgotten hearths to keep the duendes warm on frigid nights, furantulas that braided and combed one another's long hair and sang sweetly at night. And there were hundreds of wild raccoons that were just as funny and loyal as her own.

Her raccoons had been keeping a close eye on Mr. Pepperhorn, and she got word from them that he'd gone on a trip up north that very morning. They would have to wait for him to return to continue looking into his movements, but with every passing hour, Seven became more convinced that Valley's father was the other hexer. That *he* was behind the disappearances and that not even his own daughter was enough to quell his hatred of Spares.

"Ah, here," Seven said, finding the next ingredient on her list—sap from a dragon's blood tree. She would need a few more ingredients for the stone-eating sludge she was brewing to free Valley and the others, but so far so good.

Seven bottled the sap into a glass vial and tucked it safely into her rucksack before heading out of the Cursed Forest.

She made her way back home, praying to the Stars neither of her parents or, worse, Beefy, was still awake. He'd scream with happiness any time he thought Seven might be near, and that would wake up the entire neighborhood.

She made it to her house in record time, but what she saw when she got there stopped her in her tracks. There was someone, a hooded someone, peering into her living room window.

Seven put her hands up, prepared to fight, when the figure turned around and she gasped. There in front of her was someone she had not seen in person in months: Figgs Moonchild. Seven ran to him without thinking and threw her arms around him. He hugged her back, and when she stepped away, Seven's cheeks got hot. *I just hugged Figgs, oh my goats! Wait till Thorn hears about this.*

But after her initial shock at seeing him, Seven noticed how hollow his cheeks were, how dark the bags under his eyes were. Even his clothes, once pristine and well tailored, were worn and patched.

"Figgs, are you okay?" she asked.

"No." He shook his head. "I'm not. I need . . . I need . . ."

There were tears in his eyes as he took one step toward Seven, but before he could reach her, Figgs passed out cold.

CHAPTER FIFTEEN

NOT A BAD WITCH

SEVEN PACED IN THE COZY wood-paneled waiting room, in the Bluewing Infirmary, where a fireplace was crackling and a few scattered witches were drinking hot cocoa from little paper cups.

"What's taking them so long?" she asked.

Fox patted her hand. "The healers are probably just being extra cautious. Let's wait and see what they say."

Before waking her parents, Seven called Cheese to help keep Figgs warm and safe. Seven used an enchantment to turn her clothing into her nighttime clothes: a house robe in place of her cloak, pajamas in place of her pants and sweater. Then she told a tiny lie—she'd heard a noise and went downstairs to investigate, when she found Figgs outside their door, passed out. Her parents were too distressed to notice that Seven had been wearing her witch's hat with her pajamas. Fox had driven them right to the infirmary,

Talis staying behind with Beefy, and now they were waiting.

"I hope he's okay. I'm worried," Seven said.

She wished she could tell her mom about the look of pain in Figgs's eyes, how desperate he seemed.

How had Figgs gotten there? What was the matter?

"He will be all right," Fox said. "He's young and will recover, I'm sure of it. He looked a bit . . . malnourished to me. Who is Figgs living with now?"

Seven went quiet. He had made her promise over portaphone not to tell anyone about his problems. He didn't want anyone feeling sorry for him, he had said.

"I'm . . . not sure," Seven said.

"Hmm," Fox said. "Come." She patted the seat next to her. "Tell me what you're afraid will happen."

"Well . . . I'm scared Figgs won't wake up. I'm scared he's been hexed or that . . . he's going to die."

Fox considered this for a moment. "Sweet pea, I don't think he's going to die. I'm no healer, but I saw him. He was breathing normally, and the doctors said there were no major signs of a hex. I might be wrong, but my best guess is Figgs is exhausted, hungry, and maybe a bit scared. I know what happened with River must not have been easy," Fox said.

"He is having a hard time." Seven looked down. "He's having trouble finding steady work, I think. Nobody wants to hire him because of what happened in the spring. They're treating him like he's cursed or something."

"Maybe Figgs will find another family to take him in.

One that will treat him with the love and respect he and all children deserve."

Seven smiled because she was lucky to have her mother. She wanted desperately for Figgs to have someone just like her for himself. "I hope so. Figgs is so nice and hardworking and funny." Seven's cheeks went a bit hot. She wasn't sure if her mom knew about her dragon-sized crush on Figgs, but knowing her, she probably knew before Seven even did. "I don't understand why these things keep happening to him. Why does he have to have such a hard life?"

Fox put her arm around Seven and pulled her close. "That's one of those questions that never really go away in life. Why is this happening to good people, to me, to the people I love . . . I've asked myself that a lot. The truth is, sometimes there's no answer; the Stars can be cruel and uncaring. And other times . . . there are parts of our world, our towns, that aren't set up to be just. People who are the most vulnerable, like Figgs, pay the price. One thing we can't do anything about: There will always be terrible things that happen to people who do not deserve it. The other . . . well, we can try, can't we? To make right the things those around us are determined to keep broken. But we must be brave. That is the key. We must be brave and we must look out for our neighbors. There is a great magic in numbers, my little one. Never forget that you and Valley and Thorn got through last year because you relied on one another."

Seven nodded, and she wondered if her mother and

father were trying in their own ways to make things better.

"I will ask around to see if anyone can take him in. Figgs is going to be okay, Seven. He's lucky to have you as a friend."

"Thanks, Mom," Seven said, and she stood up, melting into her mother's warm hug.

"Mrs. Salazar?" A healer's assistant stood at the entrance to the waiting room. She wore a long light blue tunic with matching pants, a small envelope hat trimmed in gold.

Seven and Fox both turned to her, and Seven's heart felt like it had stopped beating.

"Yes," Fox said. "I'm here."

"Figgs is awake." The healer's assistant smiled and Seven could breathe again. "You can go in and see him now. But only for a few minutes. He still needs a lot of rest."

Seven and her mother followed the witch down a long, warmly lit hallway to his room. Seven was eager to speak to him, so worried her stomach was in knots. When they reached the door, it took her a moment to reach for the handle. Then she turned toward Fox.

"Mom, do you mind if I—"

"Go." Fox nudged Seven softly. "I'm sure seeing a friend will raise his spirits."

Seven hugged her mother.

"I'll be right here if you need me," Fox said.

Seven opened the door and found Figgs in his bed,

sitting up and drinking something—probably honey drop flower tea, by the smell of it. It had a lot of healing properties. There was a hummingheart monitor beside him, a glass box with a hummingbird made of colorful light that kept track of a patient's heartbeat. It reminded Seven a bit of Almanac, Miss Dewey's familiar. The faster the wings of the hummingheart, the faster the heartbeat. There were also magical ciphers and symbols that scrolled across the screen that only healers were trained to read.

"Hey, Figgs," Seven said.

"Hello." Figgs smiled. He put his tea on the bedside table as Seven walked closer.

"You okay?"

"Who, me? Never been better. I like coming here once a year to relax."

"Liar." Seven cocked her head to the side, giving her most unimpressed face.

"I come all the way to Ravenskill, and this is the welcome I get?" Figgs put his hands behind his head and leaned back, a charming smirk on his face. But Seven wouldn't let him get away with pretending everything was okay. Not this time.

"Figgs . . ."

"I'm fine. Promise." Figgs ran his hands through his hair and tried his best to look like his old self, but Seven could see right through it. He was ghost pale, and when he sat up, Seven saw him flinch. He was struggling and she knew it.

"You didn't *look* fine. You passed out. How did you even get to Ravenskill in the first place?"

"I . . . snuck onto the train. It was a long trip and I had to cram into a small luggage closet, but I'm okay. Just tired is all."

"Did you forget Spares are going missing right now? It's not safe for you to be wandering around alone."

"Nothing happened," Figgs said.

Seven paused, choosing her next words carefully. "I feel like you're keeping something from me. We're friends, you shouldn't keep dangerous secrets."

Figgs was quiet then but gave Seven a knowing stare. She had to change the subject. *Fast.*

"Why did you do all that? Sneak onto a train and walk through Ravenskill alone at night? It's risky, you know," she blurted out.

"You do it all the time." Figgs gave a small smile.

"That's . . . different."

"Why?"

"Because. I can't . . . it's . . ."

"A secret?" Figgs asked.

Seven sat on the chair beside Figgs's bed and looked at him sadly. "Why are you being so weird? Did I do something wrong?"

"You're right, you're right. I . . . *am* keeping secrets. I didn't just sneak onto the train . . ." Figgs took a deep breath, like he was gathering strength to say something hard. "I got chased and had nowhere else to go."

"Who was chasing you?"

"The Gran's Guard. Because I stole, if you're wondering why. I can't live off well wishes, and nobody will hire me. So, I learned how to pick pockets."

Figgs lay back on his bed and stared at the ceiling. He stayed like that for a few moments, and then a tear streamed down his face. Figgs wiped it away quickly.

"You can trust me. I just wanna help."

Figgs sat up and let out a tired sigh. "There's nowhere I feel safe." He looked down. "I live in the remnants of a fire, alone, and I'm only fourteen. Have you ever thought about what it might feel like to live alone? What it's like to spend the Festival of the Holly King or your birthday by yourself? Whenever I leave my house now, people throw insults and horrible looks at me. Witches who have known me since I was a baby, who were friends with my parents once, talk about how I deserve to die because I'm a Spare. They say I'm unnatural and I shouldn't exist. All the while, I'm just trying to find a reason to stay alive, because every moment feels more hopeless than the last."

Now Figgs was sobbing. Seven reached out for his hand but he shook his head no, wiping his tears away in vain. Seven's heart felt like it was being stomped on by a giant. There were no clever words, no plant or potion that could fix this. Seven would swim to the deep dark of the Atlantis Ocean, she would brave the coldest winds on the highest mountains, to find the magic to make Figgs happy. She would go anywhere, do anything, if it meant he'd be okay.

"Why do they hate us for something we can't control, Seven? How are we supposed to grow up and live our lives when it feels like everyone just wants us dead?"

Seven shook her head, tears streaming down her face too. "I don't know."

Figgs was shaking now, his breathing jagged and the hummingheart beside his bed beeping wildly, the wings going so fast they were a blur.

"You should drink some cold water. Getting upset like this isn't good in your condition—" Seven started to get up.

"I'm not a bad witch!" Figgs said. He was looking around the room, desperate, as though if he said it loudly enough, desperately enough, it would fix things.

"Figgs, please." Seven stood up, watching the monitor flash yellow. She did not know what that meant but it didn't look good. She should call for a healer, she could call for her mom, but she was afraid to upset Figgs even more.

"I try my hardest to be good, to be kind, even when . . . even when my parents left me, I tried." Figgs beat his chest with his fist. "But there's only so much someone can take before they break. They are breaking me, Seven. The world is breaking me. And—" He let out an indignant laugh. "Maybe they're right, maybe I shouldn't exist. I'm a burden, that's all I've ever been." Figgs buried his head in his hands and cried, his shoulders heaving with every sob. Seven put her hand on his back and Figgs hugged her. He hugged her so tightly, Seven felt she might pass out. When his breathing returned to normal and the hummingheart had steadied, he let go. Seven flourished her hand, making an ice-cold cup of water appear on the tray by his bed.

"Maybe you should drink that." Seven gestured at the water.

Figgs nodded and took a sip, then his face turned puffy and red as he politely spat a brown liquid back into the cup. "You almost got it; it's toad sludge."

"Rats!" Seven said, shaking her head. What good was conjuring when it kept going wrong?

"You know, if someone catches you conjuring like that, you're toast."

Seven waved him away. "I've got bigger jelly bean fish to fry. Everything's a mess right now."

Figgs nodded. "Not just in Ravenskill. Check my cloak pocket."

Seven shot Figgs a curious look, then walked over to the chair where his old brown cloak was laid across the back. In one of his pockets, she found a packet of small papers.

"'New leadership now . . .' 'Down with the Grans . . .' 'The Twelve Towns need a chancellor . . .'?" Seven read the flyers. "What is all this? Where did you get them?"

"When I was trying to . . . find coins for food"—Figgs's face went bright red—"I sometimes found these in the pockets of the wealthier residents of Crones Cliff Manor. There are rumors of a witches' uprising against the Grans, and some are calling for new leadership."

"A chancellor?" Seven said, shaking her head. The Twelve Towns hadn't seen a leader like that since warlock days, where just one witch would run everything. It was an awful time for the towns, and Seven didn't know why anyone would want to relive it.

Figgs coughed, and Seven began to wave her hand to conjure actual water this time when Figgs put one hand up.

"No more of your 'water,' I'm okay," he said between coughs.

Seven pulled an extra blanket from the foot of the bed over Figgs, and soon his coughing died down. With his thin, worn-out cloak and holey shoes, he'd probably caught something out in the snow.

"You okay?" Seven asked.

Figgs nodded. "I actually feel more okay than I have in a while. I'm sorry I frogged out like that."

"You don't have to say sorry for having feelings. It's not like you yelled at *me*. You're also correct about everything. It's too hard living like this. You have every right to be angry."

Figgs looked down again.

"The Oracle told me something once: The witches who are against Spares want us desperate. They want us to fight one another and stay divided. That's why they're so cruel; they are trying to beat us down so we can't fight back. And you know what? I don't think Valley, Thorn, and I would've ever gotten through the impossible task if we didn't work together. That's why everyone on the Hill can't stand us; we did the one thing they hadn't expected us to do: stick together. I think maybe that's the only way we can win. Sticking together and not letting them break us. You can vent to me whenever you want, but only under one condition."

Figgs quirked an eyebrow.

"I need you to eat. And if you don't have anything to eat, ask for help. I want you to be honest when something's wrong so your friends can help. We can't grow up or be happy or fight back against the butt-toads who want us dead if we're passing out all over the place." Seven smiled and Figgs let out a small laugh.

"You gonna be honest too?" he asked.

Seven's face went hot and Figgs laughed again. Her cheeks were probably bright pink. "Umm, I'm working on it," Seven said.

"I'll take that," Figgs said.

"Can I ask you something?"

"Sure, you've already watched me have a breakdown, so."

"Is there anything I can do to help?"

Figgs smiled softly at her, and a moth fluttered in Seven's stomach. "Can you get me a new family?" Figgs laughed. "I'm kidding, I'm kidding. Just maybe keep being my friend? Even when I'm weird?"

Seven quirked an eyebrow playfully. "When aren't you weird?"

"You still like me though. Right? I don't think I could handle losing you too." Figgs looked into Seven's eyes and she felt she might explode into a million mini raccoons. Figgs's face was red, his eyes wide as if he couldn't even believe he had said that.

Someone knocked on the door and they both let out a little startled scream. Seven turned so quickly she got dizzy. She might be sick, actually—had Figgs actually just asked her that? What was she gonna say back? Oh my goats, HAD HER MOM HEARD THEM?

"Seven?" Fox popped her head in.

"We were just talking about friend stuff!" Seven blurted out.

Figgs barely held in a laugh. "Oh," Fox said. "Hi, Figgs. Are you feeling better?"

"Yes, ma'am," Figgs said, and his smile was dazzling, despite his condition. He was trying to fool her mom, but little did he know, her name wasn't Fox for nothing.

"Hmm, we'll see." Fox checked his forehead with her hand, the way she did when Seven was running a fever.

Figgs closed his eyes, and Seven noticed when he quickly wiped away another tear. He didn't get those mom moments—your mother checking on you after a rough day at school, making sure you ate, teaching you how to cook habichuelas just right.

"You're still a bit warm but I'm sure they'll fix you up here. And I told them we'll pick you up when you're ready."

"Oh . . ." Figgs looked down. "Thank you."

"It's nothing. I'm glad you're better. I'm going to go ask the healer a few questions about home care for you and then we're going to get going," Fox said.

"Thank you, Mrs. Salazar. I don't know how to pay you back but I'll figure it out. If you ever need a Spare worker, I'm an excellent one."

Fox smiled at him warmly. "Pay me back by getting better."

Seven's mom winked at her, then left.

"Your mom is the best," Figgs said, and Seven nodded because she was. Seven knew she was lucky to have her.

Figgs yawned and Seven noticed all the markers on his hummingheart were a serene-looking blue. She didn't know for sure, but she bet that was good. Despite how tired he looked, Seven could tell that Figgs was in better spirits, and she was grateful.

"I should get going," Seven said. "School tomorrow."

"Oh yeah. How's advanced arachnid class going?"

"Oof, don't remind me! Professor Barkridge only knows two kinds of exams: difficult and impossible. That woman is a nightmare."

Figgs chuckled. "I'm sure you'll still get top marks."

"I better," grumbled Seven. "I'm glad you're okay, Figgs. I'll come by tomorrow after school to check on you, deal?"

"Deal," Figgs said, his eyes droopy with sleep.

Seven wondered what would happen if she went over and gave him a kiss on the cheek. But . . . maybe it was the wrong time. So instead, she smiled at Figgs, and gave him a little wave.

"Night," he said, already drifting into sleep.

"Night, Figgs," Seven said softly.

Seven knew then, there was no way she would leave Figgs alone for one more moment.

CHAPTER SIXTEEN

SECOND-CHANCE FAMILY

FOR AS LONG as she could remember, Seven had always walked to school. She knew the path like the warts on Edgar Allan Toad's back. She walked through her neighborhood lined with trees and the modest gardens she'd often helped her neighbors grow and keep alive; she walked past a small row of shops in town, including the Ravenskill Mudbean House, where she cherished getting a hot ponche on the coldest mornings before school. She passed the brick homes on Division Street, where Valley and her mom lived. She loved that route, walking to one of her favorite places in the world: school. Just thinking about it made her sigh wistfully, and a pang of pain pierced her heart when she remembered that was just the kind of thing to make Valley call her a Frog House nerd in disguise.

But with Spares going missing, her parents, as well as Thorn's, didn't think it was safe for them to walk anywhere alone. Instead, they had begun taking turns driving them to school. Sometimes though, they got too busy with work or Beefy and they recruited the Witchlings' *other* favorite adult. And there she was, looking as elegant as ever, leaning against a big black car.

"Miss Dewey!" Seven ran to her favorite librarian and gave her a giant hug. She hadn't seen her in days. Miss Dewey had recently joined the Ravenskill Council and was just as busy as her parents had been with the whole Spare mess. She had also been helping Ambert campaign to join the council ahead of elections next year. It was a hectic and exciting time for them, Seven was sure.

"Get in; Helio will kill us if he's late." Miss Dewey gave Seven a knowing look.

Seven laughed and got into the back seat with the Lophiifor twins. Miss Dewey normally walked around town, or zipped about on a motorized scooter, but today she was riding in Ambert's car—a tall black box of a car with the shiniest paint Seven had ever seen. It looked *expensive.*

"Morning!" Ambert said from the driver's seat. Both Tidbit, his squirrel familiar, and Almanac, Miss Dewey's bird familiar, were asleep in a small nest bed on the extra-wide rear dashboard. Miss Dewey slid in next to Ambert and kissed him on the cheek. They really were the perfect match.

"You know, I forgot to tell you this morning that you look extra handsome today," she said.

"Oh wow, really?" Dusk groaned, his head in a sketchbook.

"Sorry, sorry," Miss Dewey laughed.

"It's fine," Dusk said in his deadpan voice, but there was the smallest of sweet smiles on his face.

"Hey," Seven said to the two brothers. Dusk nodded and Helio nearly knocked her over with a hug.

"Ready for another day at the Goody Garlick Academy?!" he asked. "I am so froggin' ready for bear-lifting club after school, oh and of course charm creation lessons! Did you study for our principles of shifting class?"

"Uh, yeah I did," Seven said, taken aback. Not even she had this much enthusiasm for school this early in the morning. Now she knew how Valley felt with her and Thorn always being extra excited about everything.

She missed Valley so much.

They began the drive to school, through slow Ravenskill morning traffic, and Seven looked out the window. Her path wasn't the same from in here, but she could still see the flowers, the turning leaves of the trees, the squirrels running across their branches.

Squirrels!

Seven suddenly remembered the message sent to her from a mysterious brown squirrel last spring: *"Look for the lost one."* She hadn't thought to ask the only brown squirrel she knew personally: Tidbit! Maybe he knew something, or at least could lead Seven in the right direction.

She turned around and petted the small, sleeping creature. She hated to wake him, but this was important.

"Tidbit," Seven whispered. "Buddy."

"Good luck trying to wake him," Dusk scoffed.

Miss Dewey turned the music up and Seven was

grateful because it was kinda awkward having what seemed like a one-sided conversation in such close quarters.

Seven tried her foolproof squirrel trick, and scratched beneath his little chin. Tidbit yawned and blinked, opening his eyes sleepily.

"Hello, Uncle," he said softly.

"Tidbit, hi, I'm sorry to wake you, but do you know anything about a brown squirrel who sent me a message last spring?"

"Massage?" Tidbit asked, yawning.

"No, no, a message. The squirrel sent the message through a bird, but it told me to 'look for the lost one.' Do you have any idea what that might mean?" Seven whispered.

Tidbit blinked at Seven with a goofy smile on his face. "I lost one tooth last spring; the acorn I found was too hard. Is that what you mean?"

Seven sighed. "No, no, it was an important message from a brown squirrel."

Tidbit stretched, then shook his little head. "If you are lost, the best thing to do is stand in place and wait for an adult to find you. Books on lost things can be found in section twelve of the . . . hooonkkk shuuuu." Tidbit fell asleep and began snoring immediately.

Seven gave up. It had been worth a shot.

Miss Dewey and Ambert chatted happily, Dusk interjecting every few minutes with a soft grunt or laugh as Helio told them excitedly about his new racing toad Rhea, and Seven realized something: Miss Dewey had always wanted little Witchlings of her own but never had them. Ambert had lost his first wife, Helio and Dusk's mother, years ago. They had suffered something Seven couldn't even imagine. And yet, here they were, a new, happy blended family.

If they could all find one another, who was to say Figgs couldn't find a second-chance family of his own? An idea occurred to Seven just then. Ambert was from Crones Cliff Manor, the same town as Figgs. He had been a Golden Frog Games champion and beloved librarian. He knew everyone there; maybe he knew a family that would take Figgs in.

"Mr. Lophiifor?" Seven asked.

"Hmm?" Ambert asked, looking at her in the rearview mirror.

"Could I ask you something?"

"Of course," he said with a smile.

"You know Figgs? Moonchild?"

"Oh yes, the one that worked for the Moonfalls?" Ambert asked.

"Mm-hmm. He hasn't been able to find work because of . . . well, everything. I figured since you're from his hometown and know everyone, would you know of any family that might take him in? Not even necessarily for work . . . But, like, would someone adopt him?"

Miss Dewey clapped her hands. "Oh, I think that's a wonderful idea. It might be tough though, Seven. You're right."

"What about Ms. Nightingale?" Ambert asked.

Seven's eyes opened wide. "Quill?!"

"She's bound to be lonely right now and could probably use the company. Figgs is a great kid and would be a big help to her."

Seven leaned back into her seat. She wasn't sure if it would be an imposition or a brilliant pairing, but it wouldn't hurt to ask.

"You know, I think you made a good choice, Miss Dewey," Seven said.

Miss Dewey turned and quirked an eyebrow.

"This Ambert guy is a genius," Seven said.

Miss Dewey threw her head back and laughed, then grabbed Ambert's whole head and kissed his cheek. "I did make a good choice, didn't I? And only two weeks until our wedding."

"I can't wait," Ambert said, looking at Miss Dewey lovingly as he stopped the car to let a mother goose and her goslings cross the road.

"Seven, I really do think you should ask," Ambert said. "It might help them both."

On the rest of the ride to school, Helio studied flashcards, Dusk read an old book, Miss Dewey and Ambert talked excitedly about their wedding, and Seven wondered if she really would be able to help Figgs finally find a place to call home.

CHAPTER SEVENTEEN

WITHER OAK, ABANDONED

QUILL DIDN'T HESITATE when Seven brought up the idea to take Figgs in.

"But not as a worker," she told him in his room in the Bluewing Infirmary.

"I'd like to work. I don't want to take advantage of anyone," Figgs said.

"Oh, my sweet boy, you are still a child. It is our job to take care of you, not the other way around."

Figgs looked on the verge of tears. The relief in his eyes was enough to make Seven tear up herself. He had color back in his cheeks, the hollows under his eyes weren't quite so dark, and he was starting to look like his old self. They had been feeding him more in the infirmary than he'd eaten in months, and Seven was sure there were many four-cheese grilled cheese sandwiches in his future.

Days later, Quill, Figgs, and Seven were in Quill's apartment—Figgs stood stiffly before her, waiting for orders, a small beat-up suitcase filled with everything he had in this world beside him. Seven stood next to him for support, like he'd asked her to.

Seven had of course asked him what he thought about the idea after bringing up the topic with Quill the same way she had with Ambert and Miss Dewey. She didn't want to get his hopes up or make Quill feel backed into a corner. Valley's mom had exceeded even what Seven hoped for, suggesting Figgs stay with her without Seven having to ask directly.

"Do . . . you think she would like me? I mean, I don't know Ms. Nightingale all that well." Figgs had ruffled his hair anxiously.

"Of course she will. Plus, it's not like you have to stay there if you hate it. Think of it as a rest stop while you figure things out." Seven had smiled.

"A rest stop." Figgs had nodded. "I like that."

And so Quill and Figgs came up with an agreement: She would let him stay in their third bedroom so long as he did his chores and did his best in school. She refused to hire him, but she would, she promised, give him an allowance.

"Just money, for free?" he asked, baffled.

"Money for snacks, for a video game if you save up. You deserve to have fun too." Quill smiled.

Seven could tell it was bittersweet for Quill to have a kid to look after, and knowing Figgs, he would take care of Quill whether she liked it or not. They would hopefully be there for each other, and maybe if it worked out, Figgs could stay.

For now though, he was a temporary resident of Ravenskill, which meant he would be going to school with Seven and Thorn. It also meant Seven would get to see him every day.

In occult arts and crafts class a few days later, Seven was busy painting a jellyfish portrait—capable of poisoning an enemy with just a glance. They all had anti-hex goggles over their eyes, of course, but Figgs still looked quite nervous. He had been in and out of school since he turned twelve and wasn't used to how intense the Goody Garlick Academy could be yet.

"Am I doing this right?" he asked.

Dusk leaned over from his own easel on the other side of Seven.

"It's not bad. Maybe shade the fourth leg a bit more?"

"The top of its head looks a little like a pillow too," Poppy Mayweather said from the row behind.

"Right," Figgs said, getting back to his painting.

It was a crisp fall day out, warm enough that the occult arts and crafts teacher, Mr. Toadpuff, opened a few of the creaky wood windows in their classroom. A nice breeze weaved through the room, soft classical humdrum music playing as the seventh- and eighth-year witches in this blended class worked together. Seven felt . . . almost happy. She was a few ingredients away from finalizing the toxic stone-eating sludge cure for Valley, and now Figgs had a new home. And he was going to her school.

She looked at him out of the corner of her eye. He was wearing an ironed black shirt under a new school sweater. It was nice to see him in non-worn-out clothes. He looked . . . good. Seven smiled to herself. Maybe this coming winter would be a good one after all.

There was a knock on the door, and everyone turned to look as Mr. Wrinklecloud, a very old, very sweet half-fae witch popped his head through.

"Heyo, Poppy. Hello, Figgs, you settling in?" Mr. Wrinklecloud worked in their school's main office and knew every student by name. He even remembered their birthdays.

"Mr. Wrinklecloud," Mr. Toadpuff said, "we're in the middle of a pretty volatile poisonous paints lesson."

"Oh my, oh my, so sorry! I just had the most wonderful news and wanted to let Wither know right away."

Everyone turned to look at Wither Oak. She smiled shyly at Mr. Wrinklecloud. Wither was a younger witch, one of the newly sorted Spares, with a dark brown bowl cut and a round face with more freckles than not.

"Dear." Mr. Wrinklecloud waved his hand in Wither's direction. "The Spare housing list just came through and you got a spot! I had to pull some strings. Normally Ravenskillians your age don't live alone, but given the circumstances—"

Chatter broke out across the classroom and Wither's face went bright red. There were only two reasons why a new Spare would need housing: Their guardians died tragically, or they had been abandoned. Given that any tragic death in Ravenskill would immediately be the topic of everyone's conversation, Seven was pretty sure Wither had been abandoned.

"Mr. Wrinklecloud, can we speak outside for just a moment," Mr. Toadpuff said hurriedly, and the two older witches walked out of the classroom and closed the door.

Seven got ready to intone a spell when she noticed Mr. Toadpuff waving his hands through the little window on the classroom door, a shimmering purple light covering the two adult witches.

"Anti-chisme magic. He beat me to it," Seven said, nodding her head.

"You okay?" Figgs asked Wither, who was just a few seats down from Poppy.

"Toadally fine," Wither said, but it was obvious she was on the verge of tears.

Starlight, Poppy's butt-toad of a roommate, scoffed. "Tragic."

A few of her friends laughed meanly. Wither whipped her head around.

"What?" Starlight asked innocently.

"It's a mistake. My parents haven't abandoned me," Wither said hotly. "They wouldn't do that."

"You sure?" Starlight asked smugly.

Wither turned back around and fumbled for her portaphone as Starlight and her friends whispered gleefully. Wither dialed a number, then waited. The other side of the line was loud enough that Seven could hear the operator say the number had been disconnected.

"No . . ." whispered Wither, and tried again. Again, the disconnection message.

Starlight burst out laughing now. "Not picking up?"

"Please, stop." Wither choked back tears. She tried her parents again, and again nobody answered.

"Take it up with the Stars, *Wither.* With a name like that, who is surprised?"

Starlight's friends laughed again, and Poppy looked back at her roommate. "Aren't you failing this class? You should be working on your assignment."

Starlight's mouth flew open, her friends staring at her with amused looks on their faces. They were quick to turn on her now that *she* was the butt of the joke. Poppy caught Seven's eye and winked.

Mr. Toadpuff came back into the classroom, clearly rattled, but trying to present a calm front.

"Is it true?" Wither asked Mr. Toadpuff before he even had a chance to reach her desk.

"Wither, let's talk out in the hallway . . ."

"Tell me. I have a right to know."

"I really think it's best if we—"

"No. They're all gonna know soon anyway. I want to get it over with, please. Is it true?"

Mr. Toadpuff paused, then slowly, he nodded.

Wither's breathing came out in jagged fits, and a Goose House witch named Bramble sitting beside her put his arm around Wither's shoulders, whispering kind words to try to help her calm down.

Mr. Toadpuff was also at her side, crouched down

next to her easel, a worried look on his face.

"Mr. Toadpuff, don't our new balance and order laws prohibit any Spares living in the village from attending school here?" Starlight asked, her voice overly sweet and very clearly showing fake concern.

Balance and order, Seven nearly scoffed. What a joke. Starlight preened when she saw the approving looks from her friends. She whispered something to a friend beside her, who nodded and quickly took out her portaphone, texting someone furiously.

Seven was about ready to call the Nightbeast and let it eat Starlight.

"Starlight, that's quite enough. You pack your rucksack and go to the headmaster's now," Mr. Toadpuff said.

"I was only trying to warn her before the Gran's Guard comes for her. She should be thanking me," Starlight said through a malicious smile.

Bramble stood up, followed by the rest of the Goose House witches in the classroom. As a collective, they turned their necks toward Starlight.

Starlight scoffed and leaned back in her chair. As terrible as she was, Starlight was far from the only witch who had been acting this way. Ever since the Spare Amendment was passed, witches like her had become even more entitled and mean, their prejudices bolstered by an unjust law. They were bold and self-righteous, and it seemed anything that made Spares or their supporters upset became their life force. Witches like Starlight loved nothing more than to see others suffer.

"Students, sit down. Now," Mr. Toadpuff said.

"Wither is my friend," Bramble said slowly, ignoring their professor. "And if you don't stop, you'll be sorry."

"Excuse me?" Starlight balked. "You think I'm scared of some Goose House witches?"

Bramble chuckled. "You should be."

Starlight sneered. "Pluma."

"Oh my goats." Both Seven and Mr. Toadpuff were up and trying to shield Bramble, but the spell moved too quickly.

Bramble's face and arms broke out in tiny red blisters. The pluma spell felt like the pointiest end of a quill going into your skin over and over again. It was permitted only in a dire battle, and Starlight had just used it in a classroom.

Bramble collapsed, the pain too strong for a witch of his age to handle. "Everyone go back to your seats, now! I will be back in just a moment." Mr. Toadpuff picked Bramble up and rushed out of the classroom. If left untreated, a pluma spell could be poisonous.

They waited until he had left before the Goose House witches descended on Starlight and her friends.

"What is wrong with you!" they screeched.

"You're gonna pay, wait and see."

"I can take all of you on. I don't care," Starlight said.

"Just quit it already. Haven't you done enough?" Seven said. She didn't want to get involved, she really didn't. Her anger was too hard to rein in lately, and she was afraid of what she might do.

“Oh, not the queen of the Spares chiming in!” Starlight yelled, standing up and pushing past the Goose House witches.

“At least I’m the queen of something and not a wannabe who has to be mean to keep friends,” Seven spat.

“Oooooo,” her classmates said at the comeback, and Starlight’s face turned bright red.

“Seven, it’s not worth it,” Poppy said.

“I think she should teach her a lesson, personally,” Dusk grumbled.

Starlight walked closer. “I’m sick of you thinking you’re important. You’re noth—”

“I AM NOT NOTHING, I AM YOUR UNCLE!” The room thundered with the force of Seven’s fury.

Without realizing it, without meaning to, she had infused an amplification spell to her vocal cords. It was painful, but the searing only served to feed the fire within her.

Starlight took a step back, nearly tripping. She looked like a weasel backed into a corner, but she wouldn’t give in. “You’re nothing but a Spare to me. And I . . . I dare you to try something. I’ll have you sent to the Tombs so fast.” Starlight raised her hands and, in an instant, Poppy, Figgs, and Dusk were all by Seven’s side.

Not that she needed it. Seven had had enough.

Seven simply flicked her wrist and sent the mean witch toppling over. Starlight was covered in jellyfish paint water, thankfully not too poisonous. But Starlight would definitely have more than a few blisters in a few seconds. A just punishment for what she had done to Bramble. For humiliating Wither.

"Seven, Starlight, enough!" Mr. Toadpuff yelled as he swept back into the room.

Just then the sound of heavy boots echoed in the halls and a smug grin spread across Starlight's face as she looked at her friend who had been texting someone moments before.

The Hill Society guards barged through the door.

"What is this?" Mr. Toadpuff sputtered. "Out, all of you!"

"We've been informed of a recently abandoned Spare on school grounds," one guard said.

Seven turned to Starlight angrily. "*You* did this."

Starlight merely shrugged. "She doesn't belong here; none of you Spares do. And I can't wait for the day I watch you *all* get dragged out of here. It's her; get her out of here!" Starlight said, pointing at Wither, and the guards lunged for the young Spare.

"Stop!" Seven screamed.

"Congelar!" Mr. Toadpuff said, his hands shaking as he froze the guard in place just long enough for a tearstained Wither to grab her rucksack and run out of the classroom quicker than anyone could stop her. The other guards descended on their sweet teacher, restraining him while the rest of the class stared on in horror. As Seven tried desperately to free her teacher, she realized how wrong she had been. Things were only getting worse.

CHAPTER EIGHTEEN

A FIGURE IN THE DARK

GOING TO THE SPARE VILLAGE after dark was probably a froggin' bad idea right now, but Seven, Figgs, Dusk, and Helio decided to do just that. Besides, Seven had already been suspended from school for two days for her fight with Starlight and the Hill's Guard. What was one more thing to add to her growing criminal record?

Thorn had stayed behind to work on a big project for her advanced costura program—a brand-new poison-infused ribbon—so the unlikely quartet set off into the night to find Wither. Seven wanted to make sure she was okay, that the Hill's Guard hadn't gotten to her, and maybe to teach her a good hexing spell to glue Starlight's lips shut.

There were only a few places Seven figured Wither would be that night: at an employer's house, which was unlikely since she'd just been sorted as a Spare and allegedly abandoned. Or she'd be in the one place Spares lived when they had nowhere else to go: the Spare Village. They didn't want to knock on every door though, so Seven called in her reinforcements.

"Cheese, did you see a girl who looks like this?" Seven held up a really bad drawing of Wither for the leader of the raccoons to inspect. It was basically just a circle, with some squiggly lines for hair, two dots for eyes, a half-circle nose, and a straight line for lips. Plus, tears; Seven was careful to add big tears and a small stick-figure body. It was the best she could do.

"They're not gonna be able to tell who that is!" Helio said.

Cheese rubbed his chin, then nodded. "Yep! I saw her."

"He saw her," Seven said smugly.

"Oh." Helio cringed and Seven gave him her best "told you so" look.

"I saw her go in that direction." Cheese pointed northwest.

"I saw her in a Spare house on Acorn Street," added Breadstick.

"We can take you there," said Mozzarella Stick, and the Stick siblings led the way.

The witches and the Stick twins headed toward the northwest border of Ravenskill, the area known unofficially as Spare Village. Seven had not been through the sections of town where Spares lived often. It was usually avoided and widely regarded as "the dangerous part of town." Seven had only done what the grown-ups around her had asked her to, but now she was ashamed. Spares were the worst-treated witches in all the Twelve Towns, and she'd contributed to it. She'd believed it without a second thought. Her parents had at least tried to show kindness when they spoke about Spares, but they hadn't been immune to fear of the unknown. They had all ignored the plight of the Spares until it came knocking on their own door.

Seven could not turn back time, or change how she used to see Spares, but she could be better now. Nobody was born perfect, after all. Until you joined the dirt, sea, and Stars, there was always room to grow. They reached northwest Ravenskill, and unlike the lush greenery and warmth of the Hill, this part of town was devoid of color, the road in disrepair. There were no shops or grocers in sight, nothing but shut doors and drawn curtains in small, slipshod wooden homes. As they walked through the quiet neighborhood though, Seven noticed something else—the small flowers planted in the gnome-sized yards, the hand-painted signs pointing to the north and south of the neighborhood, the tidy porches with rocking chairs and knitting boxes, and homemade bird feeders hanging from a few of the trees. It might not be fancy like the Hill, but it seemed the witches who lived here took pride in their small neighborhood. They were trying to make it home.

Helio pulled Seven from her thoughts as they walked on.

"And you know, bear lifting is just *one* of the sports I plan to try out for in the Golden Frog Games next time. You know what Dad told me? He said I was probably a good enough toad racer, but I dunno." Helio bit his lip, a worried look on his face. "Last time I raced, I fell when I put my toad Rhea down right at the beginning of the race! I landed in toad sludge, face-first, slid all the way to the end of the track, and technically . . . I kinda won."

Figgs burst out laughing, but Dusk and Seven exchanged annoyed looks.

Helio had talked the *entire* way there. Like, the whole. Entire. Way. Seven had tuned him out after five minutes, but his cheerful voice felt like an unending drone of sound.

"Anyway, I think I just need to practice a bit more. Maybe I can ask one of the older kids!"

"Helio, if you don't quit talking, I'm gonna turn you into a racing toad myself," Dusk said.

Helio's hand flew to his mouth. "I'll stop, brother, please don't hex me again," it sounded like he said, though his voice was muffled under his hand.

"Her house is just up here," Breadstick said as they walked through the quiet streets. Seven couldn't imagine living on her own, but hopefully the things they'd brought in their rucksacks would help make it a bit easier: food, blankets, and a small mushroom lamp Thorn had donated.

"Wither's parents don't even know if their kid will become a Spare for sure," Figgs said.

"So why abandon her?"

"Just the threat of being a Spare is enough," Helio said, a disgusted look on his face.

Dusk nodded. "I bet they're keeping them there temporarily, just in case."

"As if it's contagious." Seven shook her head.

"They just want to control *everything*, so when someone is different, it frightens them," Dusk said.

There was a stormy look in his eyes and Seven appreciated that her new friends were just as protective of Spares as she was, despite not being Spares themselves. There weren't many witches who spoke this critically of anti-Spare sentiment, at least not openly. She was glad the twins had moved here. Even if Helio *was* froggin' annoying.

A chill blew through the night air and Seven closed her cloak as they walked through the small neighborhood. All the windows had their curtains drawn, warm lights glowing from within, but everything else was pitch-black, giving the area an eerie, desolate feeling. Seven pulled closer to Figgs.

Two pairs of glowing eyes appeared in the dark of a tunnel that ran under an abandoned railway line. "It's just through here," Seven said, following the Stick siblings.

They emerged in a small square patch of dirt surrounded by a few trees, and three houses facing the center of the square. The raccoons walked right up to the door of the house at the center and stood on either side with their arms outstretched like "here it is."

Seven crouched down next to Breadstick and Mozzarella Stick and patted both their heads.

"Well done," she cooed at them, giving them little snacks from her pocket.

A low flickering light came from the small house, which was really more like a cabin, and they could see right through the curtainless window: a bare room with a wooden floor and old floral wallpaper, a single lightbulb hung from a string on the ceiling. Nestled under a toad-patterned blanket on the floor, Wither seemed to be in a deep sleep. An opened bag of seaweed chips was on the floor next to her. Had that been her dinner? How was a kid supposed to live like this?

"We can leave this stuff at her door with a note and I'll come back tomorrow morning to help. She's had a long day and probably needs to sleep. I don't want to wake her," Seven said.

"Good thinking," Figgs said.

Seven politely asked the spiders on the porch to move and they very kindly did. The witches left a rucksack filled with food, a small wooden contraption that was a tinified bed frame, and dried plantain leaves stuffed into two blankets they had sewn together and closed with a button to make a mattress. Seven placed an Edgar Allan Toad plushie from the games last spring on top of the care package, and they set off toward home.

The four friends made their way back to the pathway that led to town, with the raccoons running a few toadstools ahead of them.

"So, what happens if the Gran fixes the magic and Wither turns out not to be a Spare after all?" Seven asked. "Will her parents come back like 'oopsie goosie!'?"

Figgs shrugged. "If you ask me, it should be illegal for parents to just abandon their kid like that."

"Yeah!" Seven said. "Why is that even allowed?"

As they neared the tunnel under the abandoned railway, the moon hid behind some clouds, making it darker than when they arrived. Seven was eager to get home as quickly as possible.

They were walking close together through the long tunnel when they noticed something—there was someone else ahead of them. The sound of boots on concrete echoed in the dark, and Seven tensed with fear, thinking of the veiled witches from the other day and that weirdo Master Beetle. She wouldn't want to come up against one of them in this dark tunnel. Her raccoons had already dived into the woods ahead of them, and Seven could only hope they were okay too.

"Farolito," Seven said, and a blue light appeared in her palm, illuminating a figure up ahead. Spotting them, the figure waved their arm and put the light out. And then they ran.

Seven and her friends took off after them. This might be the witch disappearing Spares, and if it was, Seven would make them pay.

"Stop!" Dusk called out.

"One more warning!" Helio yelled.

The figure was about to exit the tunnel when the twins attacked, a bright hot light and forceful wind erupting from their hands. The wind howled like a terrible storm, throwing Seven and Figgs through the air. She landed hard on her butt, then scrambled up as quickly as she could.

"What's happening?!" Figgs screamed. The light was still shining, humming weirdly. It was a familiar noise—big and all-encompassing but calm. *What was that? And why did it feel so familiar to Seven?*

And then Seven heard something horrible: Her raccoons were screeching. Her heart thundered in her chest. She had to get to them, but the twins' magic was making it impossible for Seven and Figgs to move forward and help in the fight.

"Escudo!" Seven cried out, and a shield of shadows appeared in front of her and Figgs. Seven flinched . . . this spell was supposed to be made of *light*, not shadow.

But now was not the time to be picky. They fought through the twins' bright light around them, which was simultaneously suffocating and beguiling.

Seven and Figgs reached the end of the tunnel and found the twins with their hands up, the light emitting from their palms and surrounding everything. Dusk was shaking in concentration, his dark hair pushed back from his face, his teeth bared, but Helio stood steady beside him, focused and supporting his brother. In front of them, the figure was suspended in midair, a delicate yellow scarf wrapped around their neck.

"Wait." Seven froze. "Stop!"

She took one step closer to the figure, her heart beating wildly.

"Miss Dewey?"

CHAPTER NINETEEN
THE TRUTH ABOUT MISS DEWEY

THE TWINS LOOKED back at them, horrified, then let Miss Dewey down with a thump, their light extinguishing.

"Oh my goats!" Helio said, horrified.

The four witches ran over to Miss Dewey. Seven looked around for Breadstick and Mozzarella Stick just as they emerged from the shadows in the tunnel.

"Are you two okay?" Seven asked, hugging them both.

"We are fine," the twin raccoons said. "We were screeching in solidarity."

Figgs and Dusk helped Miss Dewey up from the ground. "That was rather painful."

"Are you all right?" Helio asked.

"I didn't mean to hurt you, I swear, I would never do something like that on purpose—" Dusk was speaking hurriedly, as if he was trying to convince Miss Dewey he meant it.

Miss Dewey smiled softly and reached out to pat Dusk's hair. "I'm okay, promise. Trust me, I've been through worse."

She picked up an enormous rucksack from the ground, dusted it off, then put it on her back. She wore a pair of dark slacks, a dark cloak, and a witch's hat. She didn't look like her normal self, except for her signature yellow scarf, which she tucked back into her cloak.

"Why were you running?" Figgs asked.

Seven had been wondering just that and for a moment, panic seized her heart. She couldn't take Miss Dewey being secretly evil.

"I didn't know it was you. And I'm not exactly supposed to be, um, doing what I'm doing."

"And what *are* you doing, exactly?" Seven asked softly.

"There's no use in keeping my secret from you, I suppose, but you mustn't tell anyone," Miss Dewey said.

"We won't," Seven said.

"All right. Follow me; it's better if we don't talk out in the open. And I need to sit after that fall. Dusk, Helio, you'll have to show me how to do that," she said with a good-natured laugh.

They walked back toward a small tavern at the edge of the Spare Village. It was pretty ramshackle and old, but it was one of the only taverns in town where Spares were still allowed to go. A "*Spares Welcome Here*" sign was pinned to the door with a small dagger, something that Valley would probably stop to admire.

"Stay close. There's no danger, but Spares are jumpy right now. We don't want to worry them. They're not used to new witches coming here," Miss Dewey said.

They walked into the tavern, and everyone turned to

look at them. A few eyes opened wide at the sight of Seven, but they weren't looks of disdain, just curiosity and maybe even awe. Seven tried not to recoil when she noticed something else: *the rats*. They sat on the shoulders of Spares, curled up on their laps sleeping, sitting in miniature chairs beside them.

"What's with all the rats?"

"Oh, Spares here love them and keep them as pets sometimes. I think it's solidarity between the rejected. Not to mention, rats can help them gather food and items discreetly. Many of the rats here are highly trained."

"Interesting," Seven said. She wondered if any of them knew Cotton Swab.

"This way," Miss Dewey said as she smiled at the staring Spares.

They slid into a booth tucked in the corner of the tavern, and Miss Dewey ordered hot ponches for all of them from an old barkeep. Seven got up to use the washroom as they waited for their drinks. She had gotten dirt all over her cloak when the twins' light magic had thrown her into the air.

"Don't spill any of the beans without me," Seven said as she got up.

She weaved through the dimly lit tavern, taking in everything around her. There were signs with the town motto *"Ravenskill, a Friendly Town"* everywhere, which she had been seeing around a lot more lately. Almost as if the town was trying to convince itself that it was still true, despite treating so many of its residents like second-class witches. There were flyers about town events or job postings and, heartbreakingly, postcards with descriptions of missing Spares. There was a small drawing of Seven, Thorn, and Valley in the forest, standing on the body of the Nightbeast. Seven flinched, feeling protective of her monstruo friend. She pulled the picture down. The Nightbeast didn't deserve this slander. Laughter rumbled in her ear; the Nightbeast seemed pleased by this, amused even.

Seven found the washroom, cleaned her cloak, and splashed cold water on her face. On her way back out, a witch knocked into her, dropping a tray full of drinks on the floor.

"Oh! Sorry!" the witch said.

"Inopportuna! Careful!" someone called out.

Seven went to help Inopportuna with the spilled drinks, but she shooed her away. "No need to help me, this is the tenth tray I dropped tonight! I am used to it."

Seven chuckled awkwardly and shuffled past her and back to the booth. Just as she sat back down, the barkeep came over with their hot ponches. They had extra-big, extra-fluffy marshmallows, and Seven opened her eyes wide in surprise when she took her first sip.

"This is even better than the Mudbean House!" she said.

But maybe it shouldn't have been so surprising. After all, most Spares worked for demanding, wealthy witches who probably drank and ate the best of everything. It made sense that a Spare tavern would have only the most delicious foods.

Miss Dewey cleared her throat. "I imagine you want to know what I'm doing here."

The three younger witches leaned forward. Wait a moment, where was Helio?

"Where's Helio?" Seven asked.

"He had to go." Dusk rolled his eyes. "He's deathly scared of rats and broke out in hives."

"Understandable," Seven said, then turned back to Miss Dewey. "You were saying, Miss D?"

"Right, the short version is I run a secret organization that helps bring food, clothing, and daily necessities to Spares living in the Twelve Towns," Miss Dewey said. "Since providing aid to Spares has been made illegal after the anti-Spare laws, me being here could land me in the dungeon."

"Wow . . . really?" Seven asked. She knew Miss Dewey was great, but she didn't realize she was helping-Spares-at-the-risk-of-her-own-safety great. She could imagine more than one powerful family that would take personal offense to anyone helping Spares this way. She had seen firsthand how Thorn's family had been shunned and harassed after they gave just *one* Spare, poor Pixel, a job. She could not imagine the ire Miss Dewey would draw for helping Spares across the towns.

Miss Dewey nodded. "I've been doing it for a few years, but with these awful laws passing, things have gotten a lot worse."

"It's kind of you to help us that way," Figgs said. "Thank you."

Miss Dewey blushed. "It's . . . the very least I could do." She took a deep breath, like she was getting ready to tell them something big. Seven took another sip of her incredible hot ponche in preparation.

"You see, the truth is . . . I come from a long line of very rich and *not* very good witches," Miss Dewey said.

Seven sat back. Miss Dewey's family was bad? She couldn't imagine the family that had brought her into existence being anything but wonderful. Then again, Valley's dad was butt-toad of the century, so maybe this kinda made sense.

"They did terrible, horrible things long ago, and left me more magic and wealth than I could ever spend in one lifetime, so I've dedicated my life to two things: the library, and giving all that wealth away. I've tried to help as many witches as I could. I have a small organization, just a handful of us, dedicated to helping Spares."

"We've tried to make this somewhere worth living for the past two years. I know nothing can undo the harm my family has done to Spares like you, Seven, and you, Figgs, but I hope you know I am nothing like them."

Seven nodded. She loved and trusted Miss Dewey. Sure, it felt weird that she hadn't known this whole side of her, but at least it was something good. She knew why Miss Dewey had to keep this a secret; it would be incredibly dangerous for her if the Hill witches, or that creepy cult or Mr. Pepperhorn, found out. Seven knew all about dangerous secrets.

Miss Dewey swallowed and continued. "With Spares going missing now, everything's become more dangerous. If anyone ever found out what I do . . ."

"We won't tell," Figgs said.

"Of course, we would never," Seven said.

Dusk put his hand over his future mom's hand and smiled. It seemed he already knew all this, and something tugged at Seven's heart to see Miss Dewey as someone's mom.

"What exactly *did* your family do?" Figgs asked.

Miss Dewey let out a sigh, and she smiled sadly as if she was embarrassed. "For starters, they hoarded magic, stolen magic, from their own workers. They took advantage of them, mistreating and abusing them for years . . . stealing their family magic when they could. There are rumors that one of my great-great-grandfathers even . . . had Spares killed. Though I haven't been able to confirm it for sure."

A chill ran over Seven's body. *Killed?* They were silent then, until an older Spare who Seven did not know walked up to their table and took off his hat.

"Moira." He nodded. "Hello, young ones." He smiled at Seven, Figgs, and Dusk.

"Hello," Seven said, and the Spare's eyes went wide.

"Seven Salazar? Me oh me oh my! A pleasure to meet you indeed. I'm Walnut Neverdew." He reached out and shook Seven's hand.

"By the way, Moira dear, I know you're quite busy with the wedding coming up and all, but I thought you might like to know, we have a lot of new sign-ups this week—at least twenty!" the old witch said.

"Sign-ups for what?" Seven asked.

Walnut looked to Miss Dewey, who nodded, and the old witch placed a small card on the table.

"'Next Spare meeting—witching hour, on the sixth day, the Shaggy Rat,'" Seven read aloud.

"We were waiting for the right time to bring you in, as to not bring too much attention to it, but we've been having meetings here in the village to organize and push back against the Spare Amendment."

"Wow," Figgs said.

"We hope you'll join us for the next one," Walnut said with a smile, then walked over to the other side of the tavern just as a loud boom like amplified thunder shook the tavern violently. The room erupted in screams, Seven held on to the table, and Miss Dewey and Figgs looked around in alarm.

"Everyone, under the tables!" cried Walnut as the sound echoed and boomed again. This time Seven was worried the roof would come clean off the tavern.

Figgs and Miss Dewey did as Walnut said and ducked under the table, but Seven was on her feet, her hands up in a defensive stance. Beside her stood Dusk, hands also raised and ready to help if she needed him.

"What the hex is that?" he asked.

"No idea, but it doesn't seem like anything good," Seven said. She was on high alert now, tapped into the trees and animals that scurried around outside. She was prepared to call on her animal friends to help if she needed to. From the rafters above, the Stick siblings looked at her intently. All she had to do was give them a command and they'd be ready to strike, but it seemed the only thing to fight back against was the sky itself. Could it just be a terrible storm was descending on Ravenskill? Or were the Spares under attack?

A few witches stood against the door, holding it in place in case they were under attack, but no such strike came. Eventually, the sound subsided, and slowly, Spares began to emerge from their hiding spots.

Just then, someone pounded on the door from the outside.

"Be ready!" Seven said, but she was not sure how ready these Spares could be for a battle if that was what they were up against. How many of them knew spells that would keep them safe? Spells to strike or defend themselves with? Miss Dewey and Figgs were beside them then, hands up and ready to fight if they needed to.

"Let me in! Wither has gone missing!" someone on the other side cried out.

Seven and her friends swept out of the tavern and into the cold night, a group of Spares trailing behind them. They made it to Wither's in record time.

The door to her little house had been left open; her sleeping bag was in tatters. The single lightbulb had exploded, and the walls were blackened with soot. The seaweed chips beside her bed were still there, as was a small book and what looked like leaves, twigs, and pebbles blown in from the forest outside.

"Nobody touch anything inside," Miss Dewey said. "It might be hexed. I'll have to make sure the Gran inspects her cabin thoroughly. Everyone back to your homes, shut the doors tight, and use the protection spells we've been practicing. It is much too dangerous to be out after dark right now."

Miss Dewey and Dusk said goodbye to Seven and Figgs and they took their own paths home. As they left the Spare Village in silence and walked through the forest and back into town, Cheese caught up with them on a cobblestone road.

"Uncle Seven." Cheese tugged on her cloak and she bent down to talk to him.

"What's up, bud?"

"Mr. Pepperhorn, he has returned from a trip up north. Sopa spotted him coming out of the meat-cutting shop."

"Goosin'!" Seven said. "Did Sopa see where he went or if he met up with anyone?"

Cheese shook his head. "She tried, but there was a problem. He was being escorted by ten giant witches."

"How big we talkin'?" Seven asked.

"At least six raccoons tall," Cheese said.

"Rats!" Seven said, kicking a rainbow pebble down the road.

"What is it?" Figgs asked, and Seven stood up and explained.

"He's gotten a security detail, then," Figgs said, shaking his head.

"Lotus probably tipped him off about us, and he's going to be extra vigilant now. It'll be near impossible to follow him, and there's only so much animals can relay to me, since they can't understand him. I also worry he'll try to hurt one of them if he notices he's being watched. That witch is capable of just about anything."

"Is there any way for us to follow him without him knowing it's us?" Figgs asked.

Hmmm. Seven thought about the tavern, the Spares, their trusty and stealthy companions, when an idea came to her.

"I have a plan," Seven said. "And unfortunately for both me and Helio, it's rat-related."

CHAPTER TWENTY
RODENT PATROL

"**LISTEN UP, TRASH PANDAS**, because I'm only gonna say this once: I love you," Cheese the raccoon said, to delighted oohs and aahs from the other nine raccoons the next day.

Seven shook her head.

"Now that that's out of the way, here's what we know so far," Cheese said.

Cheese was standing in front of the raccoons, bunnybeavers, worms, and various other garden-variety monstruos and animals in Seven's backyard, and giving a rundown of the clues so far like Seven had asked him to. Seven and her friends were about to undergo a scary and dangerous mission, and they needed all the support they could get. Plus, there was only so much Seven could do at one time—putting Cheese in charge of the monstruo and animal surveillance would be a big help.

"Number one—Spares are going missing all around the Twelve Towns, purple rain, and a loud boom like a million raccoons farting . . ."

"Cheeeeesee," Seven groaned.

Cheese cleared his throat. "Apologies. A loud boom like a million raccoons *burping*?"

"Fine," Seven said.

"Spares going missing, purple rain, loud boom in the sky, nasty veiled witches, bad bad Lotus and scary Mr. Pepperhorn working together." Cheese held his little paws up. "Is that all?"

"I think so," Seven said.

As Cheese spoke, Seven, Figgs, and Thorn got ready for their part of the mission and stretched. They would need to be limber for what came next.

"Why are we stretching again?" Figgs asked.

"You'll see," Thorn said with a smile.

Figgs pointed at Thorn. "That smile is dangerous. I know it means you're trying to charm someone, which means something not so good is coming."

"Just stretch your limbs out as much as you can," Seven said. "Trust me. All right, nature friends, what we need to do now is catch Mr. Pepperhorn red-handed and find out how he's making these Spares go missing. Then, hopefully, we stop him from doing it again. Problem is, he's got a whole team of huge bodyguards with him at all times, and we need to follow him discreetly. Cheese, I need you and the other raccoons and our friends here to keep a close eye on the veiled witches. Me and my friends will take care of Mr. Pepperhorn."

"We will watch the veiled witches. Anything for Uncle Seven," said Cheese. Seven nodded at her raccoons. They had become her faithful companions, and there was almost no one she trusted and loved more than them.

The click-clack of skeleton bird wings flapped overhead, and right on time, Seven's monstruo spies brought word of Mr. Pepperhorn.

"He is heading out from his house now," one of the birds said, landing on an oak in Seven's yard.

"What direction?" Seven asked.

"Northwest," the bird replied, and Seven jumped up.

"The direction of the Spare Village; we have to move!" Figgs said.

"We have to get in our disguises first though," Thorn said.

"You're not gonna make me into a Moth House witch again, are you?" Figgs asked.

"Worse," Seven said. "Thorn is going to turn you into a rat."

"What?!" Figgs turned whiter than snow.

"Get behind this tree. It'll only hurt a little, and the stretching we just did should help," Thorn said.

Figgs winced as they found cover. Thorn handed them each a small golden ring with tiny misshapen holes in it.

"Being in an advanced costura program is coming in handy. These rings will transform you, temporarily, into whatever creature they've been enchanted with. This is a cheese ring, so you'll turn into a rat."

"How long is temporarily?" Figgs asked, a worried expression on his face.

"At least a couple of days . . ." Thorn said.

"A COUPLE OF—"

"Shhh! You want someone to hear us and blow our cover? Let Thorn finish," Seven said.

"As I was saying, a couple of days or until you take the ring off. It's up to you," Thorn said.

"Have you done this before?" Figgs asked.

"Only once, with a ladybug ring, but it worked! This is a bit bigger, but I'm confident." Thorn nodded.

"I'm ready. The sooner I turn into rat-Seven, the sooner we can get this over with," Seven said.

Seven wasn't exactly thrilled about being a rat; in fact, she was pretty sure she might cry at the thought of having a tail. But if this was the only way to find Pixel and the other missing Spares, and stop Mr. Pepperhorn, she'd do it.

"All right, on the count of three, put on your cheese rings," Thorn said.

They counted to three, slipped the cheese rings on, and began to shrink.

Down.

Down.

Down some more.

Down just a teensy bit more.

Till they were on the ground, three smallish rats. Seven was brown, with big, fluffy hair; Figgs was a slick black rat; and Thorn was a cute white-and-brown rat with a heart-shaped pink nose.

"Of course you're rat-dorable," Seven squeaked.

Thorn did whatever passed for a rat giggle, and Figgs's whole body shook from head to tail.

“This is freaky,” he squeaked.

“Tell me about it. Come on.” Seven began to run, so fast it was a bit disorienting. She was worried about not being able to move like a real rodent, but her rat instincts kicked in immediately and she was squeezing through small crevices, gliding over rocks, moving almost like liquid. It was kind of exhilarating.

“There he is,” squeaked Seven as they stood behind a lamppost on the road that led to the Hill. “Follow him but not too close.”

Mr. Pepperhorn, surrounded by his bodyguards, walked briskly past the lamppost, looking around as he did. As if he was up to no good. Which Seven knew he was, of course.

Mr. Pepperhorn stopped abruptly when a witch in heavy winter furs emerged from the wood adjacent to the road they were on. The rats were running so fast, they nearly crashed right into them. Thinking quickly, Seven dove into the bushes to their right, Figgs and Thorn following behind so they tumbled together through the brush.

“Quick, get up, get up,” Thorn squeaked.

They untangled from one another’s tails and furry bodies just in time to catch Mr. Pepperhorn’s conversation.

“*Another* ancient elder?” Mr. Pepperhorn ran his hands over his face now, looking frustrated.

“Last night,” the winter furs witch said. “That makes three from the Five Families just this year.”

The Five Families. The same phrase Lotus had used.

"Quiet, you fool," Mr. Pepperhorn said, looking around. "You want someone to overhear us?"

"Apologies, my apologies," the other witch said, bowing, a terrified look on his face.

"Inform the others. We must have a meeting soon. We're losing magic, and it won't do. Not one more drop," Mr. Pepperhorn said briskly, and walked on without saying goodbye.

What could that mean? Seven thought but did not have time to ask; they had to keep trailing Mr. Pepperhorn.

In downtown Ravenskill there were enough carts, cars, and mailboxes to weave in and out of and take cover. The rats ran, dodging witches and zigzagging over the cobblestone Ravenskill streets. Mr. Pepperhorn and his bodyguards had picked up their pace considerably. They were walking closer together, and seemed to be on high alert.

"Oh my goats," Seven squeaked when she realized where they were. In the distance, she could see little blinking eyes above the trees surrounding the big, imposing house. Mr. Pepperhorn was heading straight to the veiled witches' house.

"This way! Hurry! We have to slip in with him!"

"Where is he?" Figgs squeaked, his little rat voice panicked.

Seven looked around quickly. "What . . . I . . . we lost him?!"

One moment Mr. Pepperhorn was just toadstools in front of them and suddenly . . .

"SQUEAK!" Someone had grabbed Seven's tail and she was flying upward.

"Let me go!" Seven squeaked when she came face-to-face with Mr. Pepperhorn. Looking around frantically, she could see Thorn wriggling in Mr. Pepperhorn's other hand.

He dropped Thorn, and she landed safely on the ground, but one of his guards picked her up and put her in his pocket. Then he slammed his hand against his cloak. A high-pitched squeal came from inside the wool cloth.

"Thorn!" Seven squeaked.

"I'll take that." He slipped the miniaturized cheese ring from one of Seven's rat fingers and Seven was herself again, her hair in Mr. Pepperhorn's hand. He was pulling at it, and her scalp burned.

"I said, let me go!" she screamed.

Figgs was gone, and Seven could only hope he'd gotten far enough to save himself. Seven needed to get Thorn out of that guard's cloak.

"What exactly do you think you're doing?" Mr. Pepperhorn said, letting go of Seven but not before giving her a rough shove.

"Don't touch me again," Seven growled.

The bodyguards smirked. They were amused, Seven guessed, at this little witch's nerve. But they had no idea what she was capable of.

"I am sure the Gran will be delighted to know you've been spying on me. Isn't that against your Uncle code? Or are there no more *rules* in this town?"

Seven felt all the blood leave her face. It was in fact against Uncle code for her to use any of her powers or privileges against everyday Ravenskill citizens. *The power of the Uncle should not and will not be wielded for personal gains or projects, and to do so puts in danger your status in this important position.* Seven had all but forgotten she had rules to abide by or she could very well be stripped of her Uncle powers. She could not let that happen.

Seven took a step back and Mr. Pepperhorn smiled. "You'll find I'm not quite as clueless as you think I am, little girl."

He took a step toward her, the ten bodyguards behind her, when at the door of the house, the veiled witches emerged. There were over twenty, against one. Seven could call on her monstruos, on the Nightbeast, but what would be the consequence for her friends if she did? She could not go around fighting every adult in Ravenskill, especially not without proof.

"I will teach you a lesson, even if it means hurting one of your friends." Mr. Pepperhorn threw his hands up toward the trees surrounding them.

"NO!" Seven cried out, her hands up too late as Cheese fell from one of the trees with a loud thump.

The other raccoons were down and surrounding him in seconds—Breadstick covered his body as the others held their little paws up toward Mr. Pepperhorn and his guards, hissing.

"No, don't, don't fight him," Seven said, her heart beating wildly. She had put them in danger, she had been reckless with their safety, and now Cheese . . . oh Stars. Seven tried to run to him but Mr. Pepperhorn stood in her path.

"MOVE!" she screamed.

Mr. Pepperhorn raised his palm and blasted her with a hit of scorching magic instead. Seven was on her back and seeing stars before she could react to his attack. She scrambled to get up, to defend herself, to help Cheese, but one of the guards stepped on her cloak and she fell over again. Dirt and gravel covered her hands and went up her nose; she was humiliated and desperate. The guards laughed, and Seven tried to get up again only to be hit with another spell to the chest, something she did not recognize and was too weak, too angry to fight. In the past, her anger had helped her fight, but it had grown so big, so strong, that now it felt like she was being choked and held back by it instead. Her anger wasn't letting her see straight or focus, and worst of all it wasn't just anger. It was also fear. Mr. Pepperhorn was powerful, too powerful, and Seven was outmatched.

Just as she gathered her strength to try to fight her way out of this mess, a voice called out to her from the road.

"Seven!" the voice said again, and suddenly, a witch she was very glad to see emerged from the woods, Figgs right behind them. It was Sybell.

The guard took his foot off Seven's cloak. Seven felt like she could breathe again, but the urge to strike out against Valley's father was not subsiding. *Breathe*, she reminded herself, *your friends need you.*

She looked over to the raccoons. Cheese was sitting up, the others fawning over him, but he seemed like he was okay. The rage ebbed the tiniest bit.

"Seven, are you okay? What is going on here?" the Oracle asked as they stood between Seven and Mr. Pepperhorn. Figgs helped Seven up; his face was red and he was out of breath.

"Thanks," Seven whispered, and Figgs slipped his arm through hers.

"He has Thorn in his pocket." Seven pointed to the guard and Figgs ran over, hands out, as Sybell ordered the guard to hand over rat-Thorn.

He placed the injured rat in Figgs's hands. She was breathing but looked disoriented. *Oh, Thorn.* Seven's insides twisted with worry for her friend.

Mr. Pepperhorn cleared his throat. "Oracle, you'll find Seven here was abusing her Uncle powers and stalking a private citizen."

"She is also twelve," the Oracle said.

"And a future Uncle . . ."

"Who is still twelve. Since when is it okay for you to attack a child?" the Oracle asked.

"Wouldn't be the first time," Seven spat.

Mr. Pepperhorn's nostrils flared, his eyes wide with anger. "Don't you DARE!"

"Enough!" the Oracle said. "Figgs, take Thorn and Seven to the Gran's cottage."

Figgs pulled Seven but she stood firm. "Not yet," she whispered.

"And Mr. Pepperhorn, it will serve you to remember that regardless of wealth or status, attacking a child, let alone a future Uncle, is punishable by our laws. You do not need even more court entanglements, do you?"

Mr. Pepperhorn looked at the house, where the veiled witches stood still and silent as statues.

"Very well. But it is also my right to move freely without being surveilled."

The Oracle nodded. "I will see to it that you are."

"If there's nothing else," Mr. Pepperhorn snapped.

"Best of luck with . . . whatever you're up to." The Oracle looked at the veiled witches and smiled sarcastically.

"Guards!" Mr. Pepperhorn called, and they took off toward the house in single file.

Once he was gone, Sybell turned to Seven and shook their head. "I told you not to come back here, goats. Now you're really in for it."

The Gran had been absolutely furious, and Seven had never seen her parents so angry at her before either. It was only a few days ago that she'd been suspended from school for fighting with Starlight and now she was in trouble for abusing her Uncle powers. She wouldn't be winning any model Ravenskillian awards this year, that was for sure.

"Mr. Pepperhorn and especially those veiled witches are dangerous!" Fox had said.

"We know you're a future Uncle, we know you know your stuff, Seven, but that doesn't mean you can just put yourself and your friends in danger. It's irresponsible," her father had said.

"Yes, ma'am, yes, sir," Seven said about twelve million times that evening once the Gran had gotten through telling her off and dropped her back off at her house.

Worst of all, her plan had gotten Cheese hurt. He was mostly okay, but his little arm was in a sling, and it was all her fault. She would never forgive herself for putting her raccoons in danger.

Stuck in her room again, Seven stared at the board on her wall, red strings connecting the veiled witches to Mr. Pepperhorn to Lotus, Lotus to Valley, River, Tia, Alaric, and Mayhem—their victims. The red string crisscrossed from picture to picture, date to date. Seven had hoped it would help her untangle the spiderweb of this mystery, but right now it was only confusing her more.

There was one question that Seven kept coming back to, something that both Mr. Pepperhorn and Lotus had mentioned: Who *were* the Five Families?

CHAPTER TWENTY-ONE

BRIBING JONAFREN THE FAE

THE NEXT DAY, Seven and Thorn came up with a plan to look into the Five Families, and they needed the help of one very cranky fae to carry that plan out. The line outside the Hall of Elders complaint window was almost a mile long, like it had been ever since the Spares began to go missing. They were mostly Hill witches, and they looked very angry. Seven hoped Jonafren was okay; dealing with frustrated residents all day couldn't be easy. She also hoped he was hungry, because she and Thorn had baked him some bribe cookies to get him to talk. If anyone had information on the Five Families, it was Jonafren. Well, really, it would've been Alaric, but they hadn't been able to unstonify him, so Jonafren would have to do.

When they arrived, Jonafren was putting up a *"Be back in 60 minutes or possibly way longer"* sign, much to the crowd's dismay, but the Witchlings had come during lunch hour for a reason. Jonafren would be alone—they just had to get in through the side door without anyone noticing.

“Okay,” Seven said, “there is a small door for animal complaints on the left side of the building that leads to the Uncle office. We can crawl through there, then sneak upstairs to Jonafren’s cubicle. We have to move quickly.”

“Got it,” Thorn said, and they set off toward the animal door.

After squeezing through the tiny door, they found the lower floor of the Hall of Elders nearly empty. They went gingerly up the stairs, and weaved through the cubicles of stressed-out workers. They snuck past the guards scattered through the building, and Seven couldn’t remember a time when even on a normal day, the Hall of Elders needed protection. Ravenskill didn’t feel as safe as it once had. In fact, every day, Seven recognized her hometown less and less.

They popped into Alaric’s empty cubicle and crouched. Seven didn’t look around; she didn’t want another reminder of a friend suffering as a statue right now. It wasn’t just Valley they had to save. She shook off the sad feelings and made sure the coast was clear before standing up casually, like they belonged there.

Seven waved her hand. Papers appeared in her arms, beehive wigs on their heads, and a pair of cat-shaped glasses on both their faces. What was a good Hall of Elders break-in without disguises? Nobody would buy they were workers, but Seven hoped it at least made Jonafren laugh.

“Seven,” Thorn warned in a low tone.

“Nobody’s watching,” she whispered hurriedly.

“Eventually, you’re gonna have to explain how you can *conjure,* Seven. Because if any grown-ups ever noticed . . .”

“They won’t. Sloth out.”

“Hard to relax when one of my best friends is literally stone and the other is keeping secrets, but fine. You’ll tell me when you’re ready.” Thorn pointed a pen at her face menacingly and Seven cringed.

The pink streak in Thorn’s hair was making her channel Valley in more ways than one. Just then, more papers began materializing in their arms, shooting wildly into the air all around them.

“AH!” they both screamed.

“Cut it out!” Thorn yelled, trying to jump for the papers.

“I’m not doing anything!” Seven said, and she really wasn’t, but that didn’t stop the fake lenses in their glasses from cracking, and worse, it didn’t stop the bees . . . real bees, from buzzing in their wigs.

The Witchlings screamed, running in circles and swatting at their bee-infested wigs with paper.

“You either stop conjuring or figure out how to do it well, or so help me!” cried Thorn.

“Trust me, I want to!” Seven said. *But I don’t know how.*

“ALTO!” Thorn cried, both arms out, and the unruly magic stopped.

The papers fluttered to the ground and their fake glass

lenses fell out with a popping noise, but no fake lenses were better than cracked ones. The bees apologized to Seven before buzzing out the window, and when the Witchlings looked around, office workers were staring at them.

Seven laughed awkwardly. "It's my first day."

The office workers groaned, or shot one another knowing looks, and then turned back to the piles of paperwork on their own desks.

"Nice going, you almost got us caught!" Thorn seethed.

"It was just a little accident, no big deal!" Seven said, but she was lying. Big-time. Conjuring badly was one thing, but conjuring badly *and* involuntarily? Pathetic. Seven knew this was part of her monstruo magic acting up, she could feel it. But how could she learn to control it when there were no other monstruo witches, let alone Uncles, except for her? If only Delphinium were still around to teach her. Who knew what Seven would be capable of then?

They reached the entrance to Jonafren's cubicle and took long, deep breaths. It was time . . . to *perform*.

"Heyyyy, Jonafren!" Seven said. She and Thorn both had their biggest smiles on, trying to charm him. Not that that ever worked.

"Stop right there." He pointed at their feet. "No juvenile delinquents, sneaks, or snoopers allowed in my cubicle." With his other hand he pointed at a sign over his desk that read:

"No juvenile delinquents, sneaks, or snoopers allowed in this cubicle!"

He wasn't kidding.

"Your skin looks especially glowy today!" Thorn said.

"Have you been doing something different to your hair? It's *so* shiny," Seven said, making sure she sounded like she was really in awe.

Jonafren rolled his eyes, but he puckered his lips in the way he did when he was trying hard not to laugh. It had been a tough few days for Jonafren and the other Hall of Elders employees. Between fielding questions about the stonified witches, the Spare dilemma during the Black Moon Ceremony, and now the missing Spares, they hadn't had a moment's rest.

"I should've known I wouldn't get a second of peace today. What is it now?" He pushed his long blond hair behind one pointy ear. It really *was* shiny.

"Well, first, we brought you your favorite mudbean cookies," Seven said.

"Still fresh from the oven!" Thorn added, holding up the platter of cookies.

At this Jonafren quirked an eyebrow. "Fine, fine, come in quickly," he said, ushering them inside his cubicle without taking his eyes off the cookies.

Thorn set the baked treats down and they sat on two stools next to his desk. Jonafren took a cookie out from beneath the pink frosted glass cover and closed his eyes as he took the first bite.

"Divine," he said. "All right, what did I just get bribed for?"

"Jonafren, do you know what the Five Families are?" Seven asked quickly. She and Thorn leaned in.

Jonafren wiped his mouth daintily. "The *what*?"

"Five Families? Possibly powerful Hill witches?" Seven tried.

Jonafren shook his head no. "I've never heard of that particular group of witches before."

Seven tried again. "How about ancient elders; do you know the names of any that have passed recently?"

"We tried to look up elders with recent death days in the papers but there was nothing," Thorn said.

"Ancient elders? Why would you need to know that?"

"Just investigating a possible lead," Seven said. "For the missing Spares . . ."

"I see," Jonafren said.

Mr. Pepperhorn had seemed upset about the ancient elder's passing and had said something about losing magic. Seven wasn't sure if those elder deaths were intertwined with the Five Families or Mr. Pepperhorn's schemes with Lotus, but it gave them a place to start at least.

"Death days aren't always public knowledge; sometimes families do like privacy, you know. They'll be in individual family records, but those are off-limits to everyone except the families themselves unless it's an emergency. I could get in real trouble for even looking at that kind of thing, let alone sharing it with the two of you," he said.

"It could all very well be connected to the stone hex too, for all we know," Seven tried.

At that, Jonafren sized them up, the hoity-toity look never leaving his face despite the sadness that passed over his eyes. "You two, and Valley, are less annoying than the other children, so I will help. Besides . . . Alaric, he's still . . . well." Jonafren quickly wiped his eyes.

"Oh, please don't cry," Thorn said, handing Jonafren a handmade nose honkerchief.

"Fanks," Jonafren said as he blew his nose and the honkerchief let out a very subtle, sad *hoooonnkkkk*.

"I am fairly certain those files aren't kept here, though it's not my department so I could be wrong. Copies of family records are kept at the Twelve Towns Legacy Library, I believe. Give me one moment to confirm."

Jonafren took another cookie and then walked gracefully out of the cubicle.

The moment he was gone, Seven began snooping around.

"What are you doing?" Thorn asked in a hushed voice.

"Snoopin' around, of course," Seven said as she opened a drawer and found a pile of Enve Lopes wigs. She pointed and smiled widely at Thorn.

Thorn covered her mouth to keep from laughing. Jonafren returned and Seven quickly shut the drawer, her cheeks hot.

"If you want to borrow a wig, just say so," Jonafren said. "The ones you wore last year were *atrocious*. So are these, by the way."

"Hey, they were the best I could do on short notice!" said Thorn, crossing her arms.

"I didn't pick these," Seven said. *They just sort of appeared.*

"Next time, *don't* do rat hair wigs. Go to Curl Up and Die salon, they have the best wigs in town," Jonafren said. "As for the family records, it will take me *many* hours to process the mountain of paperwork needed to obtain them from the Legacy Library; you're gonna owe me big-time." He pointed at the Witchlings. "I can get them to you in, say, a week or two?"

Seven had hoped they'd get those records today, but it was better than nothing and she was grateful to Jonafren for helping them.

"Thanks a bunch, Jonafren, really," Seven said.

"You're the best fae we know." Thorn smiled and Jonafren smiled back.

"I'm probably the only fae you know, but I'll take it. Now I just need a name."

"The Pepperhorns, right?" Seven said, looking at Thorn. They knew from following Mr. Pepperhorn that elders had died in three of the Five Families—not to mention, Lotus had said "our" Five Families . . . like maybe she was part of them. If either of their families had ancient elders die recently, it would mean they were likely part of the Five Families themselves.

Thorn nodded. "That would be the smartest place to start, I agree, but . . ."

Jonafren narrowed his eyes at them. "Now what?"

“Could you maybe, please, pretty please, get us just *one* more?” Thorn asked sweetly.

Jonafren sighed. “You said this might help you cure the stone hex?”

“It’s . . . a possibility!” Seven said, trying to sound optimistic. They really had no froggin’ clue if it would, but they needed all the help they could get.

“What’s the other name, then? Quickly, before I change my mind.”

“The Evenstars,” Thorn said, and Jonafren opened his eyes wide.

Seven smiled. They didn’t know the identities of the veiled witches, but they did know two witches who were obsessed with balance, who would love nothing more than to get rid of every Spare in the Twelve Towns: Mr. Pepperhorn, of course, and Lotus Evenstar.

“All right, the Pepperhorns and Evenstars it is, but that’s *it*. If I get fired for this, I’m moving into your parents’ basement, Seven Salazar. And then you’ll be sorry.”

“Thanks, Jonafren, sorry, please don’t move into my house,” Seven said.

“Fine, fine. Just don’t get into any mischief,” Jonafren warned.

“Ha ha, you know you’re talking to us, right?” Seven asked.

Jonafren sighed and shoved another cookie into his mouth. “What was I thinking?”

Thorn and Seven made their way out of the cubicle,

but just as they were about to leave, the sound of heels click-clacked after them.

"Seven!" Jonafren called out, and she turned around.

"Yeah?"

"Don't stop trying to find that cure, okay? And if I find anything I think might help, I will be sure to let you know. Anything for that . . . you know, for Alaric," Jonafren whispered, then wiped another tear from his eye before turning toward a staring coworker with a scowl on his face.

"Yes, can I help you? Have you gotten those copies done I asked for an *hour* ago?" he asked meanly, and Seven smiled.

Jonafren really did like Alaric after all.

CHAPTER TWENTY-TWO
A PECULIAR MAGIC

THE NIGHT OF THE SPARE meeting had finally arrived. Seven, Thorn, and Figgs had been instructed to meet Walnut by the tunnel into the Spare Village.

When they arrived, they found Walnut already outside, looking at a worn watch on his wrist and craning his neck. When he spotted them, his face lit up.

"You came, you came, how wonderful." He patted the young witches on their backs. "Oh, the others will be thrilled!"

They followed Walnut into the tunnel beneath the old railroad tracks. Once inside, Walnut stopped and closed his eyes.

"Um, what's going on?" Thorn asked.

"Shhh," Walnut warned. Then the very old witch put his arms out and magic rippled around them. He had created a portal made of rainbow magic.

"What the—" Seven looked on in awe. She had never seen multicolored magic like this.

They followed Walnut through the iridescent rainbow wall of color and emerged into a tiny neighborhood nestled within a dense forest.

There were a few cabins with chimneys, smoke rising from them, a dirt road lined with colorful flowers, and a wooden message board covered with flyers. As they got closer, Seven could see there was one flyer with her face on it.

"This is toadally incredible," Seven whispered, to silent agreement from Thorn and Figgs. They were all a bit taken aback by this unexpected magic. A sign, painted carefully and hanging from two posts, read *"Glimmer Moon Hamlet,"* and Seven had to rub her eyes to make sure she wasn't dreaming. They were still in Ravenskill, it seemed—she could still hear and feel her animals and monstruos nearby—but somehow a tiny, hidden forest hamlet had been created within their town. A place just for Spares.

They followed as Walnut led them down a twisty dirt road. The sweet smell of the forest after rain felt like a hug around them. As they walked, a bigger structure came into view in the distance: a tavern. There were witches approaching from all directions, appearing in the middle of the woods from thin air.

"I recognize some Crones Cliff Manor Spares here," Figgs said.

Could other Twelve Towns have magic portals leading here too? After another few minutes, they reached the door of the large tavern. There was a hanging wooden sign with a disheveled-looking rat on it. "Welcome to the Shabby Rat," said Walnut with a smile.

Inside, the tavern was completely full. There were witches at every table, standing if they had to. If any of them noticed Seven, Thorn, or Figgs, they did not show it. Walnut ushered them to a table tucked into a shadowed corner.

"You can sit here and order anything you like, on the house. We'll be starting soon," Walnut said.

"Thanks," Thorn said as they settled in and took in their surroundings.

"Did you hear about the veiled cult?" said one Spare at the table beside them.

"They've been trying to bring more witches into their fold. They were knocking door-to-door on Hill houses in Ravenskill," the Spare beside her said. "Handing out flyers about a new leader in the Twelve Towns."

Seven and Figgs exchanged looks. Just like the ones he'd pickpocketed in his old town.

"Same in Blonkers," another Spare said. "Total creepsters, if you ask me."

"My employer was considering it; said they might offer a certain level of protection. Perhaps they are not wrong . . ."

"No, Olive, you mustn't say that. It's what they tell our employers but it's deceit. Especially for witches like us."

"It is, isn't it?" the other Spare said, sounding sheepish.

"We must stick together, remember."

Before Seven could eavesdrop anymore, someone with a particularly stylish witch's hat walked in and everyone quieted down.

"Spares, gather round." Everyone looked at the witch as he took his hat off, revealing spiky, flame-red hair.

Seven had to hold back a scream. *Crimson.*

"Welcome to all the new Spares here from across the Twelve Towns; thank you for joining us. And to the grand total of three non-Spare supporters, if you include me, that is—welcome." Crimson smiled and everyone chuckled. "We need to increase our efforts to recruit even more of us, but we're honored to have you here."

Crimson Riddle was one of the competitors in last spring's Golden Frog Games. Specifically, he was the teammate of Lotus Evenstar, the hexer, and River Moonfall—who'd died at Lotus's hands during the same battle that had taken Valley from them. Crimson had also been close to Tia Stardust, a fellow toad racer who was among the stone witches. Seven had tried reaching out to Crimson a few times since the spring, but aside from the odd portaphone message, it had been hard to contact him. Before Figgs had left Crones Cliff Manor, he had visited Crimson and found him in a horrible state—the tragedy of River's death at Lotus's hands driving him into a deep pit of melancholy. Seven was glad to see him in seemingly better spirits now. Crimson was an incredible witch, a master wand user, a formidable fighter, and now, it seemed, he was on the side of the Spares.

Walnut sidled over to Crimson and whispered something in his ear. Crimson's eyes opened wide and he cleared his throat.

"It seems we have extra-special guests here tonight?"

"That's our cue." Seven cringed, and she, Thorn, and Figgs stood up.

Every single witch in the room turned to them. Many of them stood up, or shouted in surprise.

"Um, hey, goats. I'm Seven."

And then Inopportuna fainted right on top of her.

CHAPTER TWENTY-THREE
THE GUILD OF SPARES

SEVEN TRIED TO HOLD Inopportuna up as other witches came to her aid.

"Oh, get up, for frog's sake!" Walnut said as Seven helped settle her into a chair and someone brought smelling snails over to wake her.

"Seven, welcome!" Crimson's eyes lit up.

Seven looked over to the teen witch and nodded. He looked much like she remembered him, with his signature red hair, smudged eyeliner, and under his cloak, safety pins adorning his probably custom-made pants peeked out. He was Moth House through and through, and the signs of his costura skills were evident in his clothing, but his black nail polish was chipped now, his black lipstick gone. He was Crimson, but he was not his full, vibrant, intimidating self. Death and loss had taken from them all.

"Thorn! Figgs!" Crimson cried, and ran to Figgs, stopping short of giving him a hug. He ruffled his black hair instead, and his eyes watered just a bit. Of the three of them, Crimson had known Figgs the longest.

The Spares who weren't tending to Inopportuna were completely silent, staring at Seven, Thorn, and Figgs. Seven shifted uncomfortably, cleared her throat, and addressed the tavern.

"I'm sorry for the chaos," Seven said.

"We are quite used to chaos!" Walnut laughed as he poured a healing tonic into Inopportuna's mouth. She had only one eye open, still half-fainted but not wanting to miss out on the drama.

"Inopportuna, are you okay with me continuing the meeting?" Crimson asked.

Inopportuna coughed. "I think so, yes," she said weakly.

Crimson nodded at Seven and took his place at the center of the room. Everyone settled in as much as they could, but it was hard to ignore the excited looks and whispers. At least they all seemed kind.

"All right, everyone, a warm welcome to our guests and maybe newest members?" Crimson quirked an eyebrow in the three witches' direction. "Let's give them a big Guild of Spares welcome!"

The room erupted in cheers, Spares patting Seven and her two friends on the back. Thorn's cheeks were pink, Figgs smirked, and Seven could not stop smiling. A *Guild of Spares*. An actual community of witches just like her, supporting one another. Seven's heart swelled with hope.

"All right, all right, settle down. The first order of

business and the reason we're gathered here today is to discuss the big strike," Crimson said.

Seven and Thorn looked at each other. *A strike?* The Hill would absolutely froggin' lose it.

"I will recap for those who missed the last meeting. We also want to make sure that there are no questions and that we all have as much protective magic as possible. Because what?"

"Safety first!" the room responded.

"Correct, safety first." Crimson smiled. "All right, the strike is still scheduled for three weeks from today. There will be no work—nothing. Not even a blade of grass will be cut. We will all meet at Twilight Square, right in front of the Ravenskill Theater, at dawn. You can pick up supplies for our protest signs right here at the Shabby Rat thanks to a generous donation from Miss Dewey."

The room clapped and Seven wondered why Miss Dewey wasn't here tonight. Probably busy with last-minute things for her wedding.

"The square will be reinforced with protective magic, a dome that will hold for at least twelve hours—one hour to symbolize each of the towns—and allow us to protest peacefully. If the Hill's Guard or any witches manage to break through the dome and try to pull us away or hurt us, we link arms and use the protective spells we worked on. Offensive spells are always a last resort. Remember, we're stronger together," Crimson said. "You'll also be very happy to know that the pamphlet dilemma has been solved. Our Goose House allies have written them up using secret squid ink, which will only reveal itself on the day of the strike so there will be no danger in you taking them with you now." Crimson pointed at a stack of boxes.

"The pamphlets outline our demands: a reversal of the Spare Amendment, of course." The room murmured in agreement or indignation. "And full rights to *all* witches regardless of coven or Sparedom. We should all have access to the same magic and resources the town provides any witch and the right to pursue any employment and education. Spares and their allies refuse to be controlled and humiliated by the few wealthy witches of our towns. We have all had enough," Crimson said, and applause broke out across the Shabby Rat.

"Lastly, I know many of you were concerned about getting to Twilight Square, but we will be adding a temporary portal from the Hill to the square, only accessible to Spares. Any allies will need to find their own way there, but I trust it shouldn't be difficult for you. Are there any questions?" Crimson said.

Seven had about a million, but she would wait to ask Crimson when everyone wasn't still sneaking looks at her, Figgs, and Thorn.

"Great. I'll be here for a few hours if you were too shy to ask out loud. Thank you all for coming!" Crimson said, and with that everyone dispersed.

The Shabby Rat settled back down, and witches gathered in small groups to have their dinner and play adventure games with little figures and maps. Soft flute music played in the background and a fire crackled invitingly, keeping the space warm and cozy. Seven, Figgs, Thorn, and Crimson sat at a table to eat together and talk. They caught up on Crimson's past few months, which mostly consisted of being in a dark room, wearing the same sleep clothes, and eating cheese circles for days on end—until one morning he woke up and decided to do something with his sadness.

"I had to avenge River, to catch whoever helped Lotus kill her," he said before taking a big swig of his drink. "I can't bring her back, as much as I wish I could, but I can make sure nobody else meets her senseless fate."

Seven nodded. "I'm really sorry about River. I'm sorry we couldn't do more to save her."

"No," Crimson said, "I should've been there. I should've known . . . I noticed Lotus being weird. Stealing away in the middle of practices and being gone all night. We just thought it was because of all the problems she was having. Lotus was in a dark place before the games, you see. Her family was being ostracized; they'd lost almost everything. She was humiliated and desperate and withdrawn. But when the games started, she also seemed happier for once. We thought she was getting better . . . but all the while she was meeting with some . . . some monster."

"Do you have any idea who it could've been?" Figgs asked, his eyes filled with rage.

Crimson shook his head. "I tried over and over again to remember something, anything that would help them catch the other hexer, but I came up with nothing. I just wish I had . . . I wish . . ."

"It's not your fault," Figgs said defiantly. "I know it's easy to try and blame ourselves, but the truth is, the only people responsible for this are the ones who did the hexing. Not us."

Thorn looked away and wiped her eyes. Figgs had been talking to Crimson, but really, it could apply to her too. And Seven. They were all grappling with guilt, blaming themselves for something they had tried hard to stop, but it wouldn't do them any good to dwell on those awful feelings when there was still a hexer out there.

"Why Lotus?" Figgs asked. "Of all the witches in the Twelve Towns, there must be a reason the hexer, the one who taught her the magic, chose her."

Crimson was quiet for a moment, a curious look in his eyes. "I've wondered that myself."

"Whoever helped Lotus and taught her to do this must be the same person behind the Cursed Toads learning archaic magic too," Seven said.

"That's been our theory for a while," Thorn explained to Crimson.

"Twice now—that we know of—whoever this witch or witches are, they picked vulnerable accomplices," Seven said.

"What do you mean?" Crimson asked.

"The Cursed Toads were Spares, like us," Figgs said, looking at the two Witchlings, who nodded at him.

"They were twelve-year-olds, trying to solve the

impossible task and probably petrified, definitely alone . . ." Seven said.

"And Lotus was desperate," Figgs said. "Her family was disgraced and broke and she was grasping for ways to save her dad from the Tombs and keep her family from being on the streets. I know firsthand how hard it is to lose everything, how it'll drive you to do things you never thought you would. Whoever is working with these witches knows that too. They're picking witches like us."

CHAPTER TWENTY-FOUR

CHISMOSAS

THE MEETING AT THE SHABBY RAT had left Seven feeling strange. The Spare strike was a good idea, even if it was risky. Seven would be there on the day of the strike, and she'd support them in any way they needed, but she also had to fight the urge to get *too* involved. She had to learn to trust in other witches' capabilities, that they could do things without Seven's help all the time.

The Spare meeting had also made Seven realize just how closely she was being watched. Miss Dewey had waited until it was safe for her and Thorn to come, for fear they'd bring unwanted attention to the cause. Seven had to dig into her bag of tricks if she wanted to keep tabs on Mr. Pepperhorn and the veiled witches too. After Cheese got hurt, Seven was unwilling to risk the safety of her animal or monstruo friends again. She decided to turn to the next best thing, her other expertise: plants.

She knew just the plant for the job—the chismosa plant. But breeding it was not an easy feat. A rare and volatile flower, the chismosa grew in pink exclusively, but could be enchanted to resemble other flowers in order to disguise them. Chismosa flowers worked like surveillance cameras . . . sort of. They had the ability to see and remember everything around them for days, and through an intense and high level of magic, they would tell you absolutely everything. As the flowers spoke, they recreated anything they had seen with millions of tiny pollen particles that resembled grainy camera footage. As useful as they were, chismosas were also considered incredibly dangerous since they were a meat-eating plant.

The chismosa flower was, strictly speaking, *super* against the rules for Seven to breed.

And now the flowers had finally bloomed, beautiful giant pink petals, and a giant, blinking eye right in the middle with a dainty mouth beneath. It was no wonder you had to disguise these things; they could be seen from a mile away. Not to mention, their glamorous looks were a tactic: Their seemingly tiny mouths could open wide enough to eat a full-grown witch, and indeed, if you got close enough, the carnivorous plant would eat you in the blink of one giant blue eye. Seven had only been able to breed three plants, so she had to be strategic about where to place them.

"You will definitely go near Mr. Pepperhorn's house on the Hill," she said as she inspected their petals, using a simple protection spell just in case one of the flowers got hungry.

"Ohhhh, I heard the Hill was a horrible place," said one of the flowers.

"You've never been there." Seven rolled her eyes.

"I have memories from my plantcestors," the plant said back.

"Uh, you're making that up," Seven said.

"Yeah," the plant giggled, and Seven shook her head. They were dramatic and gossipy and sometimes they were liars, but their surveillance visions could not lie. Thank the Stars.

"I'll put *you* near those veiled witches," she said, pointing at the second plant. "And maybe the last one . . . somewhere near Twilight Square."

Seven loaded the plants onto Thorn's trusty black wagon and made her way through town.

"Uncle Beautification Project," she had written on a banner on the back of the wagon in case anyone got curious and started asking too many questions. She had enchanted the flowers to look like a sunflower, a tulip, and a pink rose.

"I hate being a sunflower," said the first flower.

"I can make you a weed next time if that's better," Seven threatened. "Now enough complaining."

"Hmph," the flower sulked as Seven set the tall sunflower down on the balcony of the Ravenskill Theater. She was big enough to see over the stone railing and could turn her head to either side and surveil the entire square.

Seven dropped the tulip off near the veiled witches, since there were already a few of them there, and the pink rose she placed on the Hill, right at the entrance to Blood Rose Manor. It wouldn't be able to see everything, but it could see who went in and out of Valley's old place, and that would have to be enough. Maybe they'd catch Mr. Pepperhorn conspiring with whoever their master hexer was.

Finished, Seven made her way to the library to meet Thorn and Figgs. They were going to do some research on the Black Moon Ceremony and the history of Spares, and Seven was excited to hear all about Thorn's very first graded project for her costura program.

The Ravenskill Library was bustling with witches. People went there for information, or to complain to Miss Dewey, or to try to get some of her famous snacks. It seemed it wasn't just a safe space for Seven, Thorn, and Valley anymore since it was also filled with the newly minted twelve-year-old Spares. A few of them smiled at Seven when she walked in, some turned away quickly, and one, the very same witch who had waved excitedly at Seven, walked right up to her.

"You're Seven Salazar! I'm Flora. I'm a Spare too."

"For now," Seven said.

"And I hope forever. You know, I have some ideas about a Spare house. If you ever need help, I'd be happy to round up some more of us. We should get a coven house just like the others, don't you think?"

Flora was speaking loudly, and everyone around them stopped to stare. Panic rose in Seven's throat. This was not the kind of thing you could just *say*. It was like saying you wanted to feed a baby to the Nightbeast, that's how outrageous the statement seemed, because . . . it was just not something that would ever, ever happen.

"Flora," Seven whispered, "pretend to laugh, right now."

"What?" Flora opened her eyes wide. "Oh yeah!" She started laughing loudly.

"Good joke!" Seven said, and the witches around them looked back to their books, or rolled their eyes, hopefully satisfied that it *had* all been a joke.

"Something like that could get you into a lot of trouble. Don't say stuff like that out in the open, especially right now," Seven whispered.

Flora's face went bright red. "Sorry. I just thought since you were the Uncle and all . . . aren't things at least a little different now?"

"Yeah, but that's what makes it so dangerous. Most people with any power in this town don't want things to be different, and they'll do anything to keep things just like they've always been."

"Oh." Flora looked down, clearly disappointed.

"I'm not saying don't try to change things, I'm just saying don't let them know what you're doing till it's too late for them to do anything about it. Get it?" Seven winked.

Flora nodded. "I got it. Thanks, Seven." She ran off and Seven found Thorn's table.

"Where's Figgs?" Seven asked.

Thorn shrugged. "Late, I guess."

Thorn was flipping the pages of a glossy fashion

magazine and sulking, playing with the pink stripe of hair, which meant . . . something was wrong.

"How'd costura go? It's okay if you messed up. Hey, you're the youngest witch there, right? You have time," Seven tried.

"I didn't mess up," Thorn said in a small voice. "I got an almost perfect score."

"That's froggin' incredible! I knew you'd be amazing at this!" Seven said.

Thorn smiled sadly.

"What am I missing? Why aren't you happy?"

"It doesn't feel right to be happy or celebrate right now. Not when Valley and the others are still stone."

"You can't stop living because bad things happen, Thorn. Then you're giving the bad guys a double victory."

Thorn shrugged. "It's not like I want to be upset. I wish I could feel happy and excited again even for a minute, but whenever I am, it's fake. I'm going through the motions of what I would do if I were happy, but I haven't actually felt *real* happiness since before Valley got hexed. No matter what I do, I feel upset or numb. I don't think I deserve to be happy right now. It's not fair."

Seven wasn't sure what to say. She knew that what Thorn was saying wasn't true, but how could she convince her friend of something when she was feeling the same? Valley had saved Seven from turning into stone; she had jumped in front of her and taken the hex in her place. If anyone was to blame, it was Seven, but the last thing she wanted was to make Thorn feel like she had to reassure her. So instead, she put her hand on Thorn's and was silent.

"Thorn?" a voice said softly from behind them. The two Witchlings turned around to find Ambert.

"Oh." Thorn wiped her eyes. "Hi."

"I-I'm sorry, I didn't mean to eavesdrop. I was just reading up on some council bylaws and couldn't help but overhear."

"It's okay," Thorn said.

"May I?" Ambert gestured at a chair, and both Seven and Thorn nodded as the older witch sat beside them.

"I don't mean to be a, um, butt-toad, as you younger witches say, but if you don't mind, I might have some advice that could help in this precarious situation. Only if you want to hear it, of course."

Both Witchlings nodded. Seven hoped whatever Ambert said would be helpful. She would take any help she could get.

"Right. I have a bit of experience with losing people. Helio and Dusk's mother died when they were very young."

"We're sorry," Seven said. She had only heard small things from Helio.

"It was incredibly hard, as you might imagine. She passed due to a mysterious illness that I was so sure I could help cure. All the healers told me it was impossible, but I kept trying. When Marigold eventually—" Ambert paused to collect himself, running his hand over his face, taking a deep breath, and then he continued. "When

Marigold eventually passed on, I blamed myself for many years. I was so distraught, and I felt so broken that I became ill. Helio and Dusk suffered during that time, because not only had they lost their mother, they very nearly lost me too."

Seven's insides were in knots. She couldn't imagine what it would feel like to lose her mother or watch her father and Beefy suffer because of it. What would she do if everyone around her was falling apart? Immediately, she knew: Seven would be there for them. She would be strong so that her loved ones could go on.

Ambert looked at her and smiled, as if he knew what she was thinking. "It is normal to grieve something as devastating as what happened to Valley, but there are still many people here who love and care about you. What would it do to them to lose you too? How can you help Valley be cured and break free of that stone prison if you are in a prison of your own guilt?"

Tears poured down Thorn's face then, her nose red as she sniffled, and Seven put her arm around her friend. They had both been bogged down with exactly that: guilt. And Ambert putting the words to it somehow made the burden lighter.

"Thanks so very much, Ambert," Thorn said.

"It's nothing, really. Just remember what I said, and when you find yourself feeling bad again, think of what Valley would want and what Valley would do. She wouldn't want you beating yourself up over this sunrise to moonrise, and Valley would do what she could to help others. She would take risks. Do not be afraid to show them all what you're really made of."

A fire grew in Seven's heart, and she knew that Ambert was right. She had to do what she could, *all* that she could, to save Valley. Feeling sorry for herself would only slow them down. Looking at Thorn, she could tell her friend felt the same. They had to show everyone that they were legendary Spares. They would save Valley, and the missing Spares, and prove it.

Suddenly, Figgs appeared, sitting at the table with them. "Hey, sorry I'm late. Was doing some research. Hello, Mr. Lophiifor," he added. "Thanks for your help yesterday."

"Anytime." Ambert smiled. "Now alas, I have to get back to my research on the town council. The elections are soon, and I have to be prepared. I have quite the big plans for this town." Ambert winked. "I'll leave you three to it."

The older witch got up and walked to his table on the other side of the library, and Figgs leaned in, pitching his voice low. "I think I found something to help with the stone hex."

Seven and Thorn opened their eyes wide. "What?" Thorn asked.

"Have you heard of Lunar Ivy?" Figgs asked.

"No," Seven said, surprised. She knew most rare plants and roots at least by name.

"It's uncommon, especially here in Ravenskill, but it's said to grow in the deep Lunar Ponds of Bonecross,"

Figgs said. "I've been reading up on it, and it's dangerous to get, but it has miraculous healing properties. Just look at this."

Figgs took a small book from his coat pocket and showed the Witchlings an illustration—a witch holding up a plant. Next to her was a witch with a bloodied arm, a witch lying in what looked to be their deathbed, and most interesting of all, someone who looked to be hexed inside a stone cast.

"Does this mean . . . it can *cure* the stone hex?" Seven asked.

"That's what it looks like in this illustration!" Thorn said. "Where did you get this book, Figgs?"

"Have you seen the twins' library? It's froggin' giant! Last night I had a sleepover with Dusk and Helio, and we were looking for books that might help you goats with the stone hex cure when I found it. Their dad said we could borrow it so long as we're gentle. The book is fragile and supposed to be valuable," Figgs said.

Thorn nodded. "What else does the book say?"

"Well." Figgs cringed. "The Lunar Ponds are dangerous. One of us will have to dive into unknown waters. There could be anything in there."

"We'll be ready for whatever it is," Seven said, her heart nearly beating out of her chest. Could this be it, finally? Could this be the cure to save Valley?

CHAPTER TWENTY-FIVE

THE LUNAR PONDS OF BONECROSS

BONECROSS WAS NORTH of Ravenskill, a foggy town nestled within a sloping mountain range. It was only a few hours away by train but Seven, Thorn, and Figgs had gotten the okay from Crimson to use Spare portal magic to go from Ravenskill to Bonecross, so for them it would only take seconds.

"Bonecross is creepy, and it's midnight, and it's cold," Figgs pouted.

The Spare-made portal magic took months to create, and according to Crimson, each portal could only be used a few times before needing more magical reinforcement. With Spare powers being limited, they tried to use the portals, erm, sparingly, since overuse could also lead to collapse and having to build the portals from scratch. The stone hex cure was a priority for Crimson and the rest of the Guild of Spares too, it seemed, and they had granted Seven and her friends access so long as they didn't overdo it.

The moon was full as they emerged in the outskirts of Bonecross and made their way toward the Lunar Ponds. It was biting cold out, eerily quiet, and even Seven had to admit she was a bit scared. This wasn't like the Cursed Forest; here, she didn't know what to expect. They reached a tall metal gate and Figgs sighed.

"Seriously? The ponds I saw in the book weren't in a cemetery."

"These are easier to get to though, and the quicker we get the Lunar Ivy, the quicker we can leave," Seven said.

"Fine, but if I get nightmares, I'm blaming you two," Figgs said, and the two Witchlings giggled as they led Figgs into the Bonecross Graveyard.

"The ponds should be just beyond those trees, right at the center of the graveyard," Seven said. "Careful not to step on the graves, Figgs. The ghosts don't like that."

"Oh goats," Figgs's voice squeaked. "Never thought I'd say this, but I preferred being a rat."

Soon enough they reached the ponds, and they did look deep, just like the book had said. Seven had studied the book Figgs borrowed cover to cover, and was confident she'd be able to extract the Lunar Ivy easily.

"The key is to stay close to the rocky ledge on the left side of the pond as you descend, and as you come up to swim right through the center. The pressure inside will shoot you right up, but if you let it get you on the way down, it'll take a limb off," Seven said confidently.

"Are you sure you're okay going in?" Figgs asked. "I don't mind doing it; I'm a good swimmer."

"It's okay, I've got this. If there are any fish in there, my Uncle powers will come in handy." Seven smiled.

Figgs put one hand on his chest in relief and Seven laughed. As Seven took off her cloak, Thorn formed a protective circle around them, whispering, "Salvaguardia," then settling at the edge of the pond beside Figgs.

Seven wore a black diving suit, enforced with protective magic thanks to Thorn. A bit of overkill, but she knew Thorn was extra cautious after Valley, so she didn't argue.

"Tortuga marina," Seven said, casting an advanced sea turtle spell on her lungs and praying to the Stars that it worked well enough. Oh no. She had forgotten her protective eyewear!

Seven flourished one hand around the other, conjuring a trusty pair of . . . googly eyeglasses.

"Close," she chuckled awkwardly.

"Here." Thorn handed her actual goggles. "Brought these just in case. You have got to stop conjuring."

Seven nodded and put her goggles on.

"Good luck," Thorn said as she and Figgs crossed their fingers.

The spell began working; Seven's lungs felt bigger already! She plunged into the glittering blue water, surprised at its welcoming, mild temperature. Seven held on to the stony ledges as she descended, five, ten, fifteen toadstools beneath the surface. Eyes wide, she searched for the Lunar Ivy, a bright green flower with sparkling edges, according to Ambert's book. It would be impossible to miss in this darkness.

Seven continue to descend, her legs tiring slightly but her excitement at possibly being on the brink of a cure for the hex propelling her deeper into the endless pond. Suddenly, colors began to appear beneath her . . . green, to be exact . . . the flower! Seven picked up her pace, swimming faster and faster, her hand outstretched toward the Lunar Ivy. This was it: Valley would be cured soon, she'd be back with them, and they'd make up for lost time. Alaric and Tia and Mayhem could go home, and the stone hex would make it no farther toward any of their hearts.

The green blobs of color were coming into focus, almost in reach, when suddenly they shifted. Not Lunar Ivy . . . but *eyes*. Green eyes that belonged to a pale face, surrounded by seaweed and undulating aquamarine hair . . . The creature opened her mouth and sang, and the sirena song hit Seven right in the heart, a pain sharper than any she'd ever known coursing through her body in a matter of seconds.

No, no, no! Sirenas were deadly, beautiful creatures. Ancestors to the friendlier mermaids, sirenas used their song to entrap any witch foolish enough to enter their waters. And right now, Seven was that foolish witch.

Seven fought against the magic pulling her down; she kicked and thrashed and struggled. She wanted to call for Thorn or Figgs, but if she opened her mouth, the water would rush in. The turtle spell would help her withstand the deep waters, but not if the water got into her lungs.

Please, no, Seven thought as the creature swam up, her hands outstretched, her tail swishing gracefully. As much as Seven struggled, as hard as she tried to get to the center of the pond so the pressure would shoot her up and out, she could not do it. The sirena was much too strong, controlling the very water around Seven, pulling her down every time she progressed an inch, keeping her pinned against the sharp stone walls of the pond.

The lights around Seven were beginning to dim. She was losing consciousness. She wondered if Thorn and Figgs even knew anything was wrong, if they knew she was drowning, or if the water looked calm from above.

"Seven," a voice rumbled in her mind. "Do you need me?"

The Nightbeast. It would not be able to help her here, and Seven would not let another one of her friends get hurt because of her foolishness.

Seven shook her head with her last bit of strength, hoping the Nightbeast knew not to come. She felt the slimy cold hand of the sirena on her cheek, and Seven's eyes opened wide at the creature's hideous smile. The sirena opened her mouth to devour her, rows and rows of pointy teeth dipped in blood coming at her face, when from the caverns of Seven's mind, the Nightbeast roared loud and true, reverberating through the water.

The sirena screamed, fear in her eyes. She let go of Seven's face and turned faster than the blink of an eye. Her tail disappeared into the murky water, and Seven was pushed straight into the center of the pond. She shot up, faster, faster, her mind whirring, her heart beating slower than a sloth, when she broke through the surface and gasped.

"Seven!" Thorn and Figgs pulled her out as Seven coughed. "Did you get it?"

"What happened?" Figgs asked.

It took Seven a few moments to recover, but soon she was sitting up again and recounted the whole thing to Thorn and Figgs. Well, except for the Nightbeast talking to her, of course. She told them a loud noise like a wolf howling scared the sirena away.

"We didn't hear any howling," Figgs said, looking confused.

"Yeah, it was dead quiet out here. We couldn't tell what was going on at all; the water looked perfectly serene," Thorn said.

It made Seven's blood go even colder. If the Nightbeast had not howled loud enough to carry into Bonecross, then the sirena had heard the howl from Seven's mind. It was as if she had summoned the beast through her thoughts and brought it to life. Nobody had ever been able to hear the Nightbeast in Seven's thoughts except for her. Except for tonight.

"Safe to say that was a bust," Seven said as Thorn covered her in a blanket and used drying spells to get the pond water off her.

"That's an understatement; you were nearly killed." Figgs said.

Seven shook her head. "The book doesn't say anything

about sirenas. I didn't know! Besides, since when did sirenas ever live in *ponds*?"

Figgs frowned and shook his head. He was right about her almost being killed, but Seven was desperate. For all they knew, Valley's heart might already be made of stone.

CHAPTER TWENTY-SIX

A MIRROR, A MATCH

"I'M USELESS," Seven whispered.

"That's not true," Thorn said beside her.

They were cutting through the Cursed Forest, on their way home. They had already dropped Figgs off, and after their disastrous night in Bonecross, Seven had never felt more like a failure in her life. They'd tried everything to get Valley out, but even Quill hadn't been able to help them. What if this was it, and Valley would have to live the rest of her life in stone?

The thought of it took Seven's breath away and she stopped walking, holding on to the trunk of a tree to steady herself. She was dizzy with grief and pain, and the Cursed Forest seemed to spin around her, making the world a giant tornado.

"Seven!" Thorn cried out, but her voice was far away and muffled.

No . . . this wasn't just in her mind. The wind quite literally whipped around them. Leaves and branches and bramble the size of cars and dirt and snow created a vortex, trapping Seven and Thorn. The skeleton birds clacked overhead, forest creatures scurried to her aid, but Seven could not stop it. The unbearable weight of her failure had escaped her mind and her heart and was making a disaster of the Cursed Forest. She would destroy the monstruos' homes without meaning to if she did not stop. *Breathe*, she told herself, *breathe*.

But it was not until Thorn, who had fought through the raging wind and somehow reached Seven's side, put her hand in Seven's that the wind began to slow its attack. Thorn squeezed Seven's hand, and the familiar warmth reached Seven's heart; she was safe, she was always safe with Thorn. All at once the forest quieted to an eerie stillness, and Seven fell into Thorn's arms.

When they let go, Thorn looked at Seven, concerned.

"I can't do this," Seven whispered. "I can't help Valley. I failed."

"That's not true! And you never give up. So long as I've known you, Seven Nightshade Salazar doesn't quit, and neither do I. We might be Valley's only hope."

Seven shook her head. "I just . . . I don't know how. I don't know how to help her and I'm scared I'm going to let her down. And Tia, Alaric, Mayhem . . . they're all still stone and they'll never escape. They're dying and I can't figure out how to cure them."

"If you cured our baby bird, Uncle Seven, you can cure your friends," Scrape, the eldest skeleton bird, said from the branches above them.

Seven looked up. "That's different."

"What's different?" Thorn asked, and Seven explained how last year, while Thorn was battling in the costura competition, Seven had found a dying baby skeleton bird in the Cursed Forest, and somehow she'd cured it. It had cost her though, knocking her out cold for hours until her raccoons had managed to rouse her.

"You cured a skeleton bird, and they think it means you can cure the stone hex?" Thorn asked.

"I guess so."

"Think, then, think. What did you do differently that time that you haven't done with all the cure attempts?"

Seven did not have to think. She knew. She looked at Thorn and considered her options. Thorn suspected Seven's magic was behaving in unusual ways—she had seen her conjuring, after all, and even now, Seven was speaking to skeleton birds. Perhaps she did not know what it meant, but Thorn knew something was amiss, and all this time, Seven had not been able to confess the truth.

Her monstruo magic had been her biggest secret, the thing that had gotten Delphinium chased out of Ravenskill and probably killed. To tell Thorn meant risking her friend's safety, but for so long Seven had felt like she was suffocating under the weight of her secret. She knew that she had to fight her urge to take on the world alone. She could try to protect her friends, but they also had a right to protect her, didn't they? So she took a deep breath and finally, finally told Thorn the truth about her powers.

"I was able to cure the skeleton bird because I gave in to what I am."

"What do you mean?" Thorn asked, tilting her head to the side.

"There's a reason I can conjure, even if I haven't gotten the hang of it completely, a reason the Nightbeast comes to my aid and why I can talk to monstruos still even though I'm not supposed to. Thorn . . . I am a monstruo Uncle. I can talk to them. I can use magic I shouldn't be able to use. Cursed magic, hex magic, shadow magic. You've seen me do it all even if you didn't understand what I was doing."

"And when you cured the baby bird . . ."

"I tapped into that side of me, which I wasn't as used to back then. It took a lot of strength and concentration because it's . . . archaic magic."

"How long have you known?" Thorn asked.

"A few months. I hope you aren't angry at me for not telling you, but I had a good reason. There was another monstruo Uncle long before me and she told the Gran of her time and it . . . probably got her killed. I didn't want to put you in danger. I was afraid."

Thorn took a step forward and grabbed Seven's hand again, the way she always did. "I feel terrible I couldn't be there for you, but . . . I understand why you kept this secret as long as you did. Even after all this time though, you're still learning our first lesson."

Seven quirked an eyebrow.

"We're stronger together, just like Crimson said. That's

what got us through the impossible task. It's what helped us survive during the hexing spree."

"I trust you and I ask for help all the time now, not like before," Seven protested.

"But you still try to take on too much on your own, Seven. I know you're just trying to protect us, that you think it's the right thing to do to sacrifice yourself, but if something happens to you, where does that leave me, huh?"

"I'm sorry, Thorn," Seven said.

"I'm sorry too, that you've been dealing with this on your own for so long, but don't worry, we're gonna figure it out *together.* Like we always do."

"Together." Seven smiled and the Witchlings hugged.

Thorn took a step back. "So you used your monstruo magic to cure the baby skeleton bird, right?"

"Right," Seven said.

"Maybe, if you use that same magic, if you just use your monstruo Uncle magic . . . you might be able to break the hex? It's a kind of archaic magic, after all."

"I don't know. You've seen how many times I've made potions explode or how I keep conjuring the wrong thing. I still don't understand it well enough to trust myself. What if I hurt Valley or the others?"

Thorn tapped her chin, thinking. "What did you do exactly when you cured the bird?"

"I put my hand on its chest and I found what was hurting it, somehow, like I was talking to it but without words. Then once I figured out its heart was the issue, I was able to heal it."

“What if you did the same thing to the stone statues? What if you put your hand on Valley or Alaric and found the root of the hex?”

Seven’s heart began to race in tandem with her mind. Could this work? Could she really channel her monstruo magic and cure the stone witches?

“I am stronger than last spring, but it still took all of my strength to cure one skeleton bird’s heart. I don’t know if I’d be able to cure four stone witches with just my hands.”

“Wait!” Thorn’s eyes opened wide. “What if what you need is something to amplify and channel your magic?”

Seven nodded. “But . . . oh. Oh!” she said, finally understanding.

“Maybe you don’t have to use just your hands,” Thorn said conspiratorially, and Seven smiled.

“Maybe I can use a wand.”

CHAPTER TWENTY-SEVEN

THE FATE OF VALLEY PEPPERHORN

CRIMSON ANSWERED HIS PORTAPHONE on the very first ring.

"What? What happened? Are you okay?" he said, his voice still low and deep with sleep.

"Can you meet us in the Spare Village, and . . . can you bring one of your wands?" Thorn asked.

"My wands?"

"We'll explain when you get here. It's important."

"Okay, give me five minutes."

The good thing about portal magic was, there was no train from Crones Cliff Manor to take, no Cursed Forests to traverse or veiled witches to sneak past. Crimson simply found the entrance to his side of the portal and emerged on the Ravenskill end, and that's where Seven and Thorn found him. Despite the late hour and the last-minute rendezvous, Crimson wore a full silk sleeping outfit under his handmade cloak, and a witch's hat with a top that curled and twisted that was becoming the fashion now with certain witches. They met at the

Spare Village and then Walnut guided them to the Shabby Rat in Glimmer Moon Hamlet. Walnut had gotten out of bed in a bright blue sleep robe and cap and opened the pub just for them. Seven's heart stopped at every little sound; she wanted to run, to fly to Valley, and instead she had to move slowly and quietly. It felt like torture. Getting caught would be worse though. Especially when they were so very close to the thing they'd been working toward for so long.

They stood around a table in the dark tavern, with only a few candles for light. Walnut had already fallen back asleep across the bar, soft snoring noises the only sound filling the tavern.

Crimson's eyes opened wide, but he just shook his head. "You said you needed a wand?"

Seven nodded.

"I should ask what for. Not exactly a thing I should be lending out."

"We think we can cure the stone hex with one," Thorn said. "Using that and Seven's magic. But we kinda need you not to ask any more questions." Thorn smiled so cutely that Seven could practically see Crimson's guard crumbling. Thank the Stars for Thorn's not-so-secret weapon.

"All right, but I'm coming with you. These things are dangerous. Have you ever wielded a wand? I shouldn't have to ask that, the answer should be no, but knowing you two . . ."

Seven cracked a smile. "No, I never have."

"Well, that's a relief. First, you must pick your wand. Whichever calls to you, whichever feels right."

Crimson took a wand roll from his back and laid it out on the table in front of them. He hadn't just brought one wand, he'd brought a selection. There were long, skinny wands with tiny petals sprouting from them; there were wands that looked like they'd belong to a giant warlock, wrapped in tough metal; and there were dainty wands wrapped in gold or crystal.

The crystal wand reminded Seven of Valley's twin blades—and both she and Thorn pointed at it at once. Crimson took the wand out and, with both hands, handed it to Seven carefully.

It was iridescent and fit perfectly in her hand. When she held it up to the candlelight, every color in the world shone from within. She and Thorn looked at each other and nodded: This was it.

Crimson smiled. "The rosada wand? Fitting."

Rosada, pink. Thorn ran her hand softly along the pink streak in her hair and smiled. Seven's heart swelled.

"Some very quick basics, before you go. Wand wielding is a vicious business."

Crimson showed Seven how to hold her wand (steady and true), how to flick her wrist (graceful and strong), and how to channel all her magic, all her power, through the wand—something that frightened Seven quite a bit. What if something terrible happened because of her monstruo magic? What if she ended up hurting Alaric or Tia or Mayhem? What if she hurt Valley?

"Wand magic is all about feeling. You will know if your magic is spiraling out of control, just as you will know if it's not strong enough. Listen to your instincts, and most importantly, listen to your heart." Crimson held his hand to his chest.

"I can do that," Seven said, hoping it was true.

"Let's go," Seven whispered, and Thorn nodded, desperate to get to Valley. This was it.

Walnut created a portal, weaving his hands and whispering incantations Seven could not hear, and the four witches walked through, emerging on the roof of the Bluewing Infirmary. Seven led the way toward the stone witches. Walnut stayed on the roof to stand watch, though Seven suspected he would fall asleep the moment they were inside. They each took a bite of shushrooms from Seven's rucksack to quiet their steps and began their descent.

Steady and true.

Graceful and strong.

Seven repeated the words to herself over and over as they walked through the darkness and toward the stone witches. She wished her mother and father, even Beefy, were with her now. She needed their support, their assurances that things would be okay even if she failed. The weight of all four stone witches was on her shoulders and Seven was frightened that if she collapsed under their pressure, she would break too.

They looked around the corner of the long hallway that led to the rooms where Valley, Mayhem, Alaric, and

Tia were. There were Gran's Guards everywhere, but they worked in rotations, so if they timed it right, they'd be able to slip into the rooms unnoticed.

"Let's try Alaric first," Seven said. "He's already dead, so it's the least risky."

They entered the large room that held the three stone witches: Tia Stardust, Mayhem Lilitoad, Alaric . . . the ghost. What *was* Alaric's last name anyway?

The witches were all in a row, their statues the same as they'd been for months—gray stone, expressions of surprise suspended on their faces, a horrible eerie aura surrounding them. Had their hearts already been turned to stone? There was only one way to be certain.

Seven prepared herself. She held the wand out and closed her eyes, letting the monstruo magic course through her. It surged through her like raging rapids, like lightning and thunder, like the winds of a powerful storm, and when Seven opened her eyes, she knew she was ready.

She pointed the wand at Alaric's heart, and focused.

Steady and true.

Graceful and strong.

Seven's body shook with the force of the magic, the wand nearly slipping from her hand. This was it!

But Alaric's statue remained unchanged. Maybe they really were too late. She held out for a few minutes more, until her arm became numb and she had to stop. She'd failed.

Seven needed her monstruo magic; she could tell now

as she tried to cure the hex that this was the answer. The moment the magic from the wand connected to the statues, it was as if she could read their magic. She could see things she couldn't with her naked eye. She felt the hex giving way under the wand but then stitching itself up again. Seven simply did not have enough power. She did not know how to channel it correctly. The magic was the right kind, but she needed more of it. She could scream! It was so frustrating to be this close, to know the answer, but to fall short just the same.

"What happened?" Thorn asked.

"I can't . . . do it . . ." Seven shook her head. She'd been so hopeful.

"Maybe because he is a ghost, it is more difficult to break him free," Crimson suggested. "Should we try another witch?"

Seven looked at Thorn, worried. What if she killed one of them? But she hadn't even made a dent in Alaric's statue, so . . . perhaps she was worrying for nothing.

"I'll try," Seven said, and steadied herself to try again.

Tia's statue was next. The champion toad racer and October's girlfriend had been hexed during a midnight toad race, and still wore her Boggs Ferry uniform. Again, Seven poured every ounce of magic and power she could into the counter-hex and again, nothing happened.

She doubled over, sweat pouring from her face as Thorn ran over to wipe her forehead with a clean honkerchief.

"What if I try and help?" Crimson asked, but Seven shook her head.

She turned to Mayhem and tried again, ignoring Thorn's warnings to rest. Her monstruo magic connected with the hex, and she could feel her way through the stone that had taken over Mayhem's body—she could tell that Mayhem and the others were mere minutes from the stone hex taking their hearts. Seven shook, her limbs weak and her heart beating scarily fast. She gritted her teeth and held out as long as she could before she felt something wet dripping from her nose. *Blood.*

Seven lowered her wand, panting and angry. "Why can't I do this?" she cried out.

Thorn worried her cloak, her brow furrowed, and Crimson ran his hands through his hair, just as lost as they were. Valley's heart would be turned to stone. Tears spilled from Seven's eyes. They had been so close, so very close. Could this really be the end of her friend's life?

"Don't give up, Seven, please!" Thorn said. "Try Valley."

Seven looked up, struggling to breathe, and nodded. Without another word they made for Valley's room and closed the door carefully behind them, its closing echoing faintly in the large room. Hanging oil lamps cast a warm glow, making Valley look like a statue of one of the Stars instead of their friend. Flowers, cards, and offerings surrounded her still. Seven took a deep breath and tried to gather what little strength she had left.

Seven stepped up to Valley, her hands shaking. She

took the wand from her cloak and it shone in the glow of the lamps.

Steady and true.

Graceful and strong.

Seven turned her body and raised one hand, the other at her side. She did her best to keep steady. Sweat dotted her forehead, her eyes focused on the stone statue. What if she failed? What if Valley died because of her?

Her entire body trembled with fear and exhaustion, and then a warm hand took hers. Seven looked to her side, and there, as always, was Thorn. Her face fixed with determination, Thorn told Seven with just a look that she was capable.

Steady and true.

Graceful and strong.

Seven closed her eyes and pulled from the magic inside her. She felt the call of the birds overhead, the worms in the dirt many toadstools beneath the marble floor of the infirmary; she heard the buzz of the bees and the chittering of her beloved raccoons; she heard the clink-clank of the skeleton birds. Seven could even feel the electricity of the Stars looking down on her; their faces flashed before her eyes, filling her with the strength of her ancestors. The plants, the trees, the soil, it all became one with her magic in that moment.

She opened her eyes and took another deep breath, preparing to strike. Preparing to save her friend or doom her. It was all in Seven's hands and she was afraid, but more than that she was brave.

And then a whisper in her heart, a voice as clear as day, said:

I am with you too, friend. And I love you.

"Valley," Thorn choked out, and Seven knew that she could hear it too.

Seven swelled with magic; she channeled it all through her body and to the wand as Crimson had instructed her to. Right in the critical moment, right before she struck, the Nightbeast and its cubs howled high and proud. Her monstruo magic erupted.

The room around them shook with the force of a hundred stomping giants; the magic shot out of Seven's wand like a bolt of lightning and hit Valley Pepperhorn straight in the heart. This time Seven felt something she had not with the others; she was not doing this on her own, and it wasn't just Thorn helping her . . . it was . . . it was impossible! But it was. It was Valley. She felt her friend pushing out from within her stone prison, felt her chipping away at the magic. Valley was helping Seven. She was setting herself free.

A burst of magical wind and light spun around them, the flowers and trinkets flying in the air. Seven, Thorn, and Crimson stood mesmerized, their capes billowing, their hair dancing wildly, as the stone statue before them began to crack. Seven held on, shooting her magic at Valley, steady and true, graceful and strong.

The crack in the stone zigzagged, beginning at Valley's chest, then expanding outward. Seven gathered all her strength, preparing for the biggest exertion of magic she'd ever experienced, when the stone exploded.

Seven, Valley, and Crimson were thrown back with a loud BOOM. Parts of the ceiling came down all around them; dust and debris flew everywhere. Seven struggled to her feet, coughing and holding her chest from the exertion. Thorn and Crimson got to their feet beside her and the three of them ran to Valley.

They were sifting through rubble and stone when they were nearly thrown back once again as something burst out of the wreckage before them.

As the dust cleared, Seven and Thorn ran. Valley's body was slumped over on the floor, head down, her once-stone skin and hair now the peach-and-pink color she was in life, but Seven could not see her breathing. She searched for signs of life, hoping against hope that her friend was still alive, when Valley Pepperhorn looked up and smiled.

"What took you butt-toads so long?"

CHAPTER TWENTY-EIGHT

STEADY AND TRUE, GRACEFUL AND STRONG

"VALLEY!" THORN AND SEVEN threw themselves on her, knocking Valley over in the process.

Seven sobbed big, ugly sobs, her body broken from the magic, her heart in one piece for the first time in months.

"Ouch, gah, okay." Valley squirmed beneath them.

"We should take it easy on her," Crimson said. He reached out to help get them off, but Valley shook her head no.

"Just leave us here for a moment," she whispered. "I missed you goats so, so, so much."

"We missed you too," Thorn said between sobs.

The three Witchlings hugged, and cried, and held on to one another more tightly than ever before because now that they knew what it felt like to nearly lose one of them, the thought of ever being apart again felt like a venomous dart. Having Valley back felt like the biggest gift, the most beautiful blessing. Seven never ever wanted to let go again.

But eventually, they untangled from one another, and Seven really took a look at Valley, really.

She was not gray skinned like Seven thought she might be, as the Gran warned she would be. She looked as if she had just been frozen in time from the night of the Frog Ball, glittering suit, battle wounds, and all.

"Here." Thorn wiped her face and pulled a black cloak from her bag to give Valley.

Valley stood up, nearly without any help, and Seven and Thorn draped the cloak around her shoulders.

"How are you feeling?" Seven asked.

Valley cleared her throat. "A little hoarse, tired, and hungrier than a bear after hibernation," she said, and they all laughed.

"You should stay here until we cure the others," Crimson said.

"No way. I want to come. I can help," Valley said.

"Valley, you're weak, you shouldn't push yourself right now," Thorn said.

"No, I have to help. Trust me," she said, looking at Seven, and Seven knew she was right.

Seven understood that she had not done it on her own, that Valley had helped escape the stone prison she'd been condemned to. All she had needed was someone to create a crack big enough to break through.

"Then hurry, before the guards find us," Crimson said, and they left the piles of rubble, gifts, and flowers behind.

Seven drank an energy tonic from her bag and

gave one to Valley as well as she prepared to cure Alaric. The tonic helped a bit, but she was still pretty froggin' exhausted.

"Steady and true, graceful and strong," she whispered. "I hope I can do this."

"You can," Valley said. "We can do it together."

Seven nodded as Thorn took her free hand and Valley stood behind her, helping her hold the wand.

"Maybe you should let me help." Crimson tried to step in, but Seven knew it would not work. This wasn't normal magic. It wasn't the kind of power anyone was used to. It was the same magic that made the Spares different, that made Seven an Uncle and Thorn a champion and Valley strong enough to help break herself free. They had to do this together.

"We've got this," the Witchlings said in unison, and then the magic sprung from the wand, steady and true, graceful and strong.

They hit Alaric's statue right in the heart, as they had Valley, and he tumbled out, his ghostly form faded and gray instead of its normal vibrant blue. Crimson ran over and took him out of the way, while the Witchlings broke Tia free next, followed by Mayhem Lilitoad, the Goose House witch who had been the first hex victim.

All three of them were alive.

The Witchlings nearly collapsed, holding on to one another as Crimson ran out to get help.

Seven hobbled over to Alaric, Tia, and Mayhem, who were slumped against the far wall of the room.

"Seven," Alaric said weakly, smiling. "I was hoping to see you again."

Seven wrapped her arms around the ghost, and he was surprisingly warm. Maybe because he had died in a fire. "I'm glad to see you, friend. You too, Tia, Mayhem." Seven took their hands and squeezed as Thorn and Valley said their hellos.

"Is October okay?" Tia asked, her voice weak. The toad-racing champion, normally healthy and strong, looked frail, her expression desperate for news on her girlfriend.

"She's doing great, just missing you," Thorn said, and tears spilled down Tia's gray face. "She's going to be so happy to see you."

They were all varying shades of gray, all except Valley. They would need to see a healer soon, to make sure the hex was completely out of their systems and there weren't still remnants snaking toward their hearts. Then there was the matter of keeping this all a secret. They had all, perhaps with the exception of Mayhem, seen Seven wield a wand and set them free from stone. Using a wand was bad enough on its own without the Witchlings being capable of something not even the strongest healers, Grans, and Uncles of their towns could do. It would be deemed unnatural magic, an extension of Seven's Uncle powers, Thorn's cursed cape, and maybe they wouldn't be wrong.

"I have to ask something of you," Seven said. "You all know how much Spares have been persecuted, but things have only gotten worse."

"Worse how?" Mayhem asked.

"It's a lot to explain right now, but we'll catch you up on everything once you rest."

"What did you need from us?" Alaric asked.

"Would you mind not telling anyone that I broke you out of the statues?" Seven asked.

"That *we* did," Thorn said, looking at Seven.

Seven shook her head. If she could keep Valley and Thorn from getting into trouble because of this, she would.

"No, it was me," Seven tried.

"It was the three of us," Valley said. "But if they find out . . ."

"We won't say a word," Tia said, her voice raspy.

"Ghost's honor," Alaric said.

"Oh my Stars!" A group of healers poured into the room then, swarming the once-stone witches, fussing over them, marveling at their recovery and at the absolute shambles the room was in.

"I'm fine, I don't need a bed," Valley said, fighting off the healers' attempts to get her onto a stretcher.

"You at least need to be examined, young witch! We won't let you leave until you do," one of the healers' assistants said.

"Fine," Valley said, rolling her eyes.

"Room two twenty-four. If you're not there in ten minutes, we'll send the guard to fetch you."

Valley shook her head. "Sheesh, already treating me like a delinquent."

The healers carried Alaric, Tia, and Mayhem out, thankfully without any questions. For now. Seven knew though that they would come, and they had to be prepared with a good enough story. Once they were alone, Crimson hid his wand and walked out with the Witchlings.

"Thanks for your help," Thorn said.

"Don't mention it. And next time, maybe don't perform magical miracles so late at night. I need my beauty sleep," Crimson said. "Glad to have you back, Valley."

Valley smiled at the teen witch, and then Crimson tipped his witch's hat and took off.

Seven, Valley, and Thorn walked toward room 224, arms linked. It felt like a dream. Seven was afraid that any minute, she'd wake up and Valley would still be stone. She kept leaning closer to her, feeling the warmth of her arm, looking at her pink hair.

"I like your streak," she told Thorn with a smirk.

"Thanks." Thorn blushed.

"How's my mom? I can't wait to see her; I hope this exam is quick," Valley said.

"Quill is fine, but . . ." Seven's eyes went wide as she remembered.

She stopped and turned to Valley. "Um, there's something you should know before you go home."

"What?" asked Valley, looking worried.

"You, uh, sort of have a brother now."

Just nervous. And you all really need to work on your whispers."

The raccoons nodded and in unison whispered, "We will work on our whispers."

"You don't have to worry so much about me. I'm all right, I'm just . . . afraid."

The sound of little footsteps pacing behind her stopped, and Seven turned around.

"Why are *you* afraid?" asked Cheese.

"Well, I'm about to tell someone something that might . . ." Seven didn't want to alarm the raccoons. If she told them she might be in danger, they would panic, and go into battle mode, and carry her to the Cursed Forest whether she liked it or not.

"It might make others treat me differently," Seven said instead.

The raccoons looked at one another, then Cheese cleared his throat and spoke. "Others treat monstruos differently no matter what we do. Even if we are kind and helpful and do not turn over their trash bins."

The other raccoons nodded emphatically, and Cheese continued. "You do not have to be afraid. Monstruos are not afraid; they are feared."

"But I'm not . . ." Seven began to say, but then stopped. What was the difference, really, between her and a creature to be feared? Even if Spares weren't dangerous, witches were afraid of them for what they made them *feel*: discomfort, guilt, terror that just being near Spares would make them different and unwanted too.

CHAPTER TWENTY-NINE

COMING CLEAN

SEVEN SET OUT to meet the Gran at Starlight Cottage one early morning before school. She had barely slept the night before, tossing and turning in bed and debating what she should do about her big secret. Seven knew that the Gran should know the truth, not just about how she'd cured the hexed witches but about her magic. If it helped the Gran stop whoever the other hexer was, and heal any potential future victims, it was Seven's duty to tell her. Still, it made her slightly ill to think about finally telling the Gran the truth after all this time. She just hoped she didn't meet the same fate as Delphinium.

"Is she sick?" she heard the raccoons asking one another as they walked to the cottage.

"She doesn't look *not* sick," said Cheese.

"She looks awful," Breadstick said, sticking out his little tongue.

Seven held back a laugh, despite her nerves. "I'm okay.

“Monstruos are not afraid; they are feared.” She repeated Cheese’s words and the raccoons clapped.

She smiled at them, her heart warm with affection. Not for the first time, the raccoons had made her feel less alone. This time, they had made her feel brave.

That bravery propelled her on as they walked to the Gran’s cottage. In her mind, she repeated all the reasons why she had decided to tell the Gran, and she concluded that perhaps, deep down, the Gran already had an inkling of what she was. After all, Seven had summoned a Nightbeast in plain sight; she had called on the Cursed Forest to save everyone during the Frog Ball fires. Right this moment, a small army of ten raccoons followed Seven to the Gran’s cottage. There had been clues.

By the time she reached the Gran’s cottage, Seven’s body was rattling with anxiety again, but she was also filled with resolve. No matter the price, she would see this through. She was tired of secrets.

The Gran met Seven in her greenhouse just as they had arranged. She was sipping from a ceramic flower-shaped cup of something hot, looking at a group of butterflies dancing among the many flowers surrounding her. The Gran stood so still, she looked like a portrait of someone important, of someone wise. She looked so very old and so very tired. Seven’s heart lurched with worry. Was she going to make the burdens on the Gran’s shoulders even heavier?

“Seven, good morning,” the Gran said, smiling warmly. “Would you like a cup of ginger cinnamon tea?”

"I'm okay," Seven said, worried anything she ingested might be immediately thrown up.

"Have you been doing all right?" the Gran asked.

Seven nodded. "Mostly."

"Hmmm." The Gran took a sip of her tea. "Is the reason it's mostly and not yes why you're here?"

Seven nodded again. The words felt stuck in her throat. She wanted to blurt them out and run away. She wanted to tell her the truth, then be swallowed by the dirt.

Perhaps sensing the severity of Seven's topic of conversation, the Gran said, "Follow me," then walked over to an iron bench tucked in a cozy corner of the greenhouse.

They sat together, and Seven looked down at her lap, afraid to meet the Gran's eyes. She felt a hand on her chin. The Gran lifted her face.

"Whatever it is you need to tell me, you do not need to be afraid." The Gran smiled, her wrinkles deepening in her kind brown face.

Monstruos are not afraid. We are feared.

But Seven didn't want to be feared, not by the Gran. She wanted to be loved.

"I have something kind of serious to tell you, about my powers," she said.

"I'm listening," the Gran said.

Seven took a deep breath. "I can still talk to monstruos."

The Gran froze, her cup stopping just short of her lips. Seven's heart dropped, her mind racing through the seconds of silence. Was this how Delphinium had felt when she told her own Gran? The same Gran who would later kill her . . .

Knox, Seven's Gran, put her cup down beside her.

"Has it been this whole time?" she asked.

"Yes."

"And you can still speak to animals?"

"Yes. Both."

"Which monstruos have you spoken to?"

"All of them that I can think of. Skeleton birds, flor culebras . . ."

"The Nightbeast?"

"Yes," Seven said and panic rose up in her throat. Had she made a mistake? Would she put the Nightbeast and its cubs in danger? Would she meet Delphinium's fate?

The Gran nodded silently, and everything in the world, the butterflies, the raccoons standing right outside the glass greenhouse, the steam from the teapot, Seven's very heart, stopped.

"I had an inkling," the Gran said, and Seven let out a breath she didn't know she was holding.

"What will happen to me?" Seven asked.

"I think you should still be healthy, though I'll have to run some tests to see if this will affect the rest of your magic—and your mental health, of course. I imagine monstruo communication can be quite confusing."

Seven was confused, but not about monstruo communication.

"What about . . . punishment?"

The Gran sucked in a breath. "How many others know?"

"Just my coven."

The Gran nodded. "There won't be any punishment so long as we can keep this from others. Even then, I will not let them hurt you if I can help it."

Seven felt like she might explode with relief. "I won't be killed?"

"Whyever would you think something like that?"

"Because of Delphinium," Seven said, and when the Gran told her she did not know who that was, Seven told her everything about the diary she'd found, the entries that had detailed Delphinium's own monstruo powers and subsequent persecution.

"You must have been terribly frightened," the Gran said.

"You can say that again."

"I'm sorry you've been navigating this all alone, and I understand why you were hesitant to tell me, but I thank you for your trust, Seven. It is my hope we work together for many, many years, and that will work best if we confide in each other," the Gran said. "However, I think the approach you've been taking, of keeping this all a secret, is for the best. You must make sure Valley and Thorn do not tell anyone either. I will never order harm on you for this, but I cannot guarantee others won't seek to. This is a dangerous secret, Seven, and you must do whatever you can to keep it safe."

CHAPTER THIRTY
A NOT-SO-SLUMBER PARTY

VALLEY HAD BEEN DISCHARGED the very morning after she'd been cured, while the other three witches were kept in the infirmary for further care. Their skin remained gray for days, their mobility limited, and there were whispers of curiosity about Valley's condition being markedly better than everyone else's.

"It is strange this young Spare is showing no symptoms of stonification," one healer had said while Valley was being evaluated.

A few of the healers seemed suspicious of the story they were telling: that their stone-eating sludge potion attempts had finally worked. They would keep the truth to themselves, and hoped the three other cured witches would too.

When Valley got discharged from the infirmary, someone had been waiting for her right outside, standing with a pink flower in her hands.

"Graves," she said softly as the Moth House witch ran up and hugged her.

They held on for a long time, so long that Seven and Thorn almost started backing away slowly.

"Sorry." Graves let go and wiped her eyes. "I didn't hurt you, did I?"

"Nah, I'm good. Just happy to see you," Valley said.

Graves smiled and they held hands all the way to Valley's house.

There had been a lot for Valley to catch up on, not least of all the brand-new witch living in her house. Thankfully, Valley had taken the news about Figgs well. She actually seemed kind of excited about it.

"I've always wanted a brother to boss around. This will be great."

Valley needed time to settle in, spend time with her mother, rest, and get used to Figgs. In the meantime, Seven had checked on her chismosas, and Thorn had continued researching the Black Moon Ceremonies and seeing if she could find anything about the Five Families on her own. Neither had found anything useful yet, but when Valley called, they pushed everything else aside to come to her. It was time for their favorite pastime: gossip.

Quill welcomed them in with big hugs and a smile bright enough to light the world.

"Oh, come here, come here!" She pulled Seven and Thorn in for a hug and they nearly dropped their overnight bags.

"She's going to kill us!" Edgar croaked from Seven's pocket, and Seven chuckled.

Quill squeezed them tight and whispered, "How will I

ever, ever be able to thank you? Thank you for saving my Valley, thank you."

"How about an early copy of the next Witches of Heartbreak Cove?" Seven said, her face smooshed against Quill.

Valley's mother let go and wiped her eyes, laughing. "I'll put in a good word with the author. Come in, Valley's waiting and I made some grilled cheese!"

"Hex yeah," Thorn celebrated, and Seven punched the air happily. She'd been hoping for some of those.

They had been waiting for this moment for so long. Seven hadn't been sure they'd ever get to have one of their famous sleepovers again. She had even dreamed about it, the three of them together again, happy and laughing and scheming. It had felt like an impossible dream, something so good, so lovely, that there was no way it could happen. But it was happening now, and Seven felt she might explode with happiness.

They made their way to Valley's room for their slumber party, a tray of snacks and drinks ready for them, fluffy pillows and blankets, Kill Le Goose's latest album playing softly in the background. Valley was still in the shower as they settled in—Seven flopped onto Valley's bed, and Thorn sat on her furry pink beanbag. Her room was smaller than the one in Blood Rose Manor, where she used to live with her dad, but it was cozy and one hundred percent Valley. From the stuffed bats to the enchanted blinking raven in the corner, to the piles of books and magazines, it was equal parts scary and sweet, just like Valley. On her bed, there was a bright pink dress, sparkling and chic.

"That's from my mom's shop." Thorn pointed at the dress. "Valley's outfit for Miss Dewey and Ambert's wedding."

"It's beautiful!" Seven said. The wedding was the day after tomorrow, and Seven was excited for Miss Dewey, Ambert, Dusk, and Helio to become an official family. She was also excited for the wedding cake, which, like all wedding cakes in Ravenskill, would have her favorite pineapple jam filling.

Valley stormed through the door, her pink hair wrapped in a small towel, wearing black pajamas and furry toad slippers.

"Sup," she said to her friends, and they all laughed. Seven held back the urge to hug Valley again, but Thorn did not. She nearly knocked her over just like Quill had.

"Sheesh, okay, I'm still fragile, you know," Valley laughed.

"Sorry, sorry," Thorn said sheepishly.

They sat around the snack tray on the small ottoman, eating as they chatted, when something loud growled in the distance.

Seven opened her eyes wide. Was that the Nightbeast? Was something wrong?

"What was that?" Thorn asked, and Seven let out a sigh of relief that Thorn had heard it too.

"Figgs." Valley shook her head. "He snores like a walrus!"

The Witchlings giggled so hard, fizzy drink nearly came out of Seven's nose.

She had been kinda nervous about Figgs being there tonight, and she was glad he'd already fallen asleep. Seven didn't know if she wanted to deal with him seeing her in her bear-print pajamas.

"It still feels weird being back home," Valley said right before she threw a fistful of cheesy puffs into her mouth.

"Was being a stone statue like sleeping?" Thorn asked.

"Did it hurt? Are you feeling normal now?" Seven asked.

From healer checkups, to reuniting Valley with her mom, to her getting used to Figgs moving in, Valley had needed time to take everything in. All the while, they had been dying to ask her a million things, and now they finally had their chance.

Valley pulled her knees in close, resting her chin on them. There was a haunted look in her eyes, like she was remembering something terrible. "When Lotus struck me, it hurt like hex, but only for a moment."

"Valley . . . I shouldn't have let you do that. I'm so sorry," Seven began, and Valley gave her a confused look.

"What are you talking about? I just did what either of you would've done."

Seven knew it was true, but still, if she had been able to stop Lotus somehow, Valley wouldn't have lost months of her life. "I'm just sorry I couldn't protect you."

Valley shook her head. "You did as much as you could.

We're still just kids, we shouldn't have to deal with all this, but the butt-toad grown-ups of this town can't get it together. Blame them. We're all doing our best. Don't beat yourselves up. It would only make me feel worse," she said.

Thorn and Seven nodded. Seven wanted to honor what her friend asked of her, but what she knew in her brain didn't always match how she felt in her heart.

Valley continued. "After I turned to stone, everything went dark, kind of like sleeping. But after a few days, I sort of woke up. Things were still hazy, but I started to hear things. They sounded muffled, like they were far away or underwater or something. I knew all about the Spare Amendment though; some healers talked about it while they were in my room once. It was *all* they talked about for a few weeks."

"Did you hear us?" Seven asked.

"I did. I could hear you on my birthday, all the times you came to visit, your plans trying to cure me. I don't remember all of it, just bits and pieces, but your visits were the biggest comfort I had. It . . . almost would've been better if I was asleep, but being there and not being able to yell or talk or ask for help was a nightmare. I asked Alaric and Tia about it and they both said they couldn't hear anything the entire time. They stayed in the deep sleep I was in in the beginning."

"Whoa," Seven said, her mind spinning. "That sounds—"

"Like I shouldn't be able to do it? Yeah. Just like your

Uncle magic. And your cape, Thorn." Valley smiled. "Congratulations, by the way."

"Thanks." Thorn blushed. "They took my cape away though."

Valley scowled. "We'll see about that."

"How'd you help me get you out?" Seven asked.

"I tried to chip away at the stone from the inside every day. It was tiring and hard, but I blasted it with magic, bit by bit. I think it helped some."

"It for sure did. I could feel your magic pushing from inside the statue. I wouldn't have been able to do it without you."

"I'm just . . . really glad I'm out," Valley said.

"And you're totally okay, right?" Thorn asked.

"Mostly." Valley pulled the top of her sleep clothes to the side. There was a stone gash going from the top of her shoulder all the way down toward her chest. "It goes across my heart. The healers are worried I got stone in there after all, so they're still running tests. They said even if it hasn't, I might always run the risk of the hex poisoning my heart, so I have to be particularly careful with my health."

"What happens if you do have stone in your heart?" Seven asked. She felt clammy and sick at the thought of it.

"I'm . . . not sure, but I can kind of feel it. Like remember when I said I knew I could help you get the other witches out? Something happened when Lotus hexed me; unintentionally, she helped me understand archaic magic, sort of."

"Can you *do* archaic magic?" Thorn asked, eyes wide.

Valley shook her head no. "I don't know how to use it exactly. It's more like . . . an instinct. I could feel how to help heal the other witches; it was like second nature."

"That sounds sort of like my Uncle magic," Seven said. "I don't know how I know how to do it, I just do. I just get it."

Valley nodded. "It feels like that."

"What if when the hex hit you, it mixed with your magic somehow?" Seven said.

Valley looked down at her scar, then touched it carefully. "Maybe," she said softly. "But I really hope not."

The rest of the night was filled with more updates from Seven and Thorn about Uncle business, Thorn's costura program, the missing Spares, and Ambert and Miss Dewey's wedding.

"She's gonna have two sons?! Good luck," scoffed Valley.

"They're great! Well . . . Dusk is great. Helio is a little annoying," Thorn whispered.

The Witchlings giggled.

"Great or not, it's still two whole boys in your house suddenly. I have one and listen to what I'm dealing with." She gestured at the wall, where the loud hum of Figgs's snores was coming from.

Seven threw her head back and cackled as Thorn covered her face, which was red from laughter. They talked about the Nightbeast and made plans to visit it and its cubs, which Valley was absolutely thrilled about. They caught her up on the Glimmer Moon Hamlet and everything that had happened with Crimson. They even told her about becoming rats.

"Seven, you must've been sick," Valley said with a smirk.

"Don't remind me." Seven shook her head.

"There's also . . . your dad." Thorn cringed.

Seven had not been looking forward to this part.

"What about him?" Valley said, her eyes narrowed.

Thorn and Seven told Valley all about their Mr. Pepperhorn theory, about their visit to Lotus and how he had been there visiting her as well.

"You think my dad is really behind all this, huh?" Valley asked.

Thorn and Seven exchanged looks. Had they upset her? Butt-toad or not, it was hard to hear that her dad might've had a hand in her being stonified.

"I mean . . . we could be wrong," Thorn tried.

Valley shook her head. "No, I bet you're not. I'm not even a little bit surprised; it makes sense, actually."

"It's been impossible to spy on him though; he's got giant bodyguards and he already caught us once so he's on high alert," Seven lamented. "I have no idea how we're gonna prove it's him."

"I have an idea." Valley smirked. "My dad wants nothing more than for me to take over his absolute warlock of a company and be the Pepperhorn heir or whatever . . . What if I agree? I could go live with him for a few days, pretend I wanna learn *all* about magical investments or whatever it is he does, and the whole time, I can really be spying on him."

"No!" Thorn and Seven said at once.

"We can't let you go live with him, he's dangerous," Thorn said.

"I'm with Thorn here, Valley. It's way too risky and you shouldn't be living with him. What will your mom say?"

Valley bit her lip. "Think about it; I could snoop through all his stuff. His library, his paperwork, I could eavesdrop on all his secret meetings. If I can convince him I'm on his side, my dad will tell me anything he's planning, I just know it. He's obsessed with me carrying on his legacy, always has been, and he'd do anything if I promise to do just that."

"I dunno, Valley." Seven shook her head. She knew Valley was right, that she could get information out of Mr. Pepperhorn and maybe help to stop him, but what if he hurt Valley again? It wasn't safe for her to be in that house.

"It's not like you goats can stop me, if it's what I decide to do." Valley crossed her arms.

"Valley!" Thorn furrowed her brow.

"Okay, okay. What if you don't live with him but, like, have some daytime visits? That way his staff will be awake and maybe the family mage will send a witch to supervise and make sure he doesn't try anything weird," Seven suggested.

"I can make that compromise," Valley said. "I won't

hesitate to hex my father myself if I have to. I'm not the same little Valley he used to threaten and intimidate. But I like your idea, Seven. Can't hurt to have an extra layer of protection just in case."

Seven nodded. Even though she still didn't love the idea, she knew Valley would do it whether or not Seven and Thorn wanted her to.

They decided Valley would go undercover with Mr. Pepperhorn in the next few days. Maybe Valley would finally find the break in the mystery of the missing Spares they'd been looking for. The Witchlings spent the night catching up, between laughter and tears and so many snacks, until someone knocked on their door at two in the morning and a sleepy Figgs opened the door, his hair disheveled, his eyes heavy with sleep.

"Hey, goats," he said. "I haven't slept a wink. Do you have any lavender tea?"

The Witchlings turned to one another and erupted in laughter, Figgs looking confused *and* sleepy now. Then they shared some tea and snacks with him and stayed up way, way past any of their bedtimes.

CHAPTER THIRTY-ONE

A WITCH'S WEDDING

THE SAYING WENT in the Twelve Towns that if it rained while the sun was shining, it meant a witch was to be married. Well, the weather had gotten the rain part right, but there was no sunshine in sight, as a stormy morning ushered in Miss Dewey and Ambert's wedding day.

The Witchlings arrived with their parents, Grandma Lilou, Beefy, and Figgs, all dressed in their finest clothes to celebrate Seven's favorite librarians in the world. Helio greeted them at the gate to the Ravenskill Gardens, where the ceremony was being held. The garden was decorated beautifully, with crystals and giant vases with yellow flowers to match Miss Dewey's favorite yellow scarf. An enchantment had been cast over the garden, magic in the shape of an enormous shimmering umbrella, the falling rain like glitter against its surface. There were already lots of witches there, many Seven did not recognize, who must've been from Crones Cliff Manor, where Ambert used to live.

"This way." Helio ushered them to their seats, looking polished in traditional Ravenskill wedding attire—a long white shirt with four pockets and a vertical row of embroidered flowers on one side that went from the bottom hem to the top and wrapped around the collar; matching white pants; a long, luxurious silkworm cloak; and a hat adorned with flowers to match the shirt. He looked lovely, his blond hair somehow still shining on the rainy day.

"Where's Dusk?" Seven asked. She hadn't seen either of the twins in many days, and she especially missed Dusk.

"Oh, he's about. Probably helping our father. Enjoy the wedding," Helio said with a wink, and skipped off to help other arriving guests.

Seven didn't like Helio in the crush kinda way. She didn't. But she couldn't stop staring at him. When she looked at Thorn and Valley though, they were staring too.

"I bet his cloak has charming magic," Thorn said.

"Oh, yeah," Seven said, relieved that was all it was.

"This is gonna be good. I've never been to a wedding before, but I hear there's unlimited strawberry fizzy drink," Valley said.

"I'm drinking three whale-fulls of it," Seven said excitedly, giving Valley a high five.

The seats filled up and soon, it was time for the wedding. Beside the flower arch, at the front of the aisle, a musician began playing a soft, romantic version of "Ah! The Witch Is Coming! Run!" on a harp. It was time.

The guests stood up and turned toward the back of

the aisle, and in a squall of glittering white feathers, Miss Dewey and Ambert appeared. Everyone clapped at the impressive entrance.

The couple took their time walking down the aisle as Jonafren, an ordained witchtress, waited to tie their fates together. Miss Dewey's dress really was the prettiest wedding dress Seven had ever seen, with toadstools of intricate beading, glittering details, and romantic draped fabric. Ambert wore a white suit that resembled Helio's. His was made of the finest spider silk and thousands of beads. Instead of a long cloak, he wore a white dragon-scale-plated Ravenskillian warrior's cape. It was the most magnificent thing Seven had ever seen and a fitting tribute to Miss Dewey's hometown.

"Thorn, you did an amazing job," Seven said, squeezing her friend's hand, and Thorn squeezed back.

As they passed the Witchlings, Seven noticed that Ambert and Miss Dewey looked quite tired. They had bags under their eyes, like perhaps they had not slept in a few nights.

"Wedding planning *is* quite exhausting," Fox whispered to Talis.

"Welcome, all, to the marriage of Ambert Lophiifor and Moira Dewey. We are here to celebrate this wondrous day and union of two of the Twelve Towns' most beloved librarians. Now, it is time for the customary vows," Jonafren said, flourishing his arms in a reminder of his alter ego, Enve Lopes.

Miss Dewey and Ambert began to speak.

"Our souls and our hearts, bound and entwined, for all of our lives, to beyond our death day. As we become Stars, or the soil beneath the trees, I will belong to you, and you shall belong to me," the couple said in unison.

"You are now married! Congrats!"

Ambert and Miss Dewey kissed shyly, and held their arms up in triumph toward the guests, who were crying and laughing. Helio clapped wildly beside his father, but Dusk was nowhere to be found.

"We will meet you all in Goose House for the reception!" Miss Dewey said.

As they walked back down the aisle, everyone cheered, and though Seven was happy for Miss Dewey and Ambert, she could not shake the feeling that something was froggin' wrong. Dusk should be here. She knew he would not miss this wedding for the world.

CHAPTER THIRTY-TWO
THE RECEPTION

GOOSE HOUSE HAD BEEN DECORATED as if it was their last party in this world. There were toadstools and toadstools of glittering white fabric draped across the ceiling, water droplets enchanted to look like tiny dancers floated through the air, giant shimmering corals with crystal tables resting on them with every food you could think of.

They sat at one of the jellyfish-shaped tables while their waitress for the night came to bring them drinks. They had really stuck to the whole under-the-sea theme.

"Mayhem!" Seven said to the once-stone witch.

Mayhem was placing a tray teetering with drinks on the table. It seemed she would be their waitress for the night. She looked good, all the gray almost completely gone from her skin, and she was moving at her normal pace again. Seven was glad to see it.

"Oh, hi, Seven," Mayhem said, her eyes pinned to the drinks, focused.

"Great job with the decorations; you really showed House of Stars, huh?"

"We can hear you," Fox said with a playful scowl. She and Seven's dad pointed to their aquamarine amulets.

Seven waved them off with a laugh and turned back to Mayhem. "How've you been?"

"Fine, fine," Mayhem said, looking everywhere but at Seven.

"You look much better! I know I'm no match for the healers, but if you ever need any healing potions, I know a bunch of great ones."

Mayhem placed the final glass on the table with such force, the table shook. Everyone stopped their conversations to look at her.

"I'm fine, I don't need . . . thanks," Mayhem said quickly, then walked away.

"What toad pooped in her soup?" Valley asked.

"I think I annoyed her," Seven said.

"You? Annoy someone? Naaaah," Valley said, and Seven made a fist at her.

"She does seem kinda annoyed or something," Thorn said.

The three Witchlings watched as Mayhem flitted from table to table, taking orders and picking up empty glasses.

"She's just busy, I bet; don't overthink it," Figgs said, putting an impressive fifth olive into his mouth.

The Witchlings collectively turned their gaze from Mayhem and glared at Figgs.

His eyes went wide and he laughed nervously.

The rest of the evening was lovely, if a little awkward, with Mayhem serving them but being terse, bordering on unfriendly. Had Seven done something to her?

"Valley," Thorn whispered. "Did you tell your mom yet?"

Valley nodded, a distressed look on her face. "Yeah, and she hated the idea but said it was okay if I visited my dad a couple times, so long as we had supervision, which is fine by me."

"Are you sure you wanna do this?" Seven asked.

"Toadally sure. I'm going there tomorrow morning, as a matter of fact, and then the snooping will begin," Valley said.

Suddenly, Ambert and Miss Dewey were at their table.

"Miss Dewey . . . erm . . . Lophiifor?" Seven asked.

Miss Dewey laughed, and this close, Seven could see she really did look like she might be coming down with something. "Still Dewey. Thank you all for coming."

"Of course," Fox and Talis said, and they reached out for the newlyweds' hands. In each of their palms was a small satchel with a spell, or potion recipe, magic that they were gifting the couple.

"Thank you," Ambert said with a kind smile.

"Are you guys sick?" Valley asked. Thorn elbowed her and Seven stepped on her foot. "What? They look kinda sick!"

Ambert laughed. "We are incredibly tired; planning a wedding is difficult. And I do believe we came down with a case of the too-tireds, but not to worry, not contagious!"

Ahhh, that made sense. The too-tired disease did make you look like some sort of undead creature, and planning a wedding had probably taken a lot out of them. Seven relaxed a bit.

"Don't worry. We'll be good as new soon," Miss Dewey said.

Seven held her hands out toward the newlyweds.

"Oh, children don't need to—"

"I'm your Uncle," Seven said, pulling the Uncle card. "It's customary for me to give a gift."

Miss Dewey reached out, and Seven handed her the pouch of magic she, Valley, and Thorn had prepared. It was a never-ending snack tincture. Just a drop of it in water would conjure any snack your heart desired. It had reminded the Witchlings of the first time Miss Dewey helped them research the Nightbeast, how she had made sure to get all their favorite snacks. She had been one of the only adults to help them, to treat them with kindness, and they wished for nothing but kindness and love for Miss Dewey's whole life.

"Thank you," Miss Dewey and Ambert said.

"It's from the three of us," Valley said.

"Thank the three of you," Miss Dewey said, and she crouched down. The three Witchlings got up from their seats and hugged Miss Dewey all at once. She was warm, and felt like another home.

"By the way, where is Dusk?" Thorn asked.

"He's over there," Ambert said, pointing to the other

side of the ballroom. Dusk was standing alone, in a corner of the grand room, his face knitted with anger as he read a book.

"Is he okay?" Seven asked.

"He will be just fine in time," Ambert said. "This is all a lot to get used to."

"Thank you all again," Miss Dewey said, and they moved on to the next table.

Seven watched Dusk intently. She hadn't seen him at the ceremony and now he was sulking in a corner reading. Gifting hour over and dinner out of the way, witches began filling the dance floor.

"Wanna dance?" Figgs asked Seven, and her cheeks went so hot she was sure she was blushing.

"Okay, but I gotta do something first," she said, and he nodded, smiling at her sweetly.

Toads, he was cute.

Seven made her way over to Dusk. She'd noticed he hadn't eaten, so she'd wrapped some buttery rolls for him in a napkin. Before she got to him, Helio stopped in front of his brother and they began to talk heatedly. Dusk shook his head, slammed his book shut, and looked away as Helio splayed his hands out in frustration. Finally, Helio said something Seven could not make out and Dusk pushed him aside and stormed away. He was about to pass Seven when she stopped him.

"I got you these," she said.

"Huh?" Dusk asked, as if he'd been pulled out of a

deep thought. "Oh, Seven, hello. I'm sorry. Didn't see you there."

"I . . . noticed you didn't eat, and that you weren't at the ceremony earlier. Are you okay?"

Dusk was looking past her. What was everyone's deal tonight?

"I'm not hungry. I'll see you later. I have to get out of here," Dusk said, walking away. Seven noticed the book tucked under his arms. It was the memory compendium he'd gotten at the antiquers'.

"Oh, okay." Seven wrapped the rolls back in the napkin.

"Seven?" Dusk called out, and Seven turned around. "Sorry."

"Still looking for the cuentista spell?" Seven said, pointing to the book.

Dusk looked down. "Now more than ever. We'll talk later, yeah?"

Seven nodded. "Yeah."

He walked right past a concerned-looking Ambert and ignored Miss Dewey as she tried to calm him down, and went right out of the giant double doors of the ballroom.

Helio sidled up to Seven.

"Is Dusk okay?" she asked.

"Misses our mother," Helio said. "He thinks Miss Dewey is trying to replace her."

"Oh," Seven said, hitching an eyebrow. Dusk had never been anything but warm to Miss Dewey; she remembered how he had put his hand over hers at the Shabby Rat, how they'd walked away with locked arms at the end of the night. Could something have changed?

Helio went back to entertaining the guests, and Valley, Thorn, and Figgs came up to Seven. She was on the edge of the dance floor, which was packed with dancing witches now.

"Something is for sure wrong with Dusk, right?" Figgs asked.

"I think so, but I'm not sure what," Seven said.

The rest of the reception was fun. Seven danced a lot with Figgs, which reminded her of the Frog Ball and how she hadn't gotten to slow dance with him then. She made sure not to make the same mistake twice.

When the party was over, the newly married couple thanked the guests and said they would be off to their honeymoon at the Otter Sleigh Lodge in the snowy town of Castle Point, the northernmost of the Twelve Towns. Seven teared up as they left among cheers and waves. As Almanac flew out after them, she looked at Seven, who gave the light hummingbird a little wave.

The Witchlings and their parents were helping the Goose House witches clean up when Figgs appeared and cleared his throat.

"Would it be okay if I, um, walked you home?" Figgs asked.

"I should be walking *you* home," she said, still piling dessert plates on top of one another.

“Hey, I’m not completely defenseless,” Figgs muttered. “I can protect you.”

Seven looked at her parents and they both nodded, small smiles on their faces. Seven smiled back, then turned to Figgs.

She crossed her arms and smirked. “Fine. You can walk me home for a change.”

Figgs brightened up. “Really?”

“Yeah, let’s go,” Seven said.

She looked back and waved at her friends. Valley was making smooching faces at her as Thorn giggled. Seven shook her head and made her way out of the reception with Figgs.

The rain had subsided by the time the sun set, and they walked toward town in the crisp, clear night.

“How do you feel about staying at Quill’s? And Valley?” Seven asked.

“She’s kinda my sister now,” Figgs said, smiling.

“And you’re happy about that?”

Figgs hadn’t stopped smiling. “I’ve always wanted a sister. And Valley’s pretty cool.”

“I know she is,” Seven said begrudgingly. “Even if she’s annoying and loves to embarrass me.”

“Yeah, yeah,” Figgs said.

They were quiet, and it was awkward. Figgs’s hand kept brushing up against Seven’s until finally, he looked at her.

“Would it be okay if . . . I . . . um . . . held your hand, maybe?”

Seven's head whipped forward, her eyes wide. *Oh my goats, oh my goats, oh my goats.*

She cleared her throat and tried to sound as nonchalant as she could, but when she said, "Sure," her voice squeaked, and they both giggled.

Figgs took her hand, and Seven felt like she was floating. They walked hand in hand in the moonlight, through the Cursed Forest shortcut home, and Seven felt happy that Figgs wasn't afraid of the woods any longer.

"There's something I need to say," Figgs said when they reached the Strangling Figs that separated the forest from downtown Ravenskill. He let go of her hand and faced her. Seven was sweating, and trying not to be so obvious about how nervous she was.

"I wanted to say thanks," Figgs said.

Seven hitched an eyebrow. "What for?"

"You helped me find a home. You asked Ambert and Miss Dewey and then Quill, and you didn't have to do all that. It was so kind of you, and I know it must've been kinda awkward," Figgs said, his cheeks turning red.

"It was no big deal," Seven said.

"It was though. Ever since I became a Spare, people didn't . . . really help me anymore. With the exception of my old employer." He looked down. Talking about River was still difficult. "Any time I've needed help, witches turned away. Adults, witches my age, other Spares . . . it was like me needing help embarrassed *them* somehow. But not you. You just helped me. No questions asked, no weirdness. You did it because you have a good heart, and that's why . . ." Figgs cleared his throat. He shifted from one foot to another. "That's why I like you so much."

"I like you too," Seven said with a smile.

"But I mean, like, a crush like, not just a friend like. Even though I like you that way too," Figgs said hurriedly.

He was so nervous that Seven couldn't help but not be nervous anymore at all. He was adorable and sweet and perfect. He was her Figgs.

"I wanted to thank you and also, I wanted to know if it would be okay . . ." He stepped closer to her and all thoughts of not being nervous left Seven's mind. Suddenly, breathing wasn't just difficult, it was impossible.

Figgs took another step, and took her hand. "I was wondering if I had your permission . . ." He was looking down, too embarrassed or scared to look at her.

They were almost crashing into each other now, and Seven hoped her breath smelled okay. Oh gosh, what if it didn't?!

"My permission?" she asked, trying not to listen to the panicked voice in her mind, or worse, the Nightbeast's soft laughter.

"To kiss you." Figgs looked up, his dark doe eyes lit up by the moon, his eyelashes longer than an oak, his skin more lovely than a pearl.

Seven couldn't even speak, she just . . . nodded, and then he did it. Figgs kissed her. It was sweet and quick; his lips felt like two soft pillows, and when he pulled away, Figgs nearly crushed Seven with a hug.

He was laughing loudly, and Seven was completely confused.

"What? What?!" she asked.

Figgs pointed behind him. At the Strangling Figs. His eyes were alight with more than the moon; they were filled with overwhelming happiness.

"Oh . . ." Seven touched her lips with her hands.

His name prophecy.

"My first kiss was here, with you, in front of these Strangling Figs! I had always resented the name of those trees, because they felt like what my life had become, but now . . . I love them." Figgs laughed.

Seven reached out for his hand, and smiled. This likely meant their fates would be entwined for a very long time, and her heart felt so full, so happy, she might explode.

"I always figured my name was Figgs because it was my mother's favorite snack. I guess a name prophecy can change or be something different from what you first believed," he said.

"I'm glad I'm part of yours," Seven said.

Figgs took her hand again. "Me too."

Seven always wished she could fly on a broom like other witches, but now she realized, so long as she had Figgs, she didn't need that. Because this felt just like flying.

He pulled her in and gave her one more sweet kiss,

and they both smiled shyly when they pulled away, and then Figgs Moonchild walked Seven Salazar home.

Jelly bean fish fell from the sky that night. A bizarre storm that had never been seen in the history of the Twelve Towns. When they awoke the next day, a new group of Spares had gone missing.

"Spares have gone missing three times now: once after the Black Moon Ceremony when the purple rain fell, once the day Wither disappeared and there was a loud crashing sound in the sky that the whole Twelve Towns could hear, and now after the jelly bean fish storm," Seven said to Thorn and Valley on a three-way portaphone video call.

"You think they're related?" Thorn asked.

"Think about it; the three big instances of bizarre magic were followed by Spares going missing," Seven said. "It can't be a coincidence. It just can't be."

CHAPTER THIRTY-THREE

A LEGACY OF MISSING SPARES

THE FAMILY RECORDS from the Twelve Towns Legacy Library arrived the day after the wedding. Seven and Thorn were itching to go through the Pepperhorn family history and see if there was anything there about the Five Families or dying elders that might help their investigation.

"I'm worried about Valley. Have you heard from her at all today?" Seven asked as they lugged the enormous record book to Thorn's kitchen table.

Today was her first day pretending to like her dad and visiting him so she could snoop. It was a dangerous mission, but Seven trusted Valley to be careful.

"I'm worried too but I haven't heard anything from her yet either. I'm sure she'll call us later," Thorn said. "Let's get to work."

The Witchlings divided the work, Seven reading through the Pepperhorn family records while Thorn tackled the Evenstars. The books were separated by category—weddings, births, death days, announcements about everything from promotions to a particularly big crop being grown, and of course Black Moon Ceremony records, which showed the coven sortings. As they searched for ancient elder death day announcements, Seven did indeed find two, one last year, and one from just a few months ago.

"Stars, so Valley's was one of the families that lost an elder like Mr. Pepperhorn said," Thorn said.

"He seemed so cold about it." Seven shook her head. "Any dead elders in Lotus's family?"

Thorn nodded. "Yup, they passed at the beginning of the year."

"Mr. Pepperhorn said that three elders from the Five Families passed this year," Seven mused. "This backs up our suspicion that the Pepperhorns and the Evenstars are part of the Five Families—if only we knew what that meant."

As Seven wondered what to do with this information, she flipped through the Pepperhorns' Black Moon Ceremony records until she came to last year: their year. She ran her finger gently over the red mark next to Valley's name. It had been added sloppily, not like the other meticulous records kept for the other sortings. As Seven continued reading, she found something curious.

It wasn't hard to see the coven classifications, since they were color coded. There were a lot of purples for House Hyacinth, a healthy mix of Frog House green and Goose House white, some blue for House of Stars and very little Moth House black, and just one Spare in the past thirteen years. Wouldn't there normally be more Spares than that?

Seven flew back through the sorting records. By the time she reached the 1980s, there was still just the one Spare: Valley.

"This can't be . . ." she said.

"What?" Thorn asked.

"Hold on . . ."

After another few minutes of quickly scanning the pages of the Black Moon Ceremony records, Seven looked up. "Thorn, there are *no* Spares in the Pepperhorns' history before the past thirteen years."

"What?! That can't be right," Thorn said, gesturing for the book. While Thorn looked, Seven read the Evenstars' records and . . . found the exact same thing.

They had only had one Spare in the past thirteen years, and before that . . . nothing.

"No Spares," Thorn said. "But how?"

Seven shook her head just as their phones pinged. It was Valley.

"Coming over to Thorn's after nightfall," she messaged.

As Thorn kept reading, way back into the history of Spares, hours passed. Seven made them pizzas and soon the sun was setting. Valley would be arriving any minute now.

"Oh my goats, look." Thorn pointed at the pages in the large book. "The Pepperhorns and the Evenstars *did* have lots of Spares . . . before 1790! The names are so faded and old I can barely see what it says, but they had them," Thorn said. "But from 1790 on, nothing."

"Maybe this is what the Five Families is all about. Families that have gone without many Spares in their lineage. I could see witches like Mr. Pepperhorn and Lotus seeing that as some sort of blessing from the Stars," Seven said.

"But it couldn't just happen by chance. It doesn't make any sense," Thorn said.

The doorbell rang then and Thorn ran to get it. It was Valley.

She slid next to Seven, and Thorn pushed a slice of pizza in her direction, but Valley didn't touch it. She didn't even seem to notice. She looked pale and kind of frightened.

"Are you okay?" Thorn asked.

"Was he awful? Do you want me to send the Nightbeast after him?" Seven asked.

"Let's just say I hope I find whatever we need quick. It's . . . not easy being there. It was like all the old memories of how he used to treat me came flooding back in . . ." Valley shook her head. "That house feels haunted."

"Did he hurt you, because I'll . . ." Seven began.

"He didn't, no. Now that he thinks I'm on his side and want to take over as his heir, he's being nice for the first time in his life. That doesn't make it any easier though. He makes me . . . sick."

"Then you should stop. We can find whatever we need to find some other way," Thorn said.

"Yeah, Valley. You've just been unhexed after months as a statue; that's enough suffering for a whole lifetime. You shouldn't have to go back there," Seven added.

"I'm not stopping so don't even ask. It's just day trips and I'm staying in my house at night and the supervisor the mage courts sent is six toadstools and four gills tall. She watched my dad like a hawk; nothing's gonna happen to me on her watch. It's just hard being there is all."

Seven and Thorn exchanged looks. They were unconvinced.

"If you want to stop at any point though, you can. You know that, right?" Thorn said.

Valley nodded and grabbed her pizza. "I know. I also know I can probably uncover information much faster if I'm there. And we have to find the missing Spares. I hate to think what they're going through right now."

If they're even alive, Seven thought but did not say out loud. She really hoped they were okay.

"It does seem like your dad is involved in *something*," Seven said. She and Thorn caught Valley up on what they'd found in the Pepperhorn and Evenstar family records.

"What in the world?" Valley said. "How is that even possible?"

"I am pretty sure the Pepperhorns and the Evenstars are two of the Five Families. Now we need to figure out who the other three are," Thorn said.

"Not just that; we have to figure out how they made sure they had no Spares in their families." It slowly dawned on Seven as she spoke. "If they found a way to manipulate the Black Moon Ceremony, that might be the very same magic that's cracking now, the very same magic that made the sea of Spares during the last ceremony, and maybe . . . the very same magic that's making Spares disappear."

CHAPTER THIRTY-FOUR

HAPPY BIRTHDAY, THORN

"ARE WE ALMOST THERE? My dogs are killing me," Valley said.

"Told you not to wear brand-new combat boots!" Seven said.

"Thanks, Mom! Guess I forgot!" Valley said, and they scowled at each other as Thorn shook her head.

Finally, they reached the entrance to the glade. Seven opened the entrance with her Uncle magic and they entered the enchanted space.

The Nightbeast glade was adorned with streamers, a table in a clearing with finger foods and fizzy drinks, and a cake with *"Happy Born Day, Thorn"* written carefully in red icing. Seven and Valley had been here earlier, setting up for Thorn's big one-three. It had taken her half an hour, but Seven had managed to get party hats on the cubs.

"Seven," the Nightbeast said warmly, and the three cubs ran to them.

"Oh," Valley said as she crouched down and a cub ran

into her arms. Every few weeks, Seven had been coming by to expand the glade, giving them all more room to run and play, but it was Valley's first time meeting them.

They were three toadstools long already, fluffy and cute and bearlike. All three cubs' fur had turned black, one with a white stripe like its mother that had taken to Seven, one with a heart-shaped white stamp on its head that loved Thorn best, and Valley's . . . an all-black cub with pink coloring on the tips of its ears and tail.

Seven wasn't sure how the cubs could have characteristics that matched the Witchlings. Nothing in any of her Uncle training manuals mentioned this, but perhaps she would ask Cymric, one of the only Uncles who was her friend.

"I . . . love them," Valley said, her eyes filled with tears. "I don't know why I feel this way, so . . ."

"Attached?" Thorn said.

"Protective?" Seven said.

"Yeah . . ." Valley said. "Why do we feel this way?"

"I'm not sure yet," Seven said.

Valley pressed her face into her cub's fur and closed her eyes.

Seven's stomach twisted with worry. "Valley, you feeling okay?"

She hated the idea of Valley having to be anywhere *near* Mr. Pepperhorn. He was dangerous! No matter how badly they wanted to solve the riddle of the taken Spares, nothing was worth Valley getting hurt over.

"I'm all right, promise. It is weird being near my dad

and hearing all his plans for me. He's still strict—stand up straight, not too much laughter, young lady, best to be serious, lower your voice, no music!" Valley did an uncanny impression of her dad. "But he's also trying really hard to win me over and convince me to live with him full-time and leave my mom. I would never do that, obviously, but he seems really . . . worked up about something. Like he's trying to decide if he can tell me something or not. He keeps starting a grand speech, then stopping, and I'm not sure what it's about."

"Do you think he's going to confess about the Spares?" Thorn asked.

Valley shook her head. "No. It's something about the family business he keeps bringing up but then telling me it's not the time to talk about it. I just hope I find something useful soon."

"Us too," Seven said, squeezing Valley's hand just as one of the cubs sneezed so aggressively, it did an entire backward roll.

Valley and Thorn brushed the cubs as Seven petted the Nightbeast. She nuzzled it, and kissed its enormous forehead, and then they began the festivities.

"I can't believe I'm thir*teen*." Thorn shook her head.

Her family had already thrown her a small party at their bookshop, the Bruised Apple. A few witches from school had come and there had been dancing and games in an area the Larouxs had cleared out for the occasion. But Valley and Seven wanted to have a special party for Thorn, with just the three of them and the Nightbeasts, where they could really celebrate without the watchful eyes of their classmates. As kind as they tried to be sometimes, there were still horrible rumors about them spreading wildly, and the Witchlings couldn't seem to escape them no matter where they went. Except for here. And they could do something else . . . a surprise.

Seven looked at Thorn, who nodded quickly and turned to Valley.

"Oh my goats, look at what the Nightbeast cubs are doing!"

"What, what?!" Valley was up, portaphone in hand like a mother, trying to capture whatever they were doing on film.

Meanwhile, Seven pulled the box out from under the table and carefully slid Valley's own birthday cake out.

"I couldn't see anything," Valley said, turning back around, when she noticed the already lit candles on both their birthday cakes.

Valley teared up. "You goats didn't have to . . ."

"You turned thirteen this month too; you deserve cake." Thorn smiled.

"Today is supposed to be about Thorn. It's your special day, not mine," Valley protested.

Thorn scoffed. "I couldn't think of a better way to celebrate than by sharing it with you, friend," she said.

Valley threw her arms around Thorn and hugged her tightly. Seven wiped her eyes and tried to wedge herself into the hug.

"Hey, let me in."

Thorn and Valley laughed, spinning around and not letting Seven join. But Seven was not one to quit; even when the stakes were low, she had to win at all costs. They couldn't just hug without her! Not during a special moment! Seven crouched and forced herself between them with a determined look on her face. Thorn and Valley were laughing uncontrollably now. She pushed their arms apart so she was in the middle of the hug. The three Witchlings laughed and shed a few tears, grateful to have one another—grateful they'd all get to see thirteen together.

They sat down, and Valley took a closer look at her cake with a small, grateful smile on her face. "I didn't know if I'd ever get to celebrate a birthday again, and this is the perfect do-over."

"Before we keep going, let's get a picture! The sun will set soon," Thorn said.

Valley and Seven groaned.

"You and your pictures." Valley shook her head.

"We have to preserve our memories! I brought my dad's old-timey camera; it prints pictures automatically!" Thorn said.

They took a few pictures of Thorn with her cake, then Valley with hers, then of Thorn and Valley together.

"Let's get one with the cubs!" Thorn suggested.

"Who's going to take the picture?" Valley asked, and all three Witchlings looked at the Nightbeast, who was busy grooming its babies.

Seven set the old-timey camera on a tree stump and instructed the Nightbeast.

"Just hit this button, very gently, with your nose," she said.

"What is the purpose of this contraption?"

"It's to take pictures—uh, images of things," Seven said.

"Like a reflection," the Nightbeast said.

"A permanent reflection, yes," Seven said with a smile.

"It won't hurt the cubs or you?"

"Not even a bit, promise."

The Nightbeast craned its neck toward Seven and she petted it gently. She wondered how the witches in town would react if they saw her petting a Nightbeast, of all things. She knew how they would react, actually—they'd be horrified. But only because they had been taught, falsely, that all Nightbeasts were dangerous. If only they could see it this way, with its cubs, they would know the truth.

"All right, this button—remember, *gently*, very gently," Seven said.

Seven ran over to Valley and Thorn, who were standing with their cubs in their arms. Seven scooped hers up and it whined adorably at her. The Witchlings posed, and Seven yelled out at the Nightbeast.

"Okay, press the button!"

The Nightbeast booped the camera with its nose and the Witchlings laughed just as the flash of the old-timey camera went off. The camera whirred loudly and a set of three squares was spat from a small slit in the front.

Seven kissed her cub on the head, then put it down,

running to see the pictures with Valley and Thorn beside her. They each grabbed one, and Seven smiled as she saw the scene: the Witchlings together, holding their cubs, the enchanted glade behind them, all three of them with smiles big enough to light up the Twelve Towns.

Back in her room that night, Seven put the picture up on her corkboard. She was glad Thorn had thought to capture a memory of this day, even if she did complain about it.

She stepped back and admired the picture. Next to it was the crisscrossed chaos of red string, drawings, and clues she'd been adding to since the Golden Frog Games. Seven did a double take when she noticed something.

She'd drawn the Golden Frog's vision on a large scroll, each scene in a separate square, and one . . . one looked awfully familiar. The image of three witches holding foxes.

The picture of her, Valley, and Thorn holding the cubs looked almost identical, except in her picture, the Witchlings were laughing. In the fox picture, the witches had adoring looks on their faces. Seven took the photo and the scroll and sat on the floor, staring for a long, long while.

"Staring at pictures again," Edgar said from his little house. It was expanding every month; now he had his own little pond and even a slide. Soon he'd be taking over Seven's room if she wasn't careful.

“Mm-hmm,” Seven said. “You notice anything about all these pictures?”

Edgar hopped over and looked. “They all have very different colors. This one,” he said, flicking his tongue toward the picture from today, “looks quite vibrant. While this one is just a bad drawing.”

“Thanks a lot,” Seven said. She tried to remember what she knew about the fox image. She’d first seen it in the Crones Cliff Museum, before it had shown up again in her vision. It was from 1790, wasn’t it?

It was around the same time Delphinium had become a monstruo Uncle. It was the very same year that Spares had stopped appearing in the Pepperhorn and Evenstar family records. Strange. Was there something about the present that was somehow connected to that year?

“What if this isn’t the first time this has all happened? What if history is repeating itself?” Seven wondered aloud.

“History always repeats itself. Over and over. For example, historically, this is my dinnertime,” Edgar said, and Seven shook her head.

She went to get him a big helping of spicy flies. She hadn’t gleaned anything concrete from the observation, but there was a seed planted in her mind, and if there was one thing Seven was good at, it was making seeds grow.

CHAPTER THIRTY-FIVE

THE BLOOD ROSE

THE NEXT DAY, Seven left the Gran's cottage with two sore arms and a worried mind. The Gran's personal healers had run a few tests on her magic, just to make sure she wasn't in any sort of danger, but Seven couldn't help but wonder if they would know about her monstruo powers from the results and, worse, if they would tell someone other than the Gran. As she walked home, she noticed a group of witches in the distance, dressed in all black. They were walking in her direction, and when they got close enough for her to notice who they were, Seven's entire body tensed.

"Uncle Seven, should we prepare to attack?" Cheese asked from behind her.

"No, no. Don't do anything unless I say so," Seven whispered as the witches came closer.

It was Mr. Pepperhorn, a smug smile on his face as he strode with a handful of the veiled witches behind him. But it was the witch beside him who made Seven nervous.

Valley.

She wore the serious, stark black clothing she sometimes wore when she was still living on the Hill, her hair in two neat, tight plaits on either side of her face. She wore black lipstick and eyeliner, and her expression was unfamiliar, blank and focused. Valley did not look like herself. She looked like some alternate-universe version of Valley, where she was the loyal Pepperhorn heir, and had nothing to do with Seven or Thorn. Seven wished she could communicate with Valley like she could with the Nightbeast, to know if she was okay, but this had all been part of their plan and Seven had to trust her friend. A day before, Valley had overheard her father planning a meeting that sounded important for this very afternoon, and had asked if she could come along. But they'd had no idea the veiled witches were involved too.

Seven caught Valley's eye as she neared her and the raccoons, but Valley kept her gaze locked forward. Seven knew it was all part of her act, but . . . it still hurt her heart.

Mr. Pepperhorn noticed Seven and his smug smile widened. Soon the procession of Pepperhorns and veiled witches passed her, and moments later, Seven watched as the skeleton birds followed the macabre procession from the sky.

She couldn't follow Valley, but that didn't mean she couldn't keep an eye on her. Still, Seven's heart was heavy with worry the whole way home, and she called Thorn to update her.

“I’ll meet you at your house—I’m already on my way,” Thorn said.

When Seven finally got home, she was greeted by a big fat kiss on the cheek courtesy of Beefy.

“Thanks for all the spit, Beefy, you’re always so good about that,” Seven said.

“You welcome, sister. I lub you!” Beefy said.

“How did Uncle training go this morning?” her mom asked, and Seven tried not to cringe. Eventually, she was going to have to tell her parents about her monstruo magic, but not right now. She was too stressed about Valley.

“It was fine,” Seven lied, distracted.

Fox raised an eyebrow. “Gonna make some soup. You sure everything is okay?”

Seven nodded, but she was barely paying attention. She was looking out her window instead, wondering what exactly Valley was going through right now.

“Come on, Beefy. Your sister is daydreaming,” Fox said, and went into the kitchen, Beefy waddling behind her.

Seven’s stomach was in knots, and her leg bounced up and down as she waited for Thorn. It didn’t take long for Thorn to arrive, and by the look on her face, she was just as worried as Valley.

“What if something happens to her?” Seven asked.

Thorn bit her lip. “Your skeleton birds are looking out, right?”

“They are,” Seven said.

“Then we should trust they’ll let us know if something goes wrong, and we should trust Valley.”

"All right," Seven said.

Soon a whole hour had passed and Seven was pacing as she looked at her phone.

"Looking at your phone isn't going to make her get here any quicker," Thorn said from the sofa.

"Yeah, but—" The doorbell rang. Thorn's and Seven's eyes went wide, and they both ran for the door.

Standing there, out of breath, was Valley.

"What's wrong, did something terrible happen?" Seven asked.

"Did they do something to you?" Thorn asked. "Because I'll go over there right now and—!"

"No, no, nothing happened." Valley walked inside and sat down on the couch. "I'm just trying to gather my thoughts. My father had a meeting with those creeps just like he said he would. They're all panicking. They were talking about protecting the magical balance, and how they can't let another elder die, but they were yelling and saying so many things I didn't understand. It was hard to keep up. I tried to ask my dad, but he just said he'd explain it all in 'due time.' The only thing I know is they're all worried about something. They said they needed to recruit, like, a hundred guards . . ." Valley said.

"A hundred guards? What would they need that for?" Thorn asked.

"To protect something at Blood Rose Manor. My father said . . ." Valley looked around like she was trying to remember his exact words. "He said they needed the guards to protect their magic. To protect their legacy."

The Witchlings exchanged pointed looks and a chill ran over Seven. What could be at Blood Rose Manor that was so important?

"I have a feeling it might have something to do with whatever my father's business is. The veiled witches called it his responsibility, and they were arguing because many of them thought the extra guards were too extreme and would cause suspicion. Remember he kept almost telling me something about his business but never did . . . ? They're hiding something, something big, and it's in my old house."

"We have to try to get in the next time he's . . ." Seven began, but Valley cut her off.

"No, we go now. My dad will be distracted in meetings with the veiled witches for a little while longer; he didn't even notice me slipping out, I don't think. Once they hire more witches to guard the place, it'll be a lot harder to find whatever it is they're hiding. What if they move it? We have to find whatever it is right now," Valley said.

"Okay, but for the record, I'm scared," Thorn said.

"Me too," Seven admitted. She didn't like Blood Rose Manor, and the idea of Mr. Pepperhorn coming home and catching them wasn't a pleasant one.

Valley took their hands. "Me three. But we're together at least."

Seven smiled. It was true. It was easier to be brave when she had Valley and Thorn by her side.

Seven grabbed her cloak and they left, telling her parents they were just going to pick up a book from the library. Then they ran to Blood Rose Manor together, not speaking, and not knowing what they would find when they got there.

They snuck past the guards and in through the side door. Then the search began in the meticulous manor.

"There has to be something here, a book or a spell, or some sort of stockpile of magic—I dunno!" Valley said, scratching her head.

"Any idea where we should start looking?" Thorn asked.

"I'll take my father's bedroom, and you two take the study. Remember to leave everything exactly how you found it. My dad will notice if even one paper clip is out of place."

Seven gulped.

"Hurry," Valley said. "He could come home any minute."

They split up. As Thorn and Seven made their way to the study, Seven noticed just how neat Blood Rose Manor really was. There wasn't one shoe or knickknack in sight, not one speck of dust visible; everything was sparkling clean, brand-new, and painstakingly maintained. It felt more like a museum, stark white and sleek black everything, sterile and cold. It didn't feel like a home, and not for the first time, Seven was grateful Valley was out of here.

Together, Seven and Thorn began carefully riffling through books. Seven used revealing spells in every nook and book, looking for hidden objects or writing somewhere in the pages, but everything came up empty.

"Nothing on this side," Thorn said, sounding defeated.

"Here either," Seven said.

The clock was ticking, and Seven's heart felt like it was in her throat, she was so nervous.

"Seven," Valley said, suddenly at the door. "I need you."

They ran, following Valley through the echoing halls of her father's house until they reached the wing where Mr. Pepperhorn's bedroom was. Inside, the room was all black and dark purple, a four-poster bed and thick, severe-looking furniture. Everything looked expensive and, like the rest of the house, fastidiously neat.

"In the closet," Valley said, pointing but not stepping closer. Her arms were wrapped around herself, and she was shaking slightly. Thorn ran over and tiptoed to put her arm around Valley's shoulders.

"What happened?" Seven asked.

"I was rummaging in there and I . . . felt something. Like a magic repelling me; it was horrible. It sounded like . . . witches screaming. And it felt sort of like the stone hex felt. Like archaic magic."

Seven nodded. "Let me try."

She walked up to the armoire, and as she reached out for the drawer, the air crackled between her fingers and the painted black wood. Seven took a step forward and a horrible piercing sound, like witches wailing, pushed her back.

"Whoa," Seven said, looking back at Valley and Thorn.

"Scary, right?" Valley asked.

Monstruos aren't scared, Seven repeated in her mind. *We are feared.*

She stepped forward, pushing through the horrific high-pitched screams, and flourished her hand at the drawer.

"Extraer," she said, pointing toward the bottom drawer, where the screams were coming from.

The drawer shook violently, so violently the entire room shook around them, but it did not open.

"Careful, Seven!" Valley cried over the rumble of the magic.

Seven's hand shook, her palm pointing at the drawer that Mr. Pepperhorn had fortified with an archaic protection spell. If he had gone through all that trouble, there must be something important here. Something dangerous.

"Extraer!" Seven cried, and pulled from the monstruo magic inside her, until finally the drawer flew open and from inside something gold came flying right into Seven's hand. The screaming stopped and Seven caught the heavy golden metal with her outstretched hand.

"A key," she said as Valley and Thorn ran over.

It was indeed a key, made of pure gold, with a rose engraved at the top.

"Now we just need to find what this opens," Seven said.

"Ahh, but Mr. Pepperhorn might already be on his way," Thorn said nervously.

"We've come this far. And if he went through the

trouble to use such powerful magic to guard this key . . . I don't think we have any choice but to see where it leads," Seven said.

Valley took a longer look at the key and then her eyes lit up. "I think . . . I might know where to go. Come on!" The three Witchlings ran through the house, until Valley stopped in the hallway leading to the kitchen. There was black-and-purple wallpaper, with flowers that looked just like the key.

The Witchlings began to inspect every inch of the wallpaper until Seven noticed something.

"There's a tear here," she said, running her hand along the wall. It was almost imperceptible, the tiniest of rips, but in this meticulous house, the rip stood out like a bright red flag.

"There's no lock or door here though," Thorn said.

"Let me see the key," Valley said, holding the heavy golden key in her hands. She put it against the wall, pressing inch by inch until finally, impossibly, something broke loose.

Black smoke ran along the wall, making the outline of an archway.

"Oh my goats, we did it," Valley said. "Hurry."

They walked through, fear and urgency in every step. Behind them the archway closed, and they walked in near darkness, following Valley in silence.

They walked through the dimly lit tunnel until they reached an enormous black vault door and Valley used the key to open it. What met their eyes made Seven gasp.

The room inside was cavernous, with pools of what was clearly magic water everywhere around them. There were hundreds, maybe thousands of them, stretching out as far as the eye could see. In the center of the room stood a pillar with a small alcove that held, of all things . . . a book. On the other side of the pillar, a door was propped up on its side. The Witchlings walked carefully over the cobblestone ground, careful not to fall into the magical pools, until they reached the center of the room.

Seven walked around the pillar and inspected the door—it looked ancient and on the verge of falling apart. She ran her hands over it and found small markings, three lines, in one of the corners, as if a small animal had been scratching at it, trying to escape.

"What is this place?" Thorn asked.

"I don't know . . ." Valley said as she ran her hand over the pillar.

The book was surrounded by hundreds of tiny brass spikes and when she picked it up, Valley was very careful to avoid being cut. Seven and Thorn by her side, Valley opened the heavy tome.

Right in the middle of the book they found an old piece of parchment tucked between a wedding and death day announcement. It was a list of names.

"The Blood Rose Binding," it read.

"It looks like some sort of magical contract, but I can't understand these symbols. It's a complicated spell," Valley said.

"Those are witch runes," Seven said. "They don't even teach that class in school anymore, but maybe we can find an old witch to translate it?"

"Or we can look at the signatures right here." Thorn pointed at the bottom of the page. There in big, flourishing letters were five signatures, and they could read those names clearly.

Evenstar, Lophiifor, Dewey, Dimblewit, Pepperhorn.

"The Five Families!" Thorn said. "We finally have all the names."

"Ambert's family? Miss Dewey's?" Valley asked. "How—?"

"Miss Dewey did tell us her family did awful things in the olden days," Thorn said.

Seven nodded. "She told us they even killed Spares."

The air felt heavy around them. The words were too painful to say aloud just yet, but Seven would bet anything Thorn and Valley were thinking the same thing she was: *What if Miss Dewey was in on it?*

"What are all these little ponds?" Thorn asked as Valley put the book down and they walked around the cavernous space.

Seven looked closer at one of the pools, careful to not fall in. They were filled with flower petals. She walked down the narrow aisle between the pools and looked into one of them, Seven and Thorn behind her. There were words etched into the petals. No, not words . . . *names.*

"Walnut, Inopportuna," Thorn read.

"Figgs Moonchild," Seven read. *"Valley Pepperhorn."*

Seven looked up at her friends. "These are all Spare names."

"Is this the magic they were guarding? Spare magic?" Thorn said.

"Let's look in the book again; maybe there's another clue there," Seven said.

"Quickly. My dad, remember? I do *not* want to be caught here." Valley cringed and the Witchlings grabbed the book, leafing through it but finding nothing but various family records belonging to the Five Families and the indecipherable runes.

"Whatever this is, it's not a good thing. Your dad wouldn't be keeping Spare names in freaky flower ponds for decoration," Seven said.

"I know . . . but what exactly could it . . ."

"Look," Thorn said.

She was standing in front of the pillar. There, in the small alcove where the book had been, something had been etched in shining onyx letters.

A simple touch and I will bind
All your power and
Make it mine.
A name upon the petals three
Now all your magic
Will belong to me.

Thorn covered her mouth after reading the spell. Valley looked on in horror.

Seven's mind began to whir. "What if they're stealing Spare magic and this is where they keep it? Like some sort of vault for stolen powers," Seven said.

"But why?" Thorn asked. "Why would they do such an awful thing?"

"To keep a permanent less powerful class of witches, I suppose. They have us to do all their manual labor, and all the while, they get richer and richer by stealing our powers," Seven said. She had not been this angry in all her life, but she took deep breaths to temper her rage, lest all the Cursed Forest appear in the vault.

"If you're right, and I bet you are, I am never going to forgive him," Valley said, her breathing jagged. "I can't believe . . . I can't believe my family has something to do with this whole mess. The reason why we could have anything we wanted, the reason why we lived in this big froggin' house, everything is because . . . is because we were hurting others the whole time."

"It's not your fault. You didn't know," Seven said softly.

"But I know now. And if I don't do something, if I don't put an end to this, I'm just as bad as they all were. I'm just as bad as him," Valley said.

"What are you gonna do?" Thorn asked.

"I'm gonna blow this place up." Valley threw her hands up, and toward the back of the vault. "Incineradora!" Valley bellowed, her voice echoing loudly through the vault.

A burst of flame exploded many toadstools from them, in the depths of the vault, which went much farther than Seven had expected.

The ground beneath them began to rumble, the fire

coming toward them fast, and Seven yelled, "Run!"

But the vault had plans of its own. The Witchlings were sucked back with a torrent of wind and then quite literally spat out, tumbling out through the vault door and into the dark passageway.

Valley got up as quick as a rat and ran back to the door, but when she opened it this time, there was no fire. The pools of magic looked as untouched and serene as they had when they'd arrived.

They needed to find a way to destroy this wicked place, but Seven wondered what would happen if they did.

They ran to Mr. Pepperhorn's room and returned the key, going as fast as they could.

"We have to go, *now*," Seven said. "Your dad could be at the front door for all we know."

And they did need to get out of there quickly, because as much as the vault had put itself back to normal, and they had returned the key, there was one thing out of place Mr. Pepperhorn was sure to notice.

The Witchlings ran, leaving everything as they'd found it and escaping from the Hill before anyone was any wiser, the stolen book tucked safely inside Seven's cloak.

CHAPTER THIRTY-SIX

THE FIVE FAMILIES

MR. PEPPERHORN HAD INDEED noticed the missing book. He had a massive meltdown, according to Valley, and in his worry for whoever had broken into his precious vault, Mr. Pepperhorn had trunk-fulls of items moved from within his house.

"Mostly books, and ledgers," Valley said. "But also, what I suspect is that big door that was in the vault too. They took all of it to the veiled witches' house."

Valley was poring over the stolen book in Seven's bedroom, trying to find more information about the Five Families, as Seven and Thorn caught Figgs up on what they'd found.

"I can't believe the Deweys and Lophiifors are part of the Five Families." Figgs shook his head. "The twins are going to lose it if they find out. Do you think Miss Dewey and Ambert know about all this?"

"We're not entirely sure yet, but we intend to find out," Seven said. It was impossible to believe Miss Dewey was part of something so horrible, but if Mr. Pepperhorn and Lotus knew about this legacy, why not her?

"Goats, I think I found out what the connection to the ancient elders is," Valley said, putting the book down. It turned out, the tome had records of all of the Five Families, death days, coven sortings, all of it. "Thirteen years ago, ancient elders began dying in the Five Families. I've noticed that for every ancient elder in the Five Families that has died, they had that same number of Spares named in the Black Moon Ceremony that year. So last year, one ancient elder died and the Five Families got one new Spare, me."

"Oh my goats," Thorn said.

"The pattern continues like that. Every time an elder dies, a Spare appears in that ancient elder's family," Valley said. "It's happened in all but one family. There is one of the Five Families who hasn't had an elder die and who hasn't had a Spare since the 1790s . . ."

Seven, Figgs, and Thorn leaned forward.

"Ambert Lophiifor's."

"Do you think Ambert could be behind all this?" Thorn asked.

"I don't know," Valley said. "Miss Dewey knew her family was terrible and even admitted to us they used to steal Spare magic, and she was trying to make things right. But I truly don't believe she knew they were still at it. Maybe Ambert is the same."

"Also, if he were the culprit, wouldn't the weird vault with the ponds of stolen magic be in *his* house instead of Blood Rose Manor?" Seven asked. "I still think Mr. Pepperhorn is the mastermind."

Figgs threw his hands up. "What is it with this whole ordeal and evil ponds?!" Something sparked in Seven's brain.

"Wait . . . Figgs." Seven turned to him. "The book about the Lunar Ponds—how *exactly* did you come across it?"

"What does that have to do with anything?" Figgs asked.

"Just tell me," Seven insisted.

"All right, um, I was in the library with Dusk and Helio. I was telling them how we hadn't been able to find a cure and how I wished I could help and they were looking through their books with me when . . . Ambert came in the room." Figgs's eyes went wide.

"Then what?" Seven asked.

"He asked us what we were doing, and we told him, and then he . . . he was the one who pointed the book out, now that I think about it. He said I might be able to find something in it, and when I read through the book, I found the pages about the Lunar Ponds."

Seven's body was shaking now. "I think Ambert set us up. He knew there would be a sirena in those ponds, and he sent us there on *purpose*."

"What? No way." Figgs shook his head.

"Think about it. His family is one of the Five Families and he just so happened to let us borrow a book that almost got me killed," Seven said.

"Not to mention, he's well known for his knowledge of history and the Twelve Towns. You think he had *no* idea the Lunar Ponds might just be deadly?" Valley asked.

“And if you combine that with his family being the only one without Spares, the most powerful of the Five Families, it seems . . .” Thorn said.

“I think we might just have our witch.” Seven nodded.

“Do you think Miss Dewey could be in danger?” Thorn asked.

“I don’t want to be the one to say it, but how do we know she’s not in on it? Her family *is* one of the five,” Figgs pointed out.

“So is mine; that doesn’t mean I’m in on it. I don’t think anyone wants to be judged by what their family does,” Valley said, and Figgs nodded.

“You’re right, I definitely don’t.”

“Also, it’s . . . Miss Dewey. We *know* her. She has risked her own safety to give back to Spares. Why would she want to hurt us?” Thorn added.

“I agree,” Valley said. “I don’t think Miss Dewey knows what she’s mixed up in. Her family might’ve been awful, but that doesn’t mean she is. I trust her.”

Seven ran to the window and stuck her head out. “CHEESE!”

Moments later, Seven’s raccoons were out searching for Miss Dewey to make sure she was okay, or to see if, Stars forbid, she was up to no good, but Seven did not think that was the case.

She knew Miss Dewey; she was one of her favorite people in the entire world, and right now, Seven had a very bad feeling that her favorite librarian was in big froggin’ trouble.

CHAPTER THIRTY-SEVEN

THE OTTER SLEIGH LODGE

THE VERY NEXT DAY, the Witchlings skipped school and went to find Miss Dewey. It would take days for them to reach Castle Point by train, since it was the northernmost of the Twelve Towns. Unless, of course, they took the new witching hour train, but that only ran at night, and they couldn't wait that long. So they reached out to old Walnut via portaphone.

"Course you can use the portal!" he said. "The *you know what*'s in a few days, so we're trying to conserve as much magic as we can, but a couple of uses won't hurt."

"Are you certain?" Seven asked.

"If you don't use it, I'll be sad. Do you know what happens when a witch as old as I am gets sad?"

"Um . . ."

"We die." Walnut cackled.

"Uh, okay, Walnut, we'll use it, thanks!"

"Let's roll!" Valley said as Seven hung up, and they took off toward the Spare Village.

They raced to the Spare Village, found the portal, and in moments were in the snowy town of Castle Point. They knew it would be cold, much colder than they were used to, but nothing could've prepared Seven for the gust of icy wind that greeted them as they arrived.

They had come equipped with their heavy winter cloaks but had underestimated the biting cold of Castle Point, so despite the coverage, their hands, feet, and heads felt instantly numb with cold.

"Here." Seven handed each of them a hot cocoa and peppermint tonic from her rucksack. "This will heat you up in no time."

They drank the tonics and Seven could see her friends visibly relaxing. Their hands unclenched, their eyes brighter and more alert. Once they'd warmed up enough, it was time to find Miss Dewey.

"Okay, the Otter Sleigh Lodge should be just beyond that big white building there, and to the left. There's an otter statue on top of it, can't miss it. Let's go!" Seven said, and they were off.

The Witchlings pulled the hoods of their cloaks over their heads, and tried to hide their faces as much as possible. Thankfully, nobody noticed it was them, or if they did, nobody cared. As they weaved through the icy white streets of Castle Point, the chilling air whipping Seven's cloak to and fro, Seven's stomach churned with worry for Miss Dewey.

Absolutely everything in Castle Point looked like it was made of pure ice. The buildings, the fountains, even some of the trees had been enchanted to look like they were carved from the clearest, most sparkling ice ever. Instead of cars like in Ravenskill, carriages pulled by antlered beasts trotted through the streets. There were restaurants with the warm glow of candles in the windows, hot cocoa shops, and an all-night library. But in each window, and on each door, a *"No Spares Allowed"* sign was prominently displayed. There was a reason the parents of Spare children fled to the snowy town, and Seven had never seen it firsthand, but now she knew those rumors were all true.

Minutes later, they had reached the Otter Sleigh Lodge. It was owned by Ambert's family, so the Witchlings had to be extra careful.

"Don't you know any other spells?" Valley asked as she rubbed her knees. "What happened to your appearance-changing cloaks, Thorn?"

"They're at home and we rushed here," Thorn said.

Seven had turned them into old witches again.

"I don't know, I quite like being old," Thorn said, her voice sounding like an old woman's too this time. Seven's magic had gotten stronger, after all. "Look, I found a caramel candy in my pocket!"

"This is the best I got," Seven said, leading them to the exit on the roof. When she opened the door, she turned around. "If anyone asks, we're here with the Fire Quakers bird-watching club. Check your cloaks."

Valley and Thorn checked their pockets. Inside were old wooden binoculars.

"You might be a nerd, Salazar, but you know your stuff," Valley said in her old lady voice.

Seven smirked a sweet, wrinkled smirk. "Thank you, dear."

"Can we workshop the name though?" Valley asked.

"Not now, Pepperhorn. Let's go."

Miss Dewey was in room 3212, so the Witchlings made their way to the third floor, and to her door.

"What if Ambert is in there?" Thorn whispered.

"We pretend we got the wrong door, then figure out a plan B," Seven said.

Thorn and Valley nodded, then Valley knocked. They waited a few minutes, then Thorn pressed her ear to the door.

"There's no noise, but there's a light on," she said, pointing at the yellow light leaking from the bottom of the door.

Valley knocked again, harder this time. "Miss Dewey?" she called out in her old lady voice.

Shuffling from inside. Someone groaned. The Witchlings looked at one another, thoughts of plan B gone as all three of them began knocking wildly on the door.

"Miss Dewey, it's us! It's the Witchlings!" Seven cried out.

"My girls?" They heard a frail voice from within. "Help . . . help me."

That was all she had to hear.

"Miss Dewey, get away from the door! You two, take cover," Seven said to Valley and Thorn, taking a step back, her arms out. Valley and Thorn crouched behind her as Seven intoned, "Tombar!"

The door came off the hinges and fell backward into the room. The Witchlings ran through the cloud of dust, over the door, and into the room to find someone in the bed. Surely, this couldn't be Miss Dewey. This witch's skin was a deep, rich purple, pulled over her bones so tightly, it looked paper thin. Her eyes bulged from her head, as did her teeth; her hair was thin and scattered in the bed in front of her. Hovering above her bed, her familiar, Almanac, weakly flitted around, very clearly in distress and very clearly sick as well.

"Stay back," the bird said, nose-diving at Seven.

"Whoa, whoa! I'm a friend!" Seven covered her gray head of hair.

Their favorite librarian looked frightened, confused, and Seven suddenly remembered their disguises.

"We're wearing little old lady disguises again!" Seven said, still dodging Almanac. Relief bloomed on the bedridden witch's face and her familiar returned to her bedside but still eyed the Witchlings suspiciously.

"Miss Dewey? Is that really you?" Thorn whispered.

The woman nodded slowly, a sad smile on her skeletal face. "It's me, girls. Almanac, they're friends, it's okay."

"Stars," Seven said, shaking out of her trance and running over to Miss Dewey's bed.

Valley propped the door back in place. "Arreglar," she intoned, fixing the door, then joining Seven and Thorn next to Miss Dewey's bed.

"What happened to you?" Valley asked as Seven searched her rucksack for her most potent healing potions.

"That is a long story. But first, why are you old?" Miss Dewey asked, and the Witchlings laughed, Thorn and Valley pointing at Seven.

"It's the only disguise spell I'm any good at." Seven shrugged.

Miss Dewey gave a gravelly little cough. "I cannot tell you how happy I am to see you, but we must hurry. Ambert could be back any moment."

Seven shook her head. "So he *did* do this to you."

"Yes," Miss Dewey said, closing her eyes.

"We're gonna get you out of here, don't worry." Thorn patted Miss Dewey's hand.

"We need you to be a bit stronger before we take off though. Drink this." Seven gave Miss Dewey an elixir—molted flor culebra petals, rotten fruit from the Strangling Figs, and a tiny bit of raccoon fur from her friends, all ground up to make an archaic remedy that would heal Miss Dewey quickly. At least, Seven hoped it would. She knew now that to combat any kind of magic, especially the forbidden kind, you had to counter with the same kind of magic.

Miss Dewey drank the awful-smelling elixir slowly, and almost instantly, her skin began clearing from the dark purple to a lighter shade. She was now more lilac than indigo. Miss Dewey sat up a bit straighter, her eyes brightening.

"Oh, that was *not* fun to drink, but boy do I feel better," Miss Dewey said. "Thank you, Seven. Do not tell me what was in there." She picked a thick strand of fur from her mouth.

"In about fifteen minutes, the full effects will take over, but till then your legs might be jellyfish-like, so better to wait," Seven said as she administered a healing potion to Almanac as well.

"In the meantime . . . what happened with Ambert?" Thorn asked.

Miss Dewey shook her head. Her eyes were filled with tears. "Ambert was not who I believed. He had me fooled." She looked back at the Witchlings. "He had ulterior motives behind our relationship and marriage from the very first day. I was charmed by him because there was something . . . indescribable about him, like a light I could not look away from. He discovered long ago that I came from a long line of powerful witches, and his plan had always been to steal my inherited magic away. He's using archaic magic, terrible magic, to siphon my power from me bit by bit with something called a Blood Rose."

The Witchlings exchanged looks. They explained everything about the vault to Miss Dewey.

Miss Dewey looked horrified. "He told me that just a touch of that rose could bind one witch to another, and steal all their power. He said it to me like he was . . . proud. The moment we reached this resort, the illusion of who he pretended to be fell, and he attacked me after I confronted him about some suspicions I was having. I tried to fight back, to tell Almanac to call for help, but he bound his magic to this place too. Then Ambert locked me in this room and has been taking more of my magic day by day. I don't know how you even got in the door. It's enchanted," Miss Dewey said.

Seven's stomach flipped. "Uh, it's my Uncle magic, I guess. What suspicions were you having about Ambert?" she asked, both trying to change the subject and because she genuinely wanted to know what Miss Dewey knew.

"Tidbit," she said softly. "His familiar. He seemed to have rebelled against Ambert. They hadn't been getting along, that much was obvious. Tidbit never wanted to be around him, and once, I found him trying to escape. Ambert grabbed him from me before I could do anything to help. Then one day, Ambert came home with scratches on his face, just about the size Tidbit would sometimes make by accident when he got too excited about me giving him peanuts." Miss Dewey laughed softly. "When we got here, Tidbit was with us, but then two days passed, and I hadn't seen him and, well, I knew something was very wrong. Librarians don't travel without their familiars; we can barely go into the next room without missing them. I confronted Ambert about it and that's when he showed his true form."

"We need to get you out of here as fast as possible," Seven said just as her portaphone pinged. "One sec, it's Walnut."

"Don't take the portal. Guards outside, I think they're trying to get in," the old witch had written.

"Frogs!" Seven shouted.

The other three witches opened their eyes wide at the sound of Seven cursing. "Sorry, the portal is out. Guards are trying to get in," she said.

"What, how did they find out?" Miss Dewey asked, distressed.

"Don't know, but please don't get yourself worked up, you're still weak and we have to move," Seven said. "Witching hour train will be leaving soon. Can you get her there?" She looked at Valley and Thorn, and they nodded.

"Miss Dewey, do you think you'll be able to stand?" Thorn asked.

Miss Dewey nodded. "Seven's tonic seems to have helped. I'll try."

Miss Dewey's skin tone had improved even further; she looked less like a witch that was moments from death.

"We can help you," Valley said. "Thorn and I will take you to the train."

Thorn was already draping Miss Dewey's shoulders with a coat.

"What about you, Seven?" Miss Dewey asked.

"I'll meet you there shortly. I have a squirrel to find."

CHAPTER THIRTY-EIGHT
THE WITCHING HOUR TRAIN

SEVEN TRUDGED THROUGH the snow in the forest surrounding the Otter Sleigh Lodge. Her fingers and toes felt numb with cold. She rubbed her hands together and blew, but even her breath, coming out in puffs of white vapor, felt cold against her skin.

"I really hope he found a warm place to burrow," Seven said.

"He is resourceful, if not a little bit mischievous," Almanac said.

"I don't understand what happened. The times I saw him, he was always snuggled up with Ambert, happily sleeping on his car dashboard or his shoulder." Seven kicked at the snow. How could she be so close to an animal in danger and not realize it?

"The trick is in the sleeping. Ambert was sedating him with calming marbles, I believe. Until Tidbit got wise to his schemes and figured out a way to run away for good. I hope," Almanac said. "I'm going to fly up higher, see what I can see."

The brilliant blue bird flew up, up, up so high, Seven could no longer see him. She walked through the snowy forest, happy houses with chimney smoke in the distance to her right, miles and miles of unknown forest to her left. Castle Point was home to many lumber witches, who used trees to carve and make the things other Twelve Townians used. But for every tree they cut down, they planted many more, and the town was nestled in the warm embrace of nature well preserved.

It was also a town where rich Twelve Townian witches, and those outside the Twelve Towns—from troll and dwarf country, to the southern sirena islands, to vast lands beyond—came to partake in snow games and relaxation. Seven marveled at the fact that just a year ago, she didn't think much about the world outside Ravenskill, let alone the world outside the Twelve Towns. But now she wondered what lay beyond the bounds of her imagination, of her experiences in her cozy hometown. The world was big, and Seven suddenly had the urge to know more of it.

"Seven, he's here, hurry!" Almanac's birdsong voice called out to Seven, a flash of blue light appearing in the sky above her leading the way, and Seven began to run.

She ran, cold air spiking her lungs, her legs pumping as each booted foot hit the ground like a speeding train. Seven hoped Tidbit was okay, that she had not completely failed him. She hoped that Ambert had not done something unthinkable again.

"Here!" Almanac cried out, and Seven stopped.

There on the ground, in a little mound of brown fur, was Tidbit. Seven fell to her knees in front of the squirrel, whipping her rucksack off, and searched for a warming elixir suitable for very small animals.

She settled on an elderberry tonic and slowly lifted the squirrel's tiny face. His pink tongue stuck slightly out, Seven suspected because he was a senior squirrel and was missing some teeth. Thank the Stars, he was breathing, which was all that mattered right now. Seven administered a few droplets of the tonic to the squirrel, then carefully bundled him in a makeshift sling and strapped him to her chest. Edgar was, as always, in her pocket, and if she put a squirrel in there with him, he would start a colossal riot.

"Will he be okay?" Almanac said as Seven got on her feet.

"I think so." Seven checked her watch. "Come on, the train is leaving in just under ten minutes. We have to hurry."

"Veloz!" Seven cried, shouting at her feet, and the magic carried her at the same speed as Almanac's wings. They zipped through the forest, the beautiful scenery she'd seen on the way here a blur of white and green. They reached the train platform just as the witching hour train was about to depart.

Her old lady magic had long since worn out, and she

was searching for the others when her portaphone pinged.

"We're in the orange blossom car, number twenty-seven," Thorn messaged her, and Seven, Almanac, and the still-sleeping Tidbit made their way to the others.

"Hello," Seven said as she opened the car door. Miss Dewey was by the window, Thorn beside her, and Valley sat across from them, neither of them in their little old lady disguises any longer.

"Did you find him?" Thorn asked anxiously. Seven nodded.

"You look better," Seven said to Miss Dewey, and the librarian smiled.

"I feel better. Much more like myself than I have in, well, months now, I think. Whatever you put in that tonic, bottle it and sell it. You'll be rich with coin in no time." Miss Dewey winked.

She really was better. Seven smiled.

She sat down beside Valley. Almanac flitted over to Miss Dewey and rested on her lap, and Seven opened her cloak to reveal Tidbit inside the baby sling.

"Oh, poor Tidbit," Valley said, wiping her eyes. "He looks kinda like Cotton Swab when he gets all sleepy."

"He's going to be okay, but I'd feel a lot better if we got some food in him," Seven said.

"We got some stuff from the midnight snack cart," Miss Dewey said softly.

"I saved this for you, in case you were hungry." Valley handed Seven half her sandwich.

"Thanks." Seven smiled at Valley. She reminded herself again to be grateful for her friends. Just weeks ago, Valley was still a statue and now here she was, saving food so Seven would eat. Everything wasn't perfect, far from it, but Seven was thankful for these small pockets of happiness.

Seven picked out a few vegetables from the sandwich and put the rest aside.

"I think he prefers cucumber," Miss Dewey said.

Seven nodded, taking a cucumber slice and waving it gently in front of the squirrel. His nose twitched. Eyes still closed, Tidbit reached out and made grabby hands until Seven helped him take hold of the cucumber. Tidbit took quick, tiny bites until the whole thing was gone. He turned around inside the sling, burrowing into the fabric and falling into a deep, non-snoreless sleep.

"He's so cute," Thorn said, her eyes twinkling "How could anyone ever hurt such a small thing?"

Seven scoffed. "The smaller the better for some witches. Makes it easier to get away with treachery."

"I'm going to make Ambert wish he had never had a born day," Valley seethed.

"You must be careful," Miss Dewey said. "I know you witches are more than capable, but this isn't the Dimblewits or even the Cursed Toads. He is . . ."

"A big bad witch," Thorn said.

"I just wish I understood why. He seemed so . . . lovely. So kind," Miss Dewey said. "I don't know how I didn't see it."

"Nobody saw it; you're not the only one Ambert tricked," Seven said.

"He was very, very good at trickery," said a small, squeaky voice.

Seven looked down.

Tidbit the squirrel was looking right at her.

"You're up." Seven smiled.

"Oh, thank the Stars!" Thorn clapped.

"Ambert is a terrible witch, no-good, rotten," Tidbit said.

"Do you know why he's doing all these bad things?" Seven asked.

Tidbit nodded. "I can tell you everything. And there's a lot of everything to tell."

CHAPTER THIRTY-NINE

THIS IS HOW IT ALL BEGAN

"**I WILL BEGIN** at the beginning. Customarily, that is how witches tell stories, is it not? Squirrels sometimes begin in the middle, or the end, and then we make our way toward the beginning if we can remember what story we started in the first place. Does that make sense?" Tidbit asked Seven.

"Barely," Seven said. She translated the squirrel's squeaky ramblings to the others.

"Ask him which one of us he thinks is coolest," Valley said.

"Not now, Valley." Seven shook her head. "Can you tell us what you know about Ambert, from the beginning, if possible? Please."

Tidbit sighed. "Fine, I will do it the boring way."

The squirrel cleared his throat. "It began nearly five years ago, when Ambert won the Golden Frog Games . . ."

Tidbit was born for the stage. Or storytelling. Or something. Because during the five-hour train ride home, he told the story of how Ambert had been there not just from the beginning of Miss Dewey's tragic story but much, much earlier.

"When Ambert saw the Golden Frog's vision, it changed something within him. He had never been the kind witch he seemed to be, but I did not realize just how deep-down cave-droppings rotten he was," Tidbit said, scrunching up his little face in anger.

"After that, he became obsessed with finding someone: a witch with rosy cheeks and a smile like sunshine," said Tidbit as if he was reciting something.

"That's all he said about the witch?" Seven asked.

Tidbit nodded. "He would repeat it every morning like he was speaking to the Stars: rosy cheeks, smile like sunshine, rosy cheeks, smile like sunshine. I do think it has something to do with the Golden Frog's vision. Then one night he found the biggest monstruo, went all the way to the Enchanted Grim to get it . . ."

"The Nightbeast," Valley whispered.

"And he and his three rotten, scaly friends trained the biggest monstruo until it was a killing machine. That is when he found the rosy cheeks and smile like sunshine witch, I think, because we went to Boggs Ferry . . ."

"Boggs Ferry?!" Seven blurted.

"What about Boggs Ferry?" Thorn asked carefully.

Seven just shook her head, and Tidbit continued. "We went to Boggs Ferry, and I was there that night when it happened. I am sorry I could not help your brother." Tidbit turned to Thorn.

Thorn went paler than Alaric. "Ambert is the reason Petal died?"

Tidbit nodded when Seven translated, and Thorn began to sob.

Smile like sunshine, rosy cheeks. Thorn Laroux.

Hadn't she said all those months ago that the Nightbeast had launched at her and not Petal? Petal had jumped in front of his sister and saved her life while losing his own. Thorn had been the target all along. But why?

Miss Dewey patted the devastated Thorn's back as she cried. Seven could swear there was smoke coming from Valley's ears and she could not blame her.

Ambert had become one of them. They had embraced him because they loved Miss Dewey, yet he had been fooling them all along. But Thorn? Thorn had laughed with the witch who'd killed her brother; she'd been to his wedding and given him a gift. Thorn had treated him with all the love and respect he never deserved. If Thorn needed help burying him, Seven was ready with a shovel. She would plant poisonous and cursed flowers at his grave so that nobody could mourn him without knowing their wrath. He would never know peace again.

"Someone in Ambert's family, an elder, taught the Cursed Toads, the false Uncles, how to do the old evil magic. But the magic had a price.

"They were indebted to the Lophiifors, so when the time came, Ambert enlisted their help to tame and train the biggest monstruo. It was not easy; it did not want to do their bidding, and they had to purple poison it in order to control it."

"Purple poison, archaic magic," Valley said.

"When the biggest monstruo I've ever seen but would very much like to pet killed Petal, it became sick with sadness. It refused to kill Thorn; it refused to do anything until it was purple poisoned further. Ambert found cucos from the Enchanted Grim to try and soothe the beast and make it happier with its minions, but it was not easy. It wasn't until many months later when they could force it to emerge again and attack you all on the night of the waning moon," Tidbit said.

"If you knew Ambert was bad, why did you go along with it?" Seven asked. "You seem like an upstanding squirrel."

Tidbit's ears shot up and he preened. "I am honored, Uncle Seven! And yes, I am quite wonderful, but you see, Ambert is good at lying. He hypnotizes with pizzazz. I do not know how he does it, but he fooled me good. He told me you three were bad—were going to upset the balance of magic." Tidbit's chubby cheeks went slightly pink. "I am embarrassed to admit it!" He threw himself on Seven's lap, then slowly got up. "But it is my truth."

"It's not your fault. It's nobody's fault but Ambert's," Miss Dewey said once Seven translated.

"When his plan failed a second time, he came up with a new approach. He was convinced he needed someone younger, powerful and beautiful like him . . ."

"Lotus," Seven said.

Tidbit nodded. "Precisely."

The young Cursed Toads, and Lotus, were all vulnerable and desperate. Ambert chose desperate witches, and then exploited that desperation to make them do his dirty work for him. Lotus sat in the dungeon still, paying for the crimes that Ambert likely asked her to do.

"What about Dusk and Helio?" Thorn asked.

"The boys are kindhearted. Dusk in particular has been sad since his mother died, but quite liked his soon-to-be second mother." Tidbit pointed to Miss Dewey.

"All of this began because of what Ambert saw when he touched the Golden Frog. Ambert tried to kill Thorn with the Nightbeast, then with the stone hex, but each time Ambert was trying to stop *you*, Thorn. Until now. I think that's the key," Seven said.

"Why would he want to stop me? You're the most powerful one of us," Thorn said.

Seven shook her head. "Not true, first of all, but maybe it had to do with something you did, or that he saw you were going to do in the Golden Frog vision when he won. Tidbit said he changed after that; that's when he went looking for you and found the Nightbeast. He wanted to stop you from doing something, I'm sure of it."

"Winning the games? That's the only big thing I can think of that he would've wanted to stop, but why would he want to stop Thorn from winning?" Valley asked.

"More importantly, why has he stopped coming after you now? Spares are going missing, which may or may not be him too, but he hasn't tried to attack you since the games . . . it seems his target changed. Why?" Seven asked.

"Because Thorn already did the thing he was trying to stop her from doing!" Valley stood up.

Seven's eyes opened wide. "Wait . . . you're right! It's not the *games* he cared about, it was what you might learn if you won that he was scared about. That's what he didn't want you to do . . ."

"Touch the Golden Frog," the Witchlings said in unison.

CHAPTER FORTY
THE GOLDEN FROG'S VISION

"I'VE GONE OVER the vision again and again and can't make out what any of it means," Seven said.

She recited the images she'd seen out loud. "A group of witches meeting in secret; the three witches holding the foxes; Ravenskill, engulfed in flames; a bright, enchanting light underwater; a peculiar house in Ravenskill with the blurry symbol of a large animal on the front door . . ."

"It wasn't a large animal," Valley said.

"What?" Thorn and Seven asked at once.

"I didn't see a large animal on the door. I saw something else," Valley said.

"Maybe there is something Valley saw that will help you figure out the vision more clearly," Miss Dewey said.

"I have pencils and paper in my rucksack; let's draw that house again but with Valley this time," Thorn suggested, and they all agreed.

All three Witchlings drew what they saw in the vision, including Valley, who saw it in her stonified state and had to work the hardest to recall it. When they were done, they compared their drawings. They all looked quite different, Thorn's being the most artistic and beautiful, Seven's efficient, Valley's the scariest. But all three drawings portrayed the same thing. Except for one detail.

"Valley, your door looks nothing like Seven's and Thorn's," Miss Dewey observed.

Where Thorn and Seven had each drawn the outline of two completely different indiscernible animals, Valley had just drawn a shape.

"What if we put the drawings of the doors together?" Thorn suggested.

"Can't hurt," Seven said. Thorn, the best artist of the three of them, began to trace the doors, one layered on top of the other, and soon it became quite clear that it was not working.

"It looks like a three-headed dog," Valley said, shaking her head.

"It has too many ears . . . and noses." Seven scrunched her own nose as she said.

"Valley's part doesn't even look like an animal; it's just a weird shape around the blob thing," Thorn said.

"May I see?" Miss Dewey asked.

Seven pushed the paper down the table toward Miss Dewey and the librarian gasped.

"What is it?" Valley asked.

Miss Dewey pointed. "The shape Valley saw, it might not just be a shape. I think . . . it's a crest. And do you see these?"

She held up the paper, pointing to three diagonal notches on each of the four corners of the door. It was such a small, subtle detail that they hadn't noticed it, even as they'd drawn it. Besides, in each of their visions, there was only one little line on each door, not three, as there was now.

"Do those mean something?" Seven asked. "We saw a door with those lines . . . recently."

Miss Dewey nodded. "Yes. Only one type of door is made this way. These are coven house doors."

The Witchlings exchanged looks. *The door in the Blood Rose Vault.*

"The first week after the Black Moon Ceremony, when you're let into your coven house, this is one of the very first things you learn. I never thought of this, but of course Spares wouldn't necessarily know about the importance of coven house doors. These notches are a key part of the coven doors. They are infused with magic that only allows witches of that specific coven to enter at will. And only witches *from* that coven can see the coven house door markings in the first place. It's a security measure, but it's a symbol, more than anything, about the close-knit nature of each coven and the exclusivity."

"But why would the Golden Frog show us a coven door?" Valley scratched her head.

"And why would Ambert try to kill me to keep me from seeing it?" Thorn asked.

"Tidbit," Seven said, turning to the squirrel, "did you send me the message to find the lost one?"

Tidbit nodded. “I did, I did.”

Seven’s mouth fell open. “Do you know what it means? The door and that phrase, ‘the lost one’?” Seven asked.

The squirrel shrugged. “I only know that Ambert’s threats to me were getting scarier and scarier. When I overheard him saying that the most important thing was that you never find the lost one, I knew I had to warn you any way I could.”

Seven translated for her friends.

“By whom?” asked Miss Dewey.

“Why, by the Golden Frog himself, of course,” said Tidbit.

“I see,” Seven said.

“What, what is it?” Valley asked.

Seven quirked an eyebrow. “Anyone up for a little late-night break-in?”

CHAPTER FORTY-ONE
BEYOND THE WEEPING WILLOW

AS THE TRAIN PULLED into Ravenskill, fog blanketed the empty station. Empty, except for three witches in heavy black cloaks, hoods up, standing on the platform. And waiting.

Fox, Quill, and Thimble, the Witchlings' mothers, took charge of Miss Dewey as the Witchlings parted ways with their favorite librarian and ran all the way to the Hall of Elders.

"This way, hurry," Alaric said, meeting them at the door.

Their steps echoed in the vast empty corridors of the Hall of Elders. Alaric floated in front of them, holding a lantern made of pure blue light.

They had awakened the ghost from his slumber and asked if he could help them see the Golden Frog. The Golden Frog was protected by the kind of magic not even Seven could penetrate. They needed someone with the key, and it was either Jonafren or Alaric, and they didn't particularly feel like dying because they'd interrupted the fae's beauty sleep. Now they were following a ghost through the Hall of Elders and on their way to see if Seven could speak to the Golden Frog.

They stopped at a door made of pure gold. Alaric pulled an iron skeleton key from the pocket of his ghost pants, a key that Seven knew was infused with enough magic to power the entire Twelve Towns, and opened it.

They walked quietly into the room and stopped just before the tree. Whatever Seven expected to see here, it wasn't this. A willow tree as tall as a building stood before them, majestic boughs curved like the arms of a dancer, a cascade of dainty leaves creating a curtain of green.

"Here he is," Alaric said with a flourish of his transparent arm.

"Um, sorry, where?" Thorn asked.

"There, through the leaves. You'll find him once you walk through. I will keep watch out here," Alaric said.

"We'll try not to be long," Seven said. "So you can get back to sleep."

"I can sleep with my eyes open, don't worry!" Alaric said cheerfully.

"Um, what?" Seven asked, but Alaric just floated out of the room and closed the door.

Seven turned around, and when she looked at Thorn and Valley, all three Witchlings giggled. Alaric made it impossible not to. They approached the tree, and the funny energy from just a moment ago evaporated like droplets of dew. They were unsure exactly what they would find on the other side of this tree, but they did know one thing: Whatever it was, they'd face it together. The Witchlings held hands and walked through the curtain of green.

They emerged in a lagoon, the walls of the empty room no longer visible. It felt much like the Nightbeast's glade.

"This is froggin' cool," Valley whispered.

"There he is," Seven said.

On a lily pad, in the middle of a pond, sat the Golden Frog. The Witchlings stood mesmerized.

"Go." Valley nudged Seven.

"What do I say?" Seven asked.

"I dunno, you're the animal expert!"

"Is he an animal? He's, like, half statue," Thorn said.

"In that case, this is your area of expertise, Valley," Seven said.

"Too soon!" Valley said.

"Are you going to talk to me or are you going to fight until the sun rises?" the Golden Frog asked.

"Oh," Seven said.

"What?" Thorn and Valley asked in unison.

"It spoke."

Seven translated for the Witchlings and then she took a step forward, clearing her throat.

"We were wondering if you could help us with the vision you granted Thorn, please. Erm, Mr. Golden Frog."

"And you two," the Golden Frog said.

"And that you granted me and Valley, yes, sorry."

Seven laughed nervously and wiped her forehead. "Why *did* you grant us the vision too, by the way?"

The Golden Frog blinked. "A few reasons. The fate of the Twelve Towns might just rest in the mystery connected to the vision, and you three are the only witches I trusted enough to reveal it to. I would very much like to continue living, you see."

"Oh," Seven said, and relayed the message to Thorn and Valley.

"Sheesh, no pressure," Thorn said.

"Can you help us? We're trying to figure things out, but we need a hand," Seven asked.

"Before I help you, *if* I help you, you must hear the lore," the Golden Frog said.

"We don't have much time . . ."

"You must hear the lore."

"Okay, okay, we'll hear the lore," Seven said.

"Sit," the Golden Frog said.

Seven sat on the grass and motioned for Valley and Thorn to do the same. The toad began to speak, and Seven translated for her coven sisters.

"Long ago, the Twelve Towns burned. When they did, my mother, who was a normal frog, escaped from her burning home, the house of a witch she loved very much.

"Lost and alone, my mother searched for shelter, when many days of heavy rain came. Hungry, cold, and scared, my dear mother almost gave up. But then one day, she came across an elephant."

An elephant.

"The elephant took pity on the frog and created a home for her using its footprint. My mother and my brothers and sisters did not survive, but I did. When the rains stopped, something had changed. I had somehow been granted knowledge from the elephant, who is the holder of all knowledge and the keeper of memories in the animal world.

"When I looked at myself in the reflection of a pond, I saw I had been turned into gold. Any animal who touched me gained insight into their own future, and soon the witches around us took notice and captured me, making it part of their games."

"Do you want us to help you escape this place? I'm not above arson," Valley said once Seven had translated.

"I would be no safer in nature," the Golden Frog responded. "Some nefarious witch would find me, or other animals would line up sunrise to sunset to ask me questions about where to find food or defeat a rival. I am content here. I can also leave whenever I please. I know *almost* everything, you see, including where they keep the secret keys."

"The elephant, what happened to it?" Seven asked.

"It died, as all animals who do not live eternally do."

"Ask it about the door," Thorn urged.

"The door in the vision, was it . . . a coven house door?" Seven asked.

"I cannot tell you this because I do not know. I was not immune to the spells for forgetting that savaged the Twelve Towns. While I hold most knowledge of others, my own memories are incomplete. I can only tell you this . . ."

All three Witchlings leaned in so far, Seven feared they might fall right into the pond. When the frog spoke next, she very nearly did.

"The answers lie in memories."

Thunder crashed outside the Hall of Elders, startling the Witchlings. When they emerged into the night, purple rain was falling once more. Seven would bet anything more Spares had just gone missing, and she hoped against hope that her flowers had captured something.

As they ran, Seven turned over the Golden Frog's words in her mind, but she could not untangle their meaning. The only place her mind went was to her chismosas. They captured memories in a way, after all, so the Witchlings went straight to the Ravenskill Theater balcony, and checked if there was anything to be gleaned from the witch-eating flowers. Finding nothing there, they went to the location on the Hill and then finally to the flower Seven had planted near the veiled witches' house.

Seven crouched near the plant and gently tapped the flower's petals, taking her hand away quickly. The chance of a chismosa plant eating the witch who planted it is not likely, but never zero.

"Oooh, I've been waiting and waiting! This is going to be good," the plant said.

"They're funny little things, aren't they?" Thorn said, reaching out just as the plant snapped at her finger and Thorn nearly fell back.

"They are, but don't get too close," Seven warned.

"What did you see?" Valley asked.

"I only tell trusted comadres," the plant said, looking at Seven pointedly.

Seven sighed. "Did you see anything? Specifically, did you see anything moments ago when the purple rain began?"

"I thought you'd never ask!" The plant opened her mouth and a scene formed before them.

From the plant's view, you could see the house in the distance and everything in the foliage-thick fields around it. Seven looked up now, and the lights of the big house were out, thankfully.

The plant moved slightly, giving a wide-angle view of its surroundings, which was helpful. They watched for a short while before any witches came into the frame. Just one walked by, with a basket filled with what looked like breads. The bright light flashed, thunder clapped, and the witch . . . was gone.

Startled, Seven popped up from her crouched position without meaning to.

"Get back down, you big goose, they're gonna see you!" Valley pulled her and Seven sat back down.

"You got a death wish?" Valley sneered.

"The lights are off, nobody is even in there." Seven rolled her eyes.

"They probably eat dinner like that. No lights, just them in the dark smiling under those weirdo veils." Valley shivered.

"Stop talking, you're missing everything," Thorn snapped.

"Wait, who is that?" Seven asked, turning back to the scene and noticing another witch wearing a big cloak.

"This person appeared just after the witch disappeared," Thorn said. "They've just been standing here the whole time, looking for something on the ground."

The witch stopped moving, as if they'd spotted something, and then took out their portaphone.

"Father, it's done."

The witch turned and looked around, inspecting the area, it seemed—but also revealing his face. Helio Lophiifor smiled as he found a shining pebble and put it in his pocket.

CHAPTER FORTY-TWO

THE SPARES STRIKE

VERY EARLY THE NEXT MORNING, the time had come for the brave Spares of the Twelve Towns to strike. Just as they had planned, they began pouring into Twilight Square at dawn. Seven was perched atop a stone wall with Valley and Thorn, ready to protest with their fellow Spares, or fight if they needed to. Seven had been anxious to speak to the Gran, about Ambert, about Helio, about everything, but the strike had completely taken over everyone's attention. Her anxiety to learn the truth about the potential coven door, the vision and what it could mean, the Blood Rose vault, it would all have to wait. Right now, the only thing that mattered was helping to keep the Spares of the Twelve Towns safe.

Crimson was at the center of the square, organizing the Spares and helping pass out snacks and safety whistles. Soon they were marching in a circle, holding up signs like *"Spares Are Witches Too"*; *"If the Stars Hate Spares, Why Are We So Cute?"*; and *"Elder Witches for Spare Rights!"*

"How long do you think it'll take before the Hill gets wind of this?" Valley asked.

"Once they realize nobody made them their breakfast, they'll be trying to shut this whole thing down," Seven said.

"Come on, let's get down there," Thorn said, and grabbed their signs from behind the wall. *"Justice for Pixel,"* they read, and the Witchlings joined the protesters to cheers and wide smiles from the crowd.

"You made it!" Crimson said.

"We wouldn't miss this for anything," Seven said.

"Word is the Hill Society is already on their way; be ready," he said.

"We're always ready," Valley said.

Seven found her friends in the crowd, Figgs protesting beside Poppy and Graves, who ran and kissed Valley on the cheek, making her whole face go red. Her family was there too, and Thorn's, and Quill. Even Sybell made an appearance, winking at Seven as they held their sign, which read, *"The Future of Spares Is Bright, Trust Me I Know."* Everyone she knew and loved was there supporting Spares, and it warmed Seven's heart.

They marched and yelled and sang songs for an hour before the first Hill witches showed up, enraged. They demanded their Spares return to work, finding them in the crowd and trying to get to them. But they did not expect the protective dome. The witches crashed into the invisible magical barrier and were thrown several toadstools back. The Spare protesters cheered.

"That won't last forever, but toads, it's satisfying to watch," Seven said.

The Gran's Guard showed up, of course, and the Hill witches, who had grown in number by now, shrieked at them to do something, but the guard did not try to shut down the protest, of course. Protests were protected under Ravenskill law. Instead, some of the unruliest Hill witches, who had tried to blast through the dome with magic, were escorted away in magical bindings.

The Spares and their allies cheered, invigorated by these small victories, but Seven wondered what would happen tonight when the protesters had to return to their small cold rooms on the Hill, or lost their jobs altogether? They'd have to be ready for that too, and Seven vowed to herself she'd do whatever it took to help them get through it.

Reporters from the *Squawking Crow* showed up and were let into the dome to interview Crimson, Walnut, and a few other Spares. It seemed the Hill was without workers for the first time in its history. They would later learn that every store and tavern in Ravenskill, some out of necessity and some out of solidarity, shut down for the entire day. The Spares had proved the point they set out to prove: Without them, there was no Ravenskill.

There was no sign of Mr. Pepperhorn or Ambert so far, but Seven knew it was just a matter of time before they made themselves known one way or another.

Around the eight-hour mark of the protest, a large crowd had gathered outside the dome, some of them holding up protest signs of their own in solidarity with the Spares. And then, what they'd expected, the veiled witches showed up, along with a newly freed Mr. Dimblewit.

"I wish we could just fight them all now," Valley said.

"Don't worry, I'm pretty sure we'll get our chance," Seven said. "Look."

One of the veiled witches had pulled something from their cloak—a wand!

"Get down!" Crimson called, and all the Spares ducked as the veiled witch blasted the dome.

The magic cracked and shuddered, but it held. Crimson reinforced the magic with a few other non-Spares. The Oracle held their hands up and said a prayer to the Stars, and the dome shone bright, stronger than before. But they knew it would not last forever.

At the twelve-hour mark exactly, the protective dome fell away and the Hill witches stormed the square. The Spares linked arms, making a human chain as Crimson, the Witchlings, their parents, and a whole slew of non-Spare witches shielded the Spares and held the Hill witches back with their hands up.

One Hill resident got through, finding their Spare and pulling roughly on their arm, but the Spares were ready.

"Alto!" they yelled in unison. Perhaps individually, a low-level spell like that would do little to dissuade a Hill witch, but when intoned by the Spares collectively, it dealt a powerful blow to the witch, who went tumbling back and all the way into the woods. Now the veiled witches descended on them, every single one of them with a wand in hand.

"Return our workers or face the consequences," Master Beetle said.

"No froggin' way!" Valley yelled, and the Spares began to chant. "No froggin' way! No froggin' way!"

"See reason! Before it is too late!" Master Beetle said.

"Things will be as they always have been. Us above and you beneath us!" Mr. Dimblewit cried, to many protests from the crowd.

"The way it's *always* been? You sure about that, Dimblewit?" Valley said.

"You don't know what you're talking about!"

"I think your family records would show that she does, actually," Seven said.

Mr. Dimblewit's face went whiter than new snow and he raised his wand again, charging not at the Witchlings but at the Spares around them.

Coward.

Mr. Dimblewit struck Walnut and he fell to the ground.

"No!" Seven cried out, running to him.

She helped Walnut up and made sure he was okay, then prepared to jump into the fray. Spares tried to fight back, but even with Crimson and the other allies on their side, the Hill witches outmatched them. Unfortunately for the veiled witches, however, the Spares had something they did not: a witch with a heart made of stone, a Monstruo Uncle, and a champion.

Give in to who you are. It is the only way.

Seven unleashed her monstruo powers and led the Witchlings forward, descending on the veiled witches. As Mr. Dimblewit towered over a cowering Spare, Seven let her monstruo magic surge within her and blasted him with a well-timed striking spell. Seven felt the bite, the monstruo howl, behind every blow she dealt the evil witch. Her hands vibrated with the force of the gray light that emitted from them for the very first time, not quite shadow magic, but something else. Something that reminded her of the Nightbeast. Because her magic, powerful and deadly, looked like . . . illuminated fur. Mr. Dimblewit stumbled back, surprised by the force of her attack, no doubt. Seven did not let him get his bearings; she struck again and again, blasting his chest and face as battle broke out around them. Valley's twin knives were out in moments. She spun them in both hands and ran straight at the veiled witches, slashing indiscriminately at their veils, trying to reveal who was beneath them. They were no match for her skill and speed, and Valley whooped and yelled as she took on four veiled witches at once.

Thorn spun, her dress twirling around her, a pink ribbon in her hand that moved in circles and flourishes, but Seven knew all too well that it was as poisonous as it was beautiful. A veiled witch screamed as the ribbon burned straight through her cloak and reddened her skin. Thorn danced delicate circles around the veiled witches, taking them down one by one as they underestimated what the cute witch could do.

Seven's parents were fighting alongside the other Witchlings' parents. Even Beefy, stronger than most full-grown witches, punched a hole clean through a crowd of Hill witches. The battle raged on, and the Spares and their allies were prevailing, but there were many hurt Spares.

"Enough!" cried a thundering voice, and all the witches looked up. In the sky, hovering above them, was the Gran.

She floated down gracefully to the center of the square. The battle stopped as she addressed the Ravenskillians all around her.

"It might not seem like it today, but our history as Ravenskillians has been marked by the spirit of togetherness! Throughout our existence, the Twelve Towns have flourished because we have been able to see the good in one another, to push past differences, and to put an end to injustices. What the Spares and their allies did here today is a triumph," she said. At that, the Hill witches became enraged. "And I ask all of you today, what is the legacy you want to leave? Are you doing what you believe is truly right for our fair town, or are you doing what will lead to personal glory and wealth for yourself? If your children, your heirs, the witches who will come after you are long gone, were to look into your memories would you be proud of what they found? Every witch deserves dignity, happiness, a full belly, and a warm home. It is what our ancestors, what *the Stars*, have endowed us." The Gran pointed to the sky, and it shone even more brightly as she did. "Who are any of you to deny that inheritance?"

The crowd settled down, and the veiled witches retreated into the darkness of the woods.

"The memories you make now are the only legacy that matters. Let the stories your descendants learn about you be ones that will make them proud of their roots!" the Gran called out, her voice echoing into the woods after the veiled witches.

"Do you goats remember what the Golden Frog said right before we left?" Thorn asked.

"*'The answers lie in memories,'*" Valley said.

"Who is the one witch who kept talking about memories and history? The witch who seemed very upset with Ambert at the wedding? And desperate to find out what happened to his mother, who died of a mysterious illness?" Thorn asked.

Seven's eyes lit up. "Dusk," she said. "We have to find Dusk."

CHAPTER FORTY-THREE
THE CUENTISTA SPELL

THE WITCHLINGS GATHERED in Seven's room the next evening. Miss Dewey was still safe with Thorn's family, the Spare strike had been a success despite the battle that had ensued, and Ambert was nowhere to be found. Nobody knew where he was, but the Gran, the Oracle, and the council were searching for him. Now Seven, Valley, and Thorn had to figure out the truth behind the lost coven house.

They sat on Seven's bed, whispering in their sleeping clothes, Tidbit snoring softly on one of Seven's pillows. Thorn had explained her theory to the Witchlings after the Spare strike—they could find out about the lost coven house by walking through the memories of the witches who'd experienced it themselves.

"The Gran's speech reminded me of that spell Dusk was always talking about, the cuentista spell, remember? He mentioned walking in memories of his ancestors and weird stuff like that a bunch. If we could do that, maybe we could see firsthand if there really was a long-lost coven house and how they managed to get rid of it. Maybe then we could bring it back."

"The cuentista spell is not common magic anymore." Seven bit her lip. "Do you really think Dusk will help us?"

"I don't think we can trust him. How do we know he's not working with his dad?" Valley shook her head.

Seven thought back to her interactions with the moody twin, how kind he'd been, how Miss Dewey asked them to look out for him especially. She also remembered his fight with Helio. Helio had said he was upset about Miss Dewey being their new mom, but the more she thought about it, the more that story didn't make sense. Dusk *loved* Miss Dewey. He must've been upset about something else and both Helio and Ambert had lied, which meant the fight . . . was probably about *them*.

Still . . . would they be walking right into a trap?

"He is not a bad witch," a small voice said behind them. Seven turned toward the voice to find Tidbit had woken up. He was standing on Seven's bed, his fur still wild from sleep. "Dusk is a lost boy, and he is sad, but he is not evil. I know him well."

Seven looked at Valley and Thorn, and shrugged.

"Tidbit was wrong about Helio, so how can we be sure he's right about Dusk? We saw Helio at the scene of the crime, putting some sort of pebble in his pocket and calling Ambert to tell him something was done, just after Spares disappeared. He's in on this with his dad." Valley shook her head.

"Dusk is not his brother though; they can be twins and be separate people," Thorn pointed out. As a twin herself, she would know.

"Fine," Valley said. "But if he steps one foot out of line, I'm destroying him."

"Dusk's been ignoring all my messages though. How can we get him to come if he won't talk to us?" Thorn asked.

"There might be someone who can convince him to come," Seven said.

And so they called the only other friend who might be able to help: Figgs.

Shortly after their phone call to Figgs, something hit Seven's window and all three of them jumped up.

"Stay back," Seven said, slowly approaching the window.

But when she peered outside, there on the grass of her backyard was Figgs. Seven opened her window.

"You're here," she said, smiling.

"Yeah." Figgs pushed his hair back, looking sheepish. "I brought him."

From the shadows, another witch emerged: black hair, a long black sweater, dark coal-rimmed eyes.

"Hey, Dusk," Seven said. "We'll come down. There's a shed over there, wait inside. It should be open." She gave an almost imperceptible whistle and from a bush in her yard, ten raccoons rolled out, claws up. Seven smiled.

"Hey, pals, can you please go guard those boy witches?" She pointed at Figgs and Dusk, who were just closing the door of the shed. "Make sure the one that's not

Figgs isn't up to anything," Seven whispered. Better safe than sorry.

The raccoons nodded and in an instant were surrounding the shed.

"Wow, they're really always around," Thorn said.

Seven shook her head. "I keep telling them they don't have to be but they don't listen. Let's go downstairs, quick. But keep your guards up. This might be a trap."

Thorn and Valley nodded, and they crept downstairs in the near darkness.

Outside, the night was chilly, the threat of snow in the air, as one of the raccoons opened the door for them and they slipped into the shed.

The three witches stood at the entrance, their bedtime robes pulled tight to ward off the cold. All three of them crossed their arms in unison as they looked at Figgs and Dusk, who were sitting on wooden boxes. Dusk had lit a lantern with magic blue light, and they looked almost as if they were underwater.

Dusk stood up quickly, taking his winter cap off and holding it against his chest. "Hi."

"He better not try anything or you're toast when we get home," Valley said, pointing to Figgs.

Figgs laughed nervously and got up, nudging Dusk. "Go on, tell them."

"I know you're probably suspicious of me and I don't blame you, considering . . . my dad."

"Did you *know* he was terrible?" Thorn asked, her voice laced with betrayal.

Dusk shook his head. "Not until recently, I swear, but . . . my dad was good at muddling my brain, at making me believe things that I knew weren't true somehow. It's a long story, but if you let me explain, I think I can help."

Seven walked over and sat on one of the wooden boxes. The others did the same, until they were all sitting in a circle.

"All right, we're listening," Seven said.

"Speak for yourself." Valley turned to the side and stared at the wall so Dusk knew just how uninterested she was.

"I believe Ambert, my father, killed my mother," Dusk said.

Seven's heart dropped.

"He *what*?" Valley asked, turning back to him slowly.

Dusk nodded. "I've been trying to find out more about my mother since I was old enough to do spell work on my own. We barely have any pictures of her, and she died when I was really young so my memories of her aren't clear. I just . . . wanted to know more about her, you know? Every time I asked my father, he got really upset and sad, and so I started trying to find magic that would let me see her, even if it was in a memory. That's why I started looking into the cuentista spell."

"Why do you think your dad killed her though; did you see something? Did you know this whole time?" Valley asked, suddenly enthralled. "Also sorry for being so rude."

Dusk smiled. "It's fine. And no, but my dad . . . wasn't perfect. He was always so warm and bright to the rest of the world, but when we were alone he barely spoke to me. We were all sad though . . . maybe not Helio all the time, but we lived quiet, lonely lives after Mom died. I thought maybe with Miss Dewey, he would change, but then on the night before the wedding I found this."

Dusk pulled a paper from his coat. It was a page of facts, a biography, with amounts of magic in the bank, likes and dislikes, everything and anything about a list of women in the Twelve Towns. And on that list was Miss Dewey.

"What is this?" Seven asked.

"Research." Dusk shook his head. "Look at the date. It's from three weeks before my mother died. My father was already looking for a replacement and my mom was not even gone."

"Are you sure that's what this is?" Thorn asked.

"I wasn't, not totally. I fought with Helio because he just brushed it off, and my father told me I was being ridiculous, of course, but . . . I had a bad feeling. I didn't get concrete proof though until a few nights ago. He'd come home from his honeymoon early to get something for Tidbit, he claimed. And that's when I heard him . . ."

Dusk described how he overheard his father and brother whispering about Miss Dewey. They had thought him asleep, and they were together in the garden, speaking under the moonlight.

“It is almost complete,” Ambert had said. “Just as it was with Marigold.”

“Do you think Dusk suspects anything?” Helio had asked, his voice so sweet it had made Dusk retch.

“He is too soft to imagine this type of commitment. Dusk is not meant to lead, like you.”

“You’re right, Father. We will eventually need to be rid of him too,” Helio had said, as if it pained him to say it.

Horrifyingly, Ambert had put his hand on Helio’s shoulder then, and laughed. “This is why you are my heir. This is why you will inherit my legacy. And yes, someday soon our dear Dusk will have to go for good.”

“Stars,” Seven said, shaking her head.

“I’m so sorry, Dusk,” Thorn said, reaching out and patting his hand.

Valley’s face was a bright red, the kind of red that meant she was mad, not that she was embarrassed. “We can’t just let them get away with this. Your mom, the whole Spare thing, it’s too much.”

“What Spare thing?” Figgs asked.

They told them everything, about the vision and Tidbit and Miss Dewey (much to Dusk’s distress). The Witchlings told the boy witches about the Golden Frog and what they believed might be a lost coven house.

Figgs stood up, his wooden box seat toppling over. He walked back and forth in the shed, his hands in his hair, anger radiating off him in waves.

“If it’s true, how are we supposed to stop magic like

that? Magic that can change everything about our world?" Figgs asked.

"We start by telling the Gran and the Oracle," Thorn said.

"There are enough of us that have seen firsthand how horrible he is," Valley added. "That has to count for something."

"I hope that's enough. Do not underestimate my father . . . his charm, his magic. He's done horrible things, things that I can only remember the shadow of, but somehow I can never seem to remember the thing itself."

"How do you think he does it? It has to be a hex, right?" Valley asked.

Dusk shrugged. "I wish I knew."

"The best way to make sure Ambert can't hurt anyone ever again is to prove he's part of all this. We have some witnesses, but it will still be our word against his, and Ambert has a lot of people on his side. We need proof, and to get that proof, we need you, Dusk," Seven said.

"Me?"

"The cuentista spell," Thorn continued. "If we can walk through your memories as a Lophiifor, wouldn't we be able to see if your ancestors really are responsible for creating Spares?"

Dusk nodded sadly. "I'm not strong enough to let anyone inside my memories; it has to be someone more powerful who is connected to the families. We need access to an older witch's memories, someone who is at a higher magical level than we are and whose ancestors helped create Spares. That's the only way we can get the spell to work.

"The spell also requires a sacrifice," Dusk continued. "The cuentista spell will take some of your memories when you cast it. It could be something insignificant, or it could be a cherished memory. You won't be able to get it back, so you have to be sure."

"Can I help in any way?" Seven asked.

"You would be ideal to cast the spell and walk through the memories. None of the rest of us have your level of magic."

Seven thought it over for just a moment, but she knew this was the only way to get confirmation their theory was right. "All right, let's do it."

Thorn cleared her throat. "Just one little problem: We still need a witch from the Five Families so we can walk through their ancestor's past."

"It can be me," Valley said. "My family is one of the Five Families."

"Wait, Dusk, Valley still has some of the stone hex near her heart—could she get hurt if she did the spell?" Thorn asked.

Dusk cringed. "Yeah, you do not want to mess with this spell under those conditions. It has properties of archaic magic and could expand the stone or even reignite the hex."

"No!" all three Witchlings cried at once.

"Plus, as powerful as you are, I don't think a witch our age—unless it was someone like Seven, who is an

Uncle—could let us into their memories. It could really mess you up."

"Now what?" Figgs asked, and they sat in silence until Thorn spoke up.

"I think there's really only one witch we can go to, then," Thorn said, and everyone turned to look at her.

"Miss Dewey, of course."

CHAPTER FORTY-FOUR

BACK IN TIME

THEY WASTED NO TIME. The young witches ran through the night to Thorn's home, and crept to Miss Dewey's window. Thorn's parents had converted a small office that led to the enclosed garden into a cozy bedroom for their fake visiting cousin. With Ambert still on the loose, they had to make sure she was safe. Just in case.

Thorn knocked on the French doors softly as the others crouched in the garden. Almost immediately, a warm light switched on from inside. Moments later, curtains fluttered, and an unrecognizable Miss Dewey came to the door, her hands up.

"Miss Dewey, it's me," Thorn said.

Their favorite librarian put a hand on her chest. "Oh my Stars, you scared me. Did you lock yourself out, Thorn?" she asked.

"Not . . . exactly." Thorn looked behind her and the rest of the young witches stood up.

Miss Dewey covered her mouth, then opened the door. "Dusk," she said, her voice strained.

The Moth House witch ran to Miss Dewey and threw his arms around her. She hugged him back, her eyes closed, and Seven noticed a few tears fall down her face.

They pulled apart and Miss Dewey ruffled his dark hair, laughing softly. "I didn't think I'd ever see you again."

"I'm so sorry about my father. I noticed too late," Dusk said.

"You have nothing to apologize for," Miss Dewey said sharply, then looked up. "Come in, it's cold."

They all filed into the cozy bedroom, and Miss Dewey, in typical Miss Dewey fashion, got them all tea. Protests would not be listened to. Seven was worried that Thorn's family would wake up from the commotion, but no one stirred. Once they were all settling back into the bedroom, the curtain pulled tight against the night, Seven prepared to make an impossible ask.

She knew Miss Dewey was still regaining her strength, that she had just gone through something incredibly traumatizing, and here they were asking even more of her. But Seven did not see another way out of the Ambert problem. This was their one shot to get the full truth. This might be a chance to change the fate of all Spares forever.

"Have you ever heard of the cuentista spell?" Seven asked Miss Dewey.

Miss Dewey chuckled. "Why, yes, thanks to young Dusk here."

Dusk's cheeks went red. "We are going to try and cast it."

Miss Dewey put her teacup down carefully. "Does this have to do with Ambert?"

They all nodded and Miss Dewey breathed heavily. "You kids shouldn't be involved in anything he does. It's incredibly dangerous—girls, you saw what he was able to do to me."

"We know, but this might be the only way to really stop him," Figgs explained.

"I will do it. If this can help stop Ambert from hurting others, I'll do whatever it takes. Tell me what I have to do," Miss Dewey said, looking at Dusk.

Dusk nodded. "We can do it right here. It won't be loud."

Seven and Miss Dewey nodded and stood up.

"Can we help?" Figgs asked.

Dusk shook his head. "Just be vigilant in case anything goes wrong."

"Okay," Thorn said. "We'll be here."

"The three of us have to hold hands so I can guide you into the magic," Dusk said. "Seven, you will intone the spell, asking Miss Dewey for permission to talk through her ancestor's memories. Miss Dewey, you will respond with the spell to give Seven permission, and Seven, you have to funnel every bit of your magic, strength, and power into the spell, and if it works, you'll be able to walk through Miss Dewey's ancestor's past. Miss Dewey, once we intone the spell, focus on the lost coven. That will help the spell take us to the right moment in time."

"All right. Let's do it," Miss Dewey said.

Dusk taught them both the call and response spell, and once they'd memorized it, they stood in a small circle, hands clasped. Seven and Dusk began, speaking in unison, as the others looked on.

"Déjame caminar
Por los senderos de tus recuerdos
Déjame vivir los cuentos
De las brujas que te precedieron."

Miss Dewey responded.

"Te doy permiso para recorrer mi historia."

A golden light swirled around them. Valley, Thorn, and Figgs shielded themselves from the light and wind.

"Close your eyes," Dusk instructed, and as they did, Seven felt her feet give out from under her and a memory leave her mind. It was of her mother and father, holding hands. Her mother's belly was round with Beefy, and Seven was much smaller. It was the day Beefy was born—he would enter the world in just hours—and this was the last memory Seven had of just her with her mother and father. A tear trickled down her face as the memory faded and slipped through her fingers. And then it was gone.

Seven felt herself spinning through gusts of cold and hot air, every smell she could think of wafting by, laughter and screaming and singing and quiet sobs surrounding her. She felt and heard every emotion in just moments and when they stopped, she opened her eyes and found herself in Ravenskill, as it once was: dirt roads, floating carriages pulled by colorful winged horses, dresses with miles of swooping fabric that Thorn would've fainted over seeing in person, and wands. *Everyone* had a wand. There were also many witches with familiars—everything from foxes to frogs to bushy rabbits. More than Seven had ever seen. *There must be a librarian convention in town,* she thought to herself.

Seven was in front of a building she did not recognize, where the Hall of Elders should be. It was smaller, made of wooden logs. Inside, some sort of meeting was already in progress, a podium at the front of the room and rows of chairs already filled with witches. On the left sat librarians and their familiars, which made for quite a noisy meeting. On the right side of the center aisle sat witches with luxurious-looking cloaks and hats, diamonds on almost each finger, intricate jewel-encrusted wands in wrist sheaths. Seven felt herself drawn strongly toward two elegant witches sitting in the back—Miss Dewey's ancestors, she realized.

A librarian witch took the podium. "I understand the urgency of this project for your covens," said the librarian. "But we've conducted various studies that showed it would destroy more than half of the Cursed Forest if it proceeded. We simply cannot displace the creatures who call that part of Ravenskill home."

The hum of conversation rose in the room as a witch on the fancy-looking side of the aisle stood up. "And what about it? Those creatures are dangerous! We'd be doing this town a favor."

Monstruos. Seven's stomach dropped. Always reviled, even in the past.

The fancy witches clapped and nodded as the librarian at the podium asked for quiet.

"Those creatures have just as much right to live here as you or I. They have been here for many generations; it is our duty to protect them."

"What of our investment?" a Dewey ancestor cried out. "Will you be responsible for all the magic we lost?"

There were murmurs of agreement from the witches around her.

"We advised you from the start not to start the project without our approval, Arumis," the librarian said.

Hmmm. It seemed librarians had some sort of government role in this time, thought Seven. Interesting.

Arumis stood up. "We are sick and tired of waiting for your approval for everything. Do we not have a Gran? An Uncle? Why should everyone in this town submit to your will?"

"As you well know, Arumis, the Gran did have the ultimate say. But we are the keepers of knowledge," the librarian said, "and it is our duty to advise on what's best for the town."

Arumis's face turned redder than a beet and she sat back down.

The scene faded before them, turning into a million little particles of light as Seven was spun out of the memory.

Now she reappeared on a hill, a hill Seven recognized.

Five witches, maybe a bit younger than Seven's parents, one of them Miss Dewey's ancestor Arumis, were walking up the hill. They were trampling the flowers even though there was a perfectly good path of grass to walk on just beside them.

"I will show them. I will hex them all right here and now," Arumis said.

"Not in broad daylight," another witch said.

Seven realized then, there were exactly five witches stalking up the hill. Could these be witches from the Five Families?

They reached the top of the hill, and Seven gasped. There were tents everywhere, a witch taking photographs of what looked like champions. *The Golden Frog Games.*

But what Seven saw next sent chills down her spine. There, standing on the hill, were the three witches holding foxes she had seen in the photograph at the Crones Cliff Museum, the very same witches from the Golden Frog's vision. Seven felt like she was seeing old friends, or a group of famous witches. They felt so familiar to her because she had spent so many hours staring at that picture and thinking of what their significance might be.

They were even more beautiful and ethereal than the photograph had captured. One had coily brown hair and a constellation of freckles; another had luxurious honey-blond hair, and the other long red curls that reminded Seven of her mother. They each had beautiful multicolored amulets that seemed to be in fashion during this time. There was something calming about their presence, and where the group of five witches made Seven uneasy, these did not. She felt safe with them.

"I've had just about enough of you three." Arumis took a wand from her sheath and pointed it at the fox witch in the middle.

But before Arumis could attack, the fox witch on the left closed her eyes and the wand was flung from Arumis's hand and into the surrounding woods. She had protected her friend without uttering a word.

Holy goats.

"Wha— How *dare* you?!" another one of the five witches screamed.

"If you cannot be trusted with a tool of power, then should you be allowed to wield it, Lynx?" the blond fox witch asked.

"And who are you to make that judgment?" Lynx spat.

The coily-haired witch laughed. "I am but your sister, trying to keep our world one where we can all live in harmony. I should think that would be your goal as well."

"Harmony?" Lynx scoffed. "Do not be so naive."

Lynx stepped closer to the three witches, and their fox familiars jumped in front of them, teeth bared.

"You think you're better than us," Lynx said.

"We don't," said the curly-haired witch sincerely. "We do not wish to fight."

"And yet your kind continue to stand in our way. You struck down our expansion plan for my father's factories," another of the five witches said.

"Don't we *all* deserve the opportunity to thrive?"

"NO!" Lynx said. He was shaking now, and Seven was nervous he would strike the witches, or worse. "That's not how life works, that's not how business works, and that is certainly not how the Hill works."

"Well," the coily-haired witch said. "This is not only the Hill; it is all of Ravenskill."

"That may very well be," another of the five witches said. "But don't you ever forget who is truly in charge here."

The scene shifted again: They were in a house. The five witches they had just encountered were here, sitting in a circle. Standing beside them were older witches who they resembled. Perhaps their family.

"The time has come to increase our defensive measures. The knowledge keepers are overstepping their bounds," one of the older witches said.

"Do the transformation hexes no longer work?" asked Arumis haughtily.

The others all shook their head no.

Transformation hexes?

"It is not enough to get rid of some of them. It does not seem to matter, or they are not understanding the warning. They persist."

"They overcome everything we throw their way. We must find a way to fracture them. For good. And I believe I've found that way . . . it involves forgetting magic."

Seven covered her mouth. Could it be the very same magic that the Cursed Toads had used on the entire Twelve Towns once upon a time?

"What good would forgetting be? We'd need to cast it

every time we came up with a new business venture," said Lynx.

A few of the others bristled in annoyance. "Try to be less obtuse, Lynx? It is not meant to wipe their memories of our businesses; what kind of ridiculous proposal is that? It is meant to wipe the memory of *their* existence."

"Is the spell for forgetting that strong?" asked one witch.

"It is not the spell for forgetting I'm suggesting, but a modified version I've created with great care, and much of my family's magical resources," said a dark curly-haired witch who looked incredibly familiar: He looked exactly like Ambert. This was clearly the witch in charge.

"And we are most grateful to the Lophiifors for their generosity," said another witch.

The Lophiifor witch walked to the center of their circle. "The hex for forgetting requires an enormous sacrifice, and we must cast it within the next few days, or it will be too late. The Black Moon Ceremony magic is almost ready; we must cut it off at the pass."

They changed the ceremony magic? If Valley was here, she would've tried to blow this house up by now.

"We must all pick one witch to perform the hex on the full moon. Once it's done, we will siphon the magic from that wretched house and keep it in the vault of a very trusted witch," the Lophiifor witch said.

"Who is this trusted witch?"

"Prune Pepperhorn," the Lophiifor witch said.

The witch next to him smiled proudly. "I would be delighted to," Prune said.

Seven had to steady herself. This was Valley's ancestor who'd begun the Blood Rose vault. Perhaps they would give clues on how to destroy it, she hoped.

"And will all these schemes get rid of the knowledge keepers forever?" another witch asked.

"Forever. So long as the vault is running, and as long as our descendants live, we will have more power, more magic, more coin, than we could ever imagine," the Lophiifor witch said. "Tonight, as the town sleeps, the hex for forgetting will come for them in their beds. When they wake, they will no longer remember the truth of that wretched house, but our truth. The members of that house will become something I have aptly decided to call *Spares*—they will become nothing. A new coven of witches that will be treated as leftovers, less than: less magic, less power, and most importantly, less of a voice, so they will not be able to stop anything we choose to do. And generations from now, the Lophiifors and . . . your four families, of course, will control history, and what passes for truth, and we will have all the power because of it."

The other witches looked at one another and smiled.

"It seems like a sound plan to us," said another witch.

"And to us!" the rest intoned.

"It is settled, then. Pick one witch from each family to cast the spell tonight on Creeping Phlox Hill. And our little problem will finally be fixed."

CHAPTER FORTY-FIVE

THE LOST HOUSE

SEVEN FOUND HERSELF outside a coven house. It was no coven house that still existed in Ravenskill, none that she recognized. She was crouching just outside a window, beside Arumis. She was spying.

A door inside the coven house opened, and witches poured into the entrance hall. They looked distraught. Among them were the three fox witches.

"Ten of our coven have gone missing just this year," the curly-haired witch said. "What will it take for them to stop this?"

"We don't know for sure that they're behind it," said the coily-haired witch.

"You need to stop giving them the benefit of the doubt. They would love nothing more than to eradicate us."

"But they cannot. We need to figure out where all our coven members have gone, you are right, but most importantly . . ."

"We must remain one," the witches said in unison.

Some of them held hands; some of them looked at one another with deep affection in their eyes.

"We might not change how other witches see us or feel about us. But we can change the world if we stay true to one another. To our coven, and to our friendship," the blond witch said.

"Knowledge . . ." said the blond witch.

"History . . ." said the coily-haired witch.

"Friendship, above all . . ." said the red-haired witch.

Seven froze. Was that a coven house motto?

If she could only get to the front door, maybe she could finally see what the symbol was. She ran, but everything pulled her back, the memory of the witch not aligning with her movements.

Still, she pushed against the magic; she was just toadstools from the door now. If she could only . . .

And then the vision around her swirled, and they were on Creeping Phlox Hill again, under a full moon. In front of her, a group of elderly witches stood in a circle, holding hands.

"When I say, you intone the spell together," the Lophiifor witch said, with Arumis looking on beside him.

The witches nodded in understanding, and the Lophiifor ancestor stepped out of the circle and nearly right next to Seven. She froze, before remembering he could not see her.

"All right, begin," he said, and the witches' voices rose up into the night.

"Te entregamos estos sacrificios

Bajo la luz de la luna
Te damos nuestras almas
Para refundir la verdad."

A great rumbling began beneath them, and the witches started to drop to the ground, one by one. Wind swept all around them, bringing up grass and flowers and even some small trees like a tornado made of magic. And destruction. Seven watched as the wind swept over all of Ravenskill, and with it, fires began.

"Oh, Stars!" Seven cried out. Her town was on fire.

Ravenskill on fire. She remembered part of the vision and wondered, could this be what the Golden Frog had shown her?

When Seven turned back to the hill, she was met with a gruesome scene. All the witches were sprawled on the ground. Elders who looked like any of the sweet old grandparents in Ravenskill, who went to the park to feed the geese, who baked cookies for their neighbors, any one of them could've been Grandma Lilou or even the Gran, except they were not moving. Seven ran closer and crouched down beside one, when she realized they were not breathing.

"The sacrifice, it was their lives," Seven whispered to herself.

What could be so important that an entire generation, for five different families, would do something like this? Down below, Seven could see witches trying desperately to put out the fires, filling a bucket with water from a well, handing it down from witch to witch—others used water spells and wands to try and tame the fire but, like the fire during the Frog Ball, it was a purple flame that Seven knew could only be tamed with water from the Cursed Forest.

She hated not being able to help. Just standing there, powerless. But still she kept looking. She might be the only witch to know the full story of what happened on this night, so many years ago. It was important that she see it through.

"The truth of history might save us one day," she said . . . and then the sun set, rose, and set again in a matter of seconds. It was the next night and there was a crowd gathered, young witches with eager looks on their faces . . . They had arrived at a Black Moon Ceremony of the past.

Seven ran down the hill toward Twilight Square.

"And now, for the last house," the Gran said. "Clever, chaotic, mostly good . . . Goose House!"

Amulets lit up a bright white, and three witches hugged and ran to one another, while three witches looked down to see their amulets turn red.

"Well, it's the tradition," said one witch nearby.

"It's the price we pay for our magic being balanced," responded their companion.

Seven looked around, eyes wide. From one night to the next, everything had changed. Then she caught sight of them—the fox witches.

No longer did they wear flowing, beautiful gowns and no longer were they accompanied by their loyal familiars.

Instead, they wore the tattered old clothes Spares still wore to this day, a cord with a red amulet around their necks—and they were not together. Instead, each of them followed a few paces behind a Hill family, as the rich witches wrapped in their thick fur coats laughed about the night. And the worst part was, none of them seemed to remember who they were just a day before.

"No . . ." Seven whispered, reaching out just as the memory shifted once more.

Arumis and the Lophiifor witch were at the site of the burned-down coven house, looking up at the door.

"Take this down, and we're bringing it to the vault," said Arumis to two Spares.

The two Spares were looking down, and nodded, taking the door down and carrying it between them as they followed the Lophiifor witch. Seven set out to follow him, but the memory began to fade.

"No!" Seven cried out. She ran with all her might to see the symbol on the door. Everything around her turned black and white, her body pulled in every direction at once, but she had done it. Seven had managed to catch a glimpse of the door before the memory vanished completely: The symbol was a large animal carved into the wood.

All along, it had been an elephant.

CHAPTER FORTY-SIX
THE HOUSE THAT ONCE WAS

SEVEN GULPED AIR HUNGRILY as if she had been underwater for many, many minutes. She was in Miss Dewey's temporary bedroom again. Valley and Thorn were beside her, and Miss Dewey was holding out a glass of water.

"What did you see?" Valley asked.

Seven opened her eyes wide. "Everything. Thorn, can you write this all down? We have to preserve it, no matter what."

And then she retold everything, passing along the story of the history she'd witnessed firsthand to the other witches—how the Five Families had clashed with the lost coven, how they'd sacrificed their elders for power, how they'd used a hex to erase the coven and make all its witches Spares.

"My family really was involved in all this," Valley said as she stared at her lap. "I'm so ashamed. I'm sorry." She looked up at the others, tears in her eyes. "I'm so . . . very . . . sorry."

“Thorn, do you have your vision drawing here?” Seven asked.

“Yep, I’ll go grab it.” Thorn quietly left, going up to her room and coming down moments later. She handed over her drawing of their three visions, the crest at the center of the door, and Seven smiled.

“Can I?” she asked, grabbing a pencil from a nearby desk.

“Go for it,” Thorn said.

Seven added the details of what she had just seen to the sketches. Suddenly the large, indiscernible animal and the etching across the top of the door came into focus.

Seven held the drawing up, and the others gasped.

“House of Elephants,” Seven said proudly.

Valley smiled. “I love that name.”

“Me too,” Miss Dewey said.

“It’s the lost house and . . . it used to belong to Spares,” Seven said, still hardly able to believe it. “Or the witches who became Spares, anyway. They were the keepers of knowledge; they were kind and intelligent and generous. And the Five Families took that from them.”

“I can’t believe they just . . . made an entire coven disappear.” Valley shook her head. “And they’ve never had to pay for it.”

“Witches like that get away with everything. You know that,” Dusk said, looking at Valley.

“Not this time,” Valley said under her breath, and Seven was in agreement. This time, they would make them pay.

“The door in the Blood Rose Vault,” Thorn said. “Is that . . .”

Seven nodded. It was the very same door from the memories. Mr. Pepperhorn had kept the coven door under their noses all these years. And now it was with the veiled witches. No wonder he had been in such a hurry to move it.

"The witches in the memory had familiars, you said?" Miss Dewey asked.

Dusk nodded. "Each of them did. They seemed the only house to have them."

"Hmmm." Miss Dewey tapped her chin. "I wonder, then, if when their power was taken, the familiar magic was rerouted."

"Rerouted?" Thorn asked.

"When powerful magic is undone, it does not always just disappear. It has to find a place to live again. Sometimes it goes back to nature and becomes an immortal tree like the Strangling Figs, and sometimes, if it is very special, it finds a home inside other witches. In this case . . . witches like me," Miss Dewey said.

"Librarians! It explains why you have familiars, one of the great mysteries of the Twelve Towns," Dusk said.

"Precisely, my precious Dusk. And now that we have all of this information, what will we do with it?" Miss Dewey asked.

"We put things back to how they were always meant to be," Seven said.

"But how?" Dusk asked.

"Finally," Valley said. "We burn everything down."

CHAPTER FORTY-SEVEN

MAGIC, UNDONE

SEVEN WENT STRAIGHT to the Gran's cottage.

"I just knew it," the Gran said when Seven told her about what they had found in the past.

The Ravenskill Gran had tried to undo Sparedom in her first days in office, only to be shut down by the other, older Grans. But she had always felt Spares should not exist and now, finally, she was vindicated.

"Do you have any evidence, anything you can present to prove Ambert, Mr. Pepperhorn, and Lotus are in cahoots?"

Seven thought for a moment. "We have Miss Dewey's testimony and my own of the Blood Rose Vault . . ."

"But it is your word against theirs, and . . . I wish things were different, Seven, but not all the Grans will believe you," the Gran said. "For every Miss Dewey, for every Seven Salazar, there are ten Ambert supporters. He has . . . become quite popular, I'm afraid. Mr. Pepperhorn is powerful and wealthy too; many of the Grans don't like interfering with families like his, or Lotus's, for that matter."

The Gran looked into the distance, and Seven felt there was something she wasn't telling her. "If there's anything, anything you can think of that will show they are guilty . . ."

The chismosas, Seven remembered. She told the Gran all about the surveillance footage, and Helio.

"That is promising. It ties Ambert's son to the disappearances at least. Make sure you mention that to them, and be ready for the worst. I'm afraid many in the Circle of Grans are no longer on our side."

"Whatever it takes, I'm willing to help. The House of Elephants . . . it's my coven. I owe it to my coven ancestors to take up this fight," Seven said.

Knox put out an urgent call for the Grans to fly to Ravenskill, and the Circle of Grans met the very next day. Seven was called before them.

"Don't be nervous, just pretend you're presenting one of your nerd projects in class," Valley said, trying to be reassuring, as she, along with Thorn, Seven's family, and the raccoons, waited for Seven to be called in.

"Thanks," Seven said.

"We'll be right outside the door," Thorn said.

"And us," Fox said, crouching down to kiss Seven's forehead.

"Us too," Cheese the raccoon said.

It did help her to know that her friends and family were right outside.

"Seven." The Oracle emerged from the large Hall of Elders door. "They're ready for you."

Seven took a deep breath and smiled. It was all up to her now.

They walked together to the southernmost part of the hall and then took the glass employee lift box to the top floor in silence. Seven replayed what she would say over and over again in her mind.

They walked into the large meeting room, and Seven was in awe of the scene before her. Twelve Grans, ranging from old to very old, some with salt-and-pepper hair, some with bright white; some with the soft grooves of new wrinkles, and some with wrinkles as thick and permanent as the roots of trees.

"Welcome, Seven Salazar," the Blonkers Gran said. They invited her to stand before them, and Seven tried not to wring her hands and look even younger and more scared than she felt.

"Good luck," the Oracle said as Seven approached the council.

Knox, as the oldest and most powerful of the Grans, sat at the center. It gave Seven a small sense of comfort to have her there, though the Ravenskill Gran did not smile or offer her even a crumb of recognition. She needed to appear unbiased.

"You may speak," Knox said, and Seven cleared her throat.

"I am here because I believe we have solved the mystery of who has been behind the archaic magic," Seven said. "We believe we've found the group of masterminds behind the stone hexings, and the Spare disappearances as well."

The Grans murmured to one another, then looked back at Seven.

"We believe Ambert Lophiifor is the responsible party, with assistance from various witches but namely Lotus Evenstar and Mr. Lodo Pepperhorn."

Now the Grans were scandalized: Some of them seemed intrigued; some looked downright angry.

"Have you any proof?" asked the Sleepy Hollow Gran.

"I saw firsthand how Mr. Pepperhorn has been stealing magic, and we believe he has conspired with Lotus Evenstar and Ambert Lophiifor to hurt Spares and house stolen magic in the Blood Rose Vault. I have seen the vault with my own eyes, but I need approval, and help, to destroy it. It is . . . too powerful for me to do on my own," Seven said.

The Grans erupted in surprised whispers and discussion. They conferred with one another for many moments until the Irvingstar Gran cleared her throat.

"*If* what you're saying is true, and that is a very large if, destroying a vault capable of such magic will be incredibly dangerous."

"I am willing to sacrifice my life, if that's what it takes to restore the sea of Spares to their proper coven houses," Seven said. *And to restore the House of Elephants.*

"There are procedures. We cannot allow a twelve-year-old, Uncle or not, to put her life in danger to correct a hex we have no proof of, but perhaps we could gather proof?" the Bonecross Gran said.

“We could possibly search Mr. Pepperhorn’s estate ourselves,” said Knox.

“Preposterous!” said Stormville Gran. “We cannot possibly march into the home of one of our wealthiest and most important residents because of the word of . . . Miss Salazar.”

“Does the word of a future Uncle mean nothing?” the Oracle asked.

“About as much as a respected and influential member of our community,” the Castle Point Gran said.

“It is still worth a look, is it not?” the Blonkers Gran asked.

“I will not allow it!” the Irvingstar Gran said. “If we begin inspecting every resident’s house based on what amounts to a rumor, secondhand information, then when does it end?!”

The Grans began to bicker then, until the Ravenskill Gran raised her hands, a signal for them to settle down.

“There are *other* witnesses, didn’t you say?” Knox asked, prompting Seven.

“Valley Pepperhorn has seen the vaults, and Moira Dewey and Dusk Lophiifor, Ambert’s own son, can speak to his true character, not to mention prior offenses,” Seven said, thinking of the twins’ mother.

“Then we will convene at trial in a few weeks and . . .” said the Stormville Gran.

“With all due respect, a few weeks might be too long,” the Oracle said.

“Do you not realize the amount of work we have to

do? Aside from leading our towns, we have over forty missing Spares, an entire sea of Spares across the Twelve Towns. They are our priority," the Castle Point Gran said.

"It's all related though. If we can fix the magical balance, things will go back to normal," Seven said.

"Can you guarantee us that?" the Faerytown Gran asked.

Seven stuttered.

"Young Seven, what you are proposing, it is honorable, and we are grateful for your passion, but we cannot sentence you to probable death, to put your life or any other life in danger for a volatile spell, with or without proof," said the Boggs Ferry Gran.

"What about the footage of Helio?" Seven said, and then she told them about the chismosa flower and how it put Helio, Ambert's own son, at the scene of the crime.

"That might be worth investigating, but the chismosa plants are not well studied, and may be unreliable."

Seven wanted to scream. "Just because you don't understand them doesn't mean they're unreliable," she said before she could stop herself.

"We can look at the footage and we promise we will look into your proposal once, and only once, we've found our missing Spares and restored the magic of the Black Moon Ceremony . . ." the Castle Point Gran said.

"But . . ." Seven started. "You can't just delay this for no reason! There are Spares missing and we know that these witches are responsible!"

The Castle Point Gran's face turned into one of

contempt. "Ambert Lophiifor is campaigning for a new role in Ravenskill. Chancellor of Magic. Are you not aware?"

Seven's mouth fell open. *What?*

"He has quite a lot of support, you see, enough magic and backing from the witches of your town and beyond to get the votes and succeed. It would be wise for you to be cautious in how you speak about him." The Castle Point Gran's mouth curled into a cruel smile.

"He's not Chancellor yet . . ." Seven stepped forward, unafraid of this butt-toad Gran. "And I'm not backing down."

The room erupted, and Seven felt the familiar rumble of rage in her belly. The one that would call the Cursed Forest itself and let it rain down on anyone who tried to stop her. But before things got any more out of control, the gavel fell.

"The meeting is adjourned. I am sorry, Seven. I really am," the Blonkers Gran said.

The Grans began to speak among themselves as Knox, one of her trusted guards, and the Oracle walked Seven to the entrance corridor.

Seven felt like she was in a bad dream. She was numb, her brain foggy, and all she wanted to do was run back in that room and scream at them. How could the very witches tasked with protecting the Twelve Towns do more to protect the villains breaking their magic?

"What is your plan to undo the hex?" Knox whispered as they walked.

"I'm . . . not sure exactly. I tried blowing the vault up once with Valley, but it didn't work. I think we might need Thorn too."

Knox nodded. "That is likely. And an explosion will not completely undo a hex of this magnitude, but it will be a good start. I think you know by now . . . you must use your hidden powers for something like this.

"I will distract the Grans long enough for you to get there and do your best. Sybell, would you be willing—"

"You couldn't keep me from helping if you tried." The Oracle winked.

Seven's heart leapt with hope. She was unsure of her own chances of putting an end to the Blood Rose Vault, but with the Oracle by her side, they might just do this yet.

"Go," the Gran said. "Go now."

Knox swept back into the room as Seven and the Oracle walked briskly away. As they slipped through the door, Seven heard Knox say, "Oh, oh, I feel faint!"

Her plan was fainting. Frogtastic.

They met up with their friends and family outside. "We're going to the Hill. We have to finish what we started, Valley," Seven said.

"My dad won't be home now. He took off early this morning for some important meeting on the other side of town. We have to hurry," Valley said.

"Get on," Sybell said, grabbing their broom from the parking spot on the side of the building. "We'll get there faster by flight."

CHAPTER FORTY-EIGHT

ATTACK ON BLOOD ROSE MANOR

"WHAT SPELL ARE WE GOING TO USE?" Fox asked as they flew to the Hill.

Seven flew with Fox, Valley was with the Oracle, and Thorn with Talis.

Seven gulped and tightened her arms around her mother's waist. "We can't use a spell. We have to use a, um . . . a hex."

"And *you* are going to use a hex?" Fox asked. "I don't think so, young lady."

See, this was why Seven didn't like when her parents came along on adventures.

"Mom, first of all, I'm an Uncle, and second of all . . . I am capable of a lot more than you know. I am good at monstruo magic, for example."

Seven waited for her mom to dive straight down and take her home, but she was just quiet for a moment. "As in . . . you can speak to monstruos as well as animals?"

"Exactly like that."

It was scary to tell the truth after keeping it to herself for so long, but it was also a relief.

"Why hadn't you told me?" Fox asked, her voice tinged with hurt.

"I was afraid if you knew, you might get hurt. I didn't want anything bad to happen to you or Dad or Beef," Seven said, hugging her mother's waist tighter. "Please, please, don't see me differently. Please don't stop loving me," she whispered.

Fox put one of her hands on Seven's. "I know you are an Uncle, that you will have responsibilities I can only ever imagine, but I am still your mother. It is your father's and my job to protect you too, do not forget that. You're growing up, we only have so much time left together, so . . . let us be there. But no matter what happens, or who you become . . . I will never, ever stop loving you."

Seven could tell by the way her mother's voice had hitched up that she was crying. Seven hugged her even tighter, tears spilling down her face. She should have told her parents; she should have told them right away, but she had been so *scared*.

"We're here," the Oracle called out, and they began to land on the glittering Hill below. The moment they touched the ground, the group of witches walked briskly to the gates of Blood Rose Manor.

"We must not raise suspicion," the Oracle said. "Seven, do you have an action plan?"

"I'll go in with you, Valley, and Thorn. Mom, you can

stand guard outside with the raccoons when they all get here. Dad, you know what to do," Seven said, and Talis nodded, kissing her forehead, hugging Fox before taking off to meet with Leaf and Crimson like they'd planned the night before. She felt weird giving them orders, especially her parents, but they both looked just as determined as Seven to see this through.

"My dad and the others will meet us after they get the coven door from the veiled witches' house for the next phase of the plan."

They walked to the side of the estate, avoiding Mr. Pepperhorn's guards successfully, and got into the house through a side door. Once they were inside, Valley ran to her father's bedroom, retrieved the key, and then led them to the vault.

"I will be right here, guarding the entrance," Fox said, stopping outside the vault. "Please be careful."

She patted Seven's curls softly and Seven smiled. "I'll be fine, don't worry."

"I will make sure she is safe," the Oracle said.

With that, Seven, Valley, Thorn, and the Oracle swept into the vaults. When they reached the enormous pools of magic, the Oracle's jaw dropped. They tapped the shimmering magical water lightly with one finger and shivered.

"I cannot believe this was here all along, just under our noses," the Oracle said.

"Tell me about it. Try having a bedroom above all this," Valley said.

"All right, Seven, tell us what to do," Thorn said.

"We must move quickly," the Oracle added.

Seven nodded. "Sybell, we need a hex, something like an explosion where I'll be able to channel my, erm, unusual magic."

"Hmmm." Sybell tapped their chin. Asking the Oracle for advice had more than one advantage. They were a skilled witch, with a vast knowledge of spells and hexes, yes, but they were also an Oracle, a Seer, and would likely be able to predict what hex had the best chance of succeeding.

"The arcane rush hex," the Oracle said finally. "The three of you must pour your magic into the hex, but the majority of power will come from Seven."

"Why don't you do it? You're more powerful," Valley said.

"Too true; however, hexes are not my expertise. Seven here seems to be an expert though." The Oracle quirked an eyebrow.

"It's a long story." Seven shook her head. The Oracle taught them the hex, and then they got in position at the entrance to the vaults.

Seven lifted her hands and closed her eyes, feeling the monstruo power, the Cursed Forest, course through her veins. She held her arms steady and tried to connect with the Oracle, Valley, and Thorn, to feel their own magic, to pull what little bits of the archaic also dwelled inside the two younger witches. Just as she prepared to intone the hex, Ambert burst through the door.

Seven's heart seized with fear. Was her mother okay? Why had she let him pass?

"Stop, stop! Seven, Valley, Thorn! What are you children doing here! This place is dangerous!" cried Ambert.

He had no idea they knew, did he? He was still trying to play the hero.

"I don't think so," Valley cried out before Seven could think of how to handle the situation, and struck out at Ambert.

"Valley, what are you doing?!" Ambert easily, too easily, blocked Valley's attack.

He looked to the Witchlings, his eyes filled with tears, and Seven began to have second thoughts. What if they were wrong? All they really knew was what they'd heard from a tale-telling squirrel . . .

But then she remembered what Dusk had said—that his father was too good at trickery, at lying and making you believe what was right in front of you wasn't really there.

Then she noticed something she had not seen before. His face was covered in scratches, his black shirt was ripped almost to ribbons, and beneath, Seven could see blood . . . The raccoons had attacked him! And they would not have if he hadn't tried to hurt her mother to get in.

Her heart was pounding relentlessly against her chest, her thoughts faster than a hummingbird's wings. She had to get past Ambert, destroy this place, and make sure her mother was okay.

"You can't fool us anymore," Seven said, turning to Ambert, hands up. Valley was on him too, as was Sybell. As powerful as he might be, could he fight back against an Uncle, a Stoneheart, and an Oracle? Ambert backed toward the door, hands down, a pleading look on his face as they cornered him. He was up against the exit now, and Seven's entire body yearned to push past him and make sure her mother was okay, but she had to finish what she had started.

"You don't know what you're doing! The harm it will cause to Spares!" Ambert's eyes were wide as he looked past them to the pools of magic. "Please. Please don't do this."

"Esposas," the Oracle said, and iron rings appeared on Ambert's wrists and clicked together. "We will take you to the Committee on Magical Misdeeds and they and the Grans can figure out what to do with you."

Ambert looked down and shook his head.

"Seven, come on, let's intone the hex," Valley said, and Seven nodded.

They were about to put an end to this injustice, this unfairness, to the idea that someone could even be a left-over witch, a Spare, once and for all.

"I have tried to reason with you," Ambert said, shaking his head. "I only want what's best for the Towns."

"And you can explain all that to the Grans." The Oracle gestured for Ambert to walk but he didn't move.

His head still down, Ambert shook his wrists. "I don't think I will do that, Sybell."

The iron rings fell away, and before any of them had a moment to react, Ambert attacked.

"Rayo de furia!"

Ambert threw a blast of light at them.

It was like nothing Seven had ever felt.

The blast sent Seven skidding across the stone floor of the vault, every toadstool feeling like the most intense pain she'd ever experienced. It was like being dragged through a fire, everything from her feet to her forehead so hot, Seven worried she might just explode.

An archway stopped her with a sickening thump, and Seven fought through the intense pain and got up. Valley and Thorn were toadstools ahead, running straight at Ambert, the Oracle right beside them.

Seven struggled to run; she felt something wet on her back and was pretty sure it was blood. The Oracle put their hands up and a hum of music rang through the vault. It sounded like a chorus of voices, and it stopped another incoming attack from Ambert long enough for Valley to get at him with her twin blades.

Valley jumped and slashed, clipping Ambert's face and eliciting a screech of pain from the witch. She scuttled backward, her feet weaving in and out like an intricate dance as she flourished her arms and prepared to strike again. As she did, Thorn unraveled her poison ribbon. She spun it around her head, then shot it toward Ambert, wrapping it around his shoulders quicker than a snake, so that Valley could do damage.

"Arder," Valley whispered into each of her blades, and

rushed Ambert once again. Taking advantage of her shorter height to get down low, she pierced one leg and then another.

Ambert fell to his knees now, screaming in pain, the burning spell combined with the cut of Valley's expert blades enough to incapacitate him.

"Go! Now!" Sybell screamed.

Seven, Valley, and Thorn recited the arcane rush hex, the one that would put an end to this place once and for all.

"Orbe de fuego caótica," Seven recited.

"Ira arcana," Valley answered.

"Fuego de destrucción," Thorn said.

"Furia de venganza!" they all intoned together.

The three witches focused their magic on bringing the incantation alive. They closed their eyes, brows furrowed in concentration, sweat dripping from Seven's forehead in buckets as she focused all her power, all her magic, into keeping the hex steady. A small ball of light, the size of a chipmunk or maybe a rat, grew between the three Witchlings. They balanced the magic between them, back and forth, back and forth, trying their best not to let the thread of magic drop. Ambert had fallen over, completely knocked out, and just in time; it was the Oracle's turn to convert the spark of the hex into an explosion.

"Now!" Seven cried through gritted teeth, and the Oracle raised their hands and began to levitate.

"Estrellas, escúchenme!" the Oracle called to their ancestors, to the very Stars in the sky, their voice like a chorus of a thousand witches singing more beautifully than any bird or sirena ever could.

Everything from the Oracle's fae dust–powdered face to their holographic cape to their long pointy nails lit up with the power of a thousand stars. Light shone from their mouth like a flashlight made of the galaxies, and the voice of a thousand ancestors erupted, a cacophony of haunting voices, terrifying and beautiful all at once. It shook the walls of the vault and brought pillars down around them. The Oracle had done their part. It was working!

Ambert screamed and somehow broke free of the magic binding him.

But before he could strike, the Oracle flourished their hand and shot bolts of magic at Ambert as he tried to match their speed and power.

"Inmolar!" Ambert managed to get one hand free and shot fire at the Oracle.

Though it made contact, Ambert's fire spell did nothing.

In fact, Sybell seemed to absorb them, growing stronger and more feral with every hit.

Ambert was desperate, looking around at the pools of magic as if they were his precious children.

"Strike down this witch!" they said. "In the name of the Stars, STRIKE HIM DOWN!"

A relentless shock wave of magic, incandescent with the power of the Stars, hit Ambert straight on.

"AHHHHH!" he screamed, blood dripping from his eyes as he fixed his gaze on the Oracle.

“You have your Stars,” he screamed, “but I too have my ancestors to call upon . . . inundaciones!”

A windstorm crashed around them. Seven screamed as an onslaught of water from Ambert’s attack hurtled at them from all angles.

“Take cover!” Valley cried, and they anchored themselves to the few remaining pillars, all the while trying to keep the magic volleying between them like a delicate ball of light. It was growing in size, Seven could feel it, but it was not yet ready to be let go. The Oracle and Ambert exchanged blows as the vault filled with water.

Sybell parted the rushing waves and continued to strike Ambert, taking hit after hit from him in return. The water reached Seven’s shoulders, then chin, and soon they were going to be inundated.

“Swim toward the Oracle. Don’t let go of the spell!” Seven cried just moments before being submerged. The walls of water came crashing down, sending Seven head over foot, flipping over and over again underwater, until she came face-to-face with Ambert.

Underwater, he shone as bright as the Oracle, directing the water at them. No longer hurt and struggling, he seemed to intensify his powers. A familiar light underwater—the very same light from the Golden Frog’s vision!—appeared before her. Then teeth broke through the light, rows and rows of teeth, pointy and small, chomping toward her face.

Instead of panicking, Seven was enraptured. She tried to resist but her body floated ever closer to Ambert instead. What was this strange, hypnotic pull? She could not seem to break free of it, just like the purple archaic fire. So spellbound was she that Seven did not even realize when she began to drown.

She had long since run out of air and was clutching at her throat with one hand, the other up and desperately trying to hold on to the magic. But still, she had not let go of the spell, and neither had Valley or Thorn. She could still feel it, growing between them as she kicked her feet and struggled to reach the surface.

What she found instead was Valley and Thorn, eyes wide and running out of breath, just as desperate as Seven. But suddenly she felt it. The spell was ready.

Seven used the last of her strength to nod wildly at them. The three Witchlings held hands, closed their eyes, and released the explosive magic.

Boom.

The vault came crashing down all around them.

CHAPTER FORTY-NINE
AMULETS

TIME STOPPED. They were suspended in a dome of colorful lights. The red from a rose, orange like the bill of a goose, the yellow of a goldfinch, green like the emerald grass on the rolling hills of Ravenskill, blue like the water of the Boggy Crone River, indigo and violet like the flowers on Creeping Phlox Hill, glimmered around them.

Water drained rapidly from the vault, and the pools of magic with the Blood Roses within were washed away. They had done it. Ambert lay motionless in a corner, Thorn was rubbing her eyes, and Seven reached out for Valley, who was beside her on the ground. She strained to grab her friend's hand when Valley sat up, coughing.

The vault was in ruins, piles of stone and rubble covered the ground, but the walls had not collapsed completely, and they were mercifully all alive. They looked around, in awe of the light show around them.

"What is this?" the Oracle whispered, but when Seven found Sybell's eyes, she realized they were not looking at the lights around them but at Seven, Valley, and Thorn.

The lights were coming from their amulets.

The Witchlings got to their feet, just as Cheese came running in.

"My mother . . ." Seven started.

"She is safe. We carried her to the healers," Cheese said.

"Thank you, thank you." Seven bent down and hugged her furry pal.

"I will restrain Ambert so he can cause no more harm," the Oracle said, getting to work with magical binding. "I will alert the Gran of what happened here. We'll need support soon."

"Good idea," Seven said.

Seven, Valley, and Thorn stood in a circle, mesmerized by the new color of their amulets.

"Does this mean it worked?" Valley asked.

"No idea," said Thorn, "but let's get out of here."

The Witchlings made their way out.

"You sure you don't need any help?" Seven asked the Oracle, who had wrapped several layers of light around the unconscious witch.

"Already done." The Oracle waved their hand and Ambert, motionless but still breathing, began to float behind them as they walked over the rubble and destruction of the vault and upstairs to Valley's old home.

The once-pristine manor was in shambles. Bookcases were overturned, windows blasted out from their frames. Seven wondered what Valley was thinking. This had been her home for twelve years, after all.

"Are you all right?" Thorn asked.

Valley nodded. "I thought I'd feel upset seeing this place ruined, but I just feel . . . kinda relieved." Valley smiled. "Like I can finally put that part of my life behind me."

Thorn squeezed Valley's hand, and then took Seven's as they walked over the threshold of where the enormous double doors of Blood Rose manor used to be. What they found outside was like something out of a strange and beautiful dream.

Residents of the Hill were all standing outside their homes, or in front of the destroyed manor. The explosion had brought out the entire neighborhood, but that wasn't the shocking part. What Seven had to rub her eyes to believe were the many rainbow amulets lighting up the night. All around them, Spares . . . no, former Spares . . . *House of Elephants* witches, stood looking up at the Witchlings.

They were all silent, as if they were waiting for something. They wanted to know what in the hex was going on. Seven took a step forward, ready to face the growing crowd of witches in front of her. She felt Valley step beside her.

"You don't have to . . ." she began, but Valley raised one hand.

"It was our choice to undo this magic, together. And this was my family's doing. I am just as, if not more, responsible for providing answers as you are," Valley said.

Thorn stepped up on the left. "Don't even think about telling me not to. I will always be by your side."

Seven smiled at her brave friends, and she did not fight them on it. Instead, she let their strength propel her, and Seven Salazar began to speak.

"Tonight, something momentous has happened. We discovered that through trickery and evilness, long ago, witches stole magic. Magic that once belonged to Spares."

The crowd murmured in shock; the wealthy Hill witches exchanged looks. "What magic would Spares even have to steal?" scoffed a Hill witch.

"We . . . were not always Spares," Seven said. "We had our own coven house. It was called the House of Elephants. We found a vault beneath Blood Rose Manor filled with that stolen magic. And by destroying the vault, tonight that magic has been freed."

"Preposterous," cried a Hill witch.

As the crowd erupted in equal parts anger and shock, the former Spares began stepping closer to Seven, Thorn, and Valley, their eyes filled with tears, smiles on their tired faces.

"Does this mean we are no longer Spares?" one witch asked.

Seven smiled. "Yes, you are no longer Spares. You have full powers now; you won't live in the shadow of the other covens any longer, because you have your very *own* coven. You are House of Elephant witches—knowledge, history, friendship above all . . ." Seven said, just as the Gran should've on their Black Moon Ceremonies.

"An elephant never forgets!" Valley, Thorn, and

Seven cried out together, and their coven members, their brothers, sisters, and siblings cheered.

The newly minted House of Elephant witches embraced, some of them cried, one or two of them told off their employers, but the wealthy Hill witches would not accept this easily, just as Seven suspected they would not.

"And on whose authority are you performing such a heinous act?!" one such witch cried out.

"I don't need anyone's authority; nature has done it for us. Look at our amulets for yourself," Seven said.

"It is trickery!"

"No, what was trickery was that these witches were robbed of their Stars-given magic," the Oracle said. "There shall be a full investigation into any families who've participated in this inconceivable act of violence against our very own Ravenskillians, and all the other families who stood to benefit from their malicious schemes."

"The Five Families, more specifically," Seven said, and now a few of the Hill witches' faces really did go pale with fear.

"Without a coven house door, you can have no coven! You cannot simply make a coven from thin air because you wish it to be so. Fanciful wishes and dreams won't do; you need the real work our ancestors put into our true covens," said another witch.

"That shouldn't be a problem." Seven smirked and gestured toward four witches walking through the crowd—Figgs, with a newly rainbowed amulet, Talis,

Leaf, and Crimson; between them they were carrying an enormous wooden door.

They propped the door up, their hands raised in defense just in case, as they let the crowd observe the wooden slab. The elephant symbol, the notches on the corners, and all along the edge of the door, words in old script—*"An Elephant Never Forgets."*

As expected, a flash of light came from somewhere in the crowd. A desperate Hill witch was trying to destroy the door but Crimson was too quick, and blocked the attack.

"You will find the door is protected by magic, from the Gran herself," Crimson said.

The Hill witches were very clearly reeling, but the surprises of the night were not over.

"You cannot do this!" a Hill witch said, his hands up. All around them, witches turned their hands on the House of Elephants witches, ready to attack, to put them back in their place. But these were not the same witches of a few hours ago; these witches could finally fight back.

"We will not return to being your beaten-down servants!" cried a former Spare, throwing her hands up.

Before anyone knew what hit them, the Hill witches and the House of Elephants witches began to fight.

Seven ran to help them, but . . . they did not need her help. In fact, they outnumbered the Hill witches three to one—one gardener, cook, and cleaner for each house *at least*—and they were filled with a palpable rage. It was a rage fueled by years and years of deceit, of missed opportunity, of a life filled with unnecessary struggle because of pure, unchecked greed. It was a rage fueled by the Spares who never got to see their full potential, who had left this earth and become ancestors, never knowing who they truly were. That rage made them unstoppable in this moment, and Seven let them defend themselves.

From the edges of the battle, former Spares appeared, dazed and pale. They left the houses of the Hill witches, and then one very familiar witch appeared in the crowd.

"Pixel!" cried Thorn as the witch waved at her from the other side of the battle.

They ran to each other and hugged.

"Are you okay?" Seven asked.

"I . . . think so. One moment I was running to get my gloves on the balcony, and the next I was . . . on top of a nest. A pigeon woke me up with gentle little pecks. Thank goodness . . . I didn't destroy her eggs."

Seven looked at Pixel and her mind reeled as she realized, finally, where Pixel had been along.

"The pebbles," Seven said in shock. "They turned you into pebbles. That's what we saw Helio pick up in the vision, it was a rainbow pebble like the one Blueberry used on her nest. The little rock inside Wither's house. They turned you into stone."

"I want to join the fight," Pixel said.

"Do you have enough strength?" Thorn asked, concerned.

"Never felt stronger." Pixel nodded. "We've got this!"

In the distance, Graves appeared, a troop of the Gran's Guard behind her. They would diffuse the fight and make sure no one was seriously hurt. With the crowd distracted, the Oracle brought Ambert out. Together, Seven and the Oracle ran toward town. Leaf, Talis, Dusk, Figgs, and Crimson followed behind them, carrying the door. The door had to be properly placed. They had to make sure the House of Elephants returned.

Downtown Ravenskill was no less hectic than the Hill, with new Elephant House witches walking out of the shops in a daze, and confusion and chaos in the streets as people pointed up to the still-billowing smoke and flashes of light from the Hill.

As they ran toward the spot Seven had recalled from the memory, Dusk and Miss Dewey, still in her disguise, joined them.

Seven turned to Leaf, Talis, Figgs, and Crimson. "We have to get the door to the clearing at the end of the coven house row—it's fifty toadstools south of Moth House. That's where the coven house was in the memory," Seven said. "Once the door is placed, the magic of our coven will be cemented. It will be a lot harder for them to just do away with it again. Nothing matters more than putting this where it belongs." The four witches nodded.

"We'll meet you there soon. Have to make sure we get Ambert safely to the Gran before anything happens," Seven said, and the door team took off through the woods toward the coven house road.

Just as Seven lost sight of them through the forest, a blinding golden light flashed, and someone screamed.

When the light faded, Seven already knew what she would be met with: Helio.

He had come from the woods, waiting for the perfect moment to strike. Helio descended on them. He threw his hands up quicker than a spark, and pummeled Seven and the others with a scorching blast of magic. His light threw Seven and her friends back; they crashed into trees or boulders or into the cold, hard ground. In an instant, Helio had untied his father. Ambert was free. Instead of fighting, they both ran for the woods.

"Where are they going?!" Thorn screamed as they took off after them.

"To the door. They're going to try and destroy it!" the Oracle said, out of breath as they ran through the dark forest. The Witchlings, Dusk, Miss Dewey, and the Oracle ran as quickly as they all could, but Seven was afraid it was not quick enough.

"Veloz!" she shouted at her feet. The others followed suit, running faster than the wind as they weaved through the maze of bramble, fallen leaves, and logs. The sound of rustling in the woods ahead of them and the occasional flash of Helio's stark blond hair let them know they were still on the two witches' trail.

But then suddenly everything was deadly quiet. Seven got a sinking feeling in her stomach. They were in the middle of the forest, far from their allies . . . Had they been led out here on purpose? Was this some sort of trap?

As if he could hear her thoughts, Ambert laughed in the distance. "I'm afraid this little game is over. Veneno peligroso!" he cried.

The venomous hex snaked toward them at the speed of light, but before it could get close, the Oracle deflected it with their own counterspell, sending it hurling through the sky and far away from them.

"Descubrir y convocar!" cried the Oracle—another double-sided, high-level spell.

Ambert appeared, a spotlight over him in the woods. The spell pulled him to them like a rag doll, screaming the whole time. Helio had vanished.

"Seems you haven't learned your lesson, but I've got time for extra credit!" the Oracle said, and blasted Ambert, throwing him against a tree.

Ambert recovered and rushed at them, his steps infused with a magic so potent their various attacks could not stop him. But when Ambert's eyes found Dusk, he halted, his face unrecognizable with rage.

"Dusk, my son. What are you doing? Come to this side!" he said.

"No," Dusk said, though his voice was shaking. "I know who you really are. You killed my mother!"

Ambert rubbed his face, then looked at Dusk apologetically. "Sometimes, these things must be done."

"What?" Dusk asked. "You're just going to . . . say it like it's nothing?"

"It *was* nothing. She was nothing once I took her magic. Of course, Marigold came from a prestigious, powerful family. Otherwise, I would not have wasted my time on her. But once I was done taking all the good out of her, what use was she to *either* of us? Son, I did you a favor. Don't you see?"

"No!" A scream of pure agony ripped through the air as Dusk fell to his knees. "Why? Why couldn't you just let her live?" Dusk asked between sobs.

"It was only natural. I had gotten what I needed from her, just as I had from my wife before her, and the two before her . . ."

Ambert hadn't just killed the twins' mother and nearly killed Miss Dewey; he had been killing his wives and stealing their magic all his grown-up life, it seemed.

"And as you had planned to do to your wife after." Miss Dewey waved her hand, and the disguise fell away.

Ambert took a step back, his face one of true bafflement.

"Moira, my love."

"Do not call me that, *ever* again!" Miss Dewey screamed.

"Very well," Ambert said with a pleasant smile, then turned from her and toward Dusk. "Dusk, come here. This is your final warning."

"Listen carefully," Dusk said, his voice low with the threat of a storm. "I will never come back to your side again. I will never acknowledge you as my family again. Neither you nor Helio. I am alone in this world, and that is preferable to being a Lophiifor."

Ambert was shaking with rage now, and he could do nothing but laugh, a maniacal laugh, his eyes wide and terrifying. "No, no, no. You are my blood, my legacy! And my legacy is *everything*! I will not allow this!"

"You will not be alone," Miss Dewey said, stepping next to Dusk and helping him up from the ground. "If you'd like, you can be my family."

Dusk looked over to Miss Dewey, nearly her height already at just fourteen, and he smiled gratefully.

Seven did not lower her hands the whole time, ready to attack the moment she had to, ready to call all the monstruos and animals to help them take Ambert and Helio, wherever he was, down.

"You are my SON!" Ambert raged. "And you will not go with this witch!"

He moved faster than a bolt of lightning, till he was right in front of Miss Dewey, his hand up to her chest.

Seven cried out, the Oracle, Valley, and Thorn all intoned spells to repel him, but Ambert was stronger than any of them knew. *Do not underestimate my father.* The words came back to Seven just as he called out a spell that none of them would be able to stop.

"LA MUERTE!" Ambert screamed. The death spell.

Once someone as powerful as Ambert cast the death spell, there was nothing anyone could do to stop it. The silhouette of a woman in a billowing dress and robe appeared in the woods, and Miss Dewey shook her head.

"No, no, please!" she cried.

The silhouette rushed forward like a violent gust of wind. Valley slashed at her with twin blades, but it did nothing. Thorn tried to stitch the folds of her robe and trap her in its shadowy fabric, but that did little. Seven and the Oracle both shot a searing burst of magic at La Muerte, and for a moment, the silhouette of death stumbled. But even against an Oracle and an Uncle, she pushed on. Dusk tried to pull Miss Dewey from where she stood, but Ambert kept her there with his own magic, his face straining against his son's power, as La Muerte stood in front of Miss Dewey and prepared to end her life.

Seven had seen Lotus attempt this spell in the spring, but she had managed to repel it. Lotus had not been as powerful, as skilled as Seven. That was not the case with Ambert.

Seven, Valley, Thorn, the Oracle, and Dusk threw spell after spell at Death, but she would not stop.

Death would not relent for anyone.

Not even the kind, patient, wonderful Miss Dewey.

La Muerte held a scythe made of shadows and slashed across Miss Dewey; the magic hit her directly, and as if in slow motion, her body fell to the forest floor. Someone screamed. La Muerte turned around and floated away, her shadows blending with the forest until eventually, she was gone.

Seven could not speak; she could not move. She could only stand there watching as one of her favorite people in the whole world lost her life. Miss Dewey, who had been one of the only adults to believe in them. Miss Dewey, who always knew their favorite snacks, and helped Seven through her friendship breakup with Poppy. Miss

Dewey, their favorite librarian, a kind witch. A good witch. Miss Dewey was gone.

Dusk's agonized screams snapped Seven back to the present. He was draped over Miss Dewey's body, shaking with every sob, as a glittering white light, the color of her Goose House coven, left her body and spun into the night sky.

"I will try to bring her back, somehow, perhaps as a ghost if I can manage," the Oracle said, already on their knees beside Miss Dewey's lifeless body and a sobbing Dusk. "Go, do not let Ambert escape."

Ambert was running through the woods. Helio had returned and was helping him get away. But hurt and tired, Ambert could not move as fast as usual. All three Witchlings threw their hands toward the retreating Ambert.

"DETENER!" they cried, locking Ambert's legs in place.

With a tremendous amount of pain in her heart, Seven walked away from Miss Dewey, and lobbed spell after spell at Ambert and Helio. With Valley and Thorn at her side, she advanced on the two witches. Already, Ambert had managed to break free of the Witchlings' leg-binding spell, but he and Helio were no longer running. Instead, they were blocking spells and walking calmly forward.

Do not underestimate my father.

Once they were just toadstools away from each other, Ambert threw his hands up and began to glow. His whole body looked almost . . . translucent, and a wind so violent Seven could not see swept across the forest. The wind pushed them back; Thorn almost got picked up into the air, it was so strong, but worst of all, they could see nothing.

The Oracle's voice bellowed in the night sky, a spell to try and calm the wind, but Ambert was strong enough on his own, and with Helio? He seemed unstoppable. They were too strong even for the Oracle, who had almost bested Ambert once but was now so worn out, Seven noticed the strength of their spells waning. Ambert was again as strong, as powerful, as hours before. He was a true monstruo, a terror.

The wind swept around them, so hot that Seven worried the forest would catch on fire. She cried out for the animals to retreat, but she doubted they could hear her. She was only glad her raccoons weren't by her side, that she had had the foresight to leave Edgar home this time. Seven was not sure if she would survive this attack. Perhaps she was about to meet Miss Dewey among the stars.

CHAPTER FIFTY

FRAMED

"WHERE ARE WE?" the Oracle asked.

The wind stopped abruptly, and through the trees, the orange rays of the rising sun broke through. How long had they been trapped in the tornado? What had Ambert just done?

Something else was wrong. Dusk was no longer where he'd once been, mourning over Miss Dewey. Instead, he stood where Ambert had been, the dark purple smoke of archaic magic coming from his hands.

"What . . . what is this?" Dusk asked as he held his own hands up to his face.

Ambert lay motionless at Dusk's feet as Helio emerged from the woods. He ran toward them, and Seven raised her hands to fight before noticing he had a large crowd of witches behind him, including the Gran.

"There! It was my brother! He killed my new mother and hurt my father. Help us!" Helio cried.

"That's not what happened!" Seven cried. "He's lying!"

The Gran surveyed the scene, but the faces of the Ravenskillians around her were not so impartial. They looked at Dusk with disgust; some cried over the sight of Miss Dewey's lifeless body or Ambert lying there like a butt-toad. Seven wished she could kick him, make them realize he was faking it. At least, she thought he was. It couldn't be that whatever hex he'd cast had knocked him out, could it?

"It seems very clear what's happening here!" a witch said.

"Arrest that boy!" said another.

"Wait!" Valley said. "We have proof Dusk isn't the culprit! Right?" She looked at Seven hopefully.

Of course. The chismosa footage showed Helio at the scene of the crimes. Once they showed that to the Gran, to the town, they'd have no choice but to agree he was up to no good, that his word could not be trusted. The Gran's Council had already agreed to look it over too.

But just as she prepared to speak, Dusk's hand flew to his face.

"Ah!" he cried out, and when his hand came away, the sunburst birthmark that had always been on his skin had disappeared.

"No . . ." whispered Thorn, shaking her head. "How?"

Dusk looked at the Witchlings with tears in his eyes. "This is my fault. I told Helio about the flowers, about everything. I thought he could help us . . . be on our side. Instead, he turned out to be just like our father."

Helio touched his cheek slightly, the sunburst

birthmark freshly stamped onto his skin. Now anyone who watched the footage would clearly see one of the twins' faces, both sides of his profile, but no birthmark. It would incriminate Dusk and not Helio.

"Sybell?" Seven asked. "Tell them!"

"I—" The Oracle shook their head. "I can't remember what happened, Seven. Not . . . in any way that would be helpful to Dusk." They whispered the last part so only Seven could hear.

Somehow, Ambert had cast the hex for forgetting once more, making Sybell remember what he wanted them to: that Dusk had killed Miss Dewey and injured Ambert, that he had been behind everything.

They had played into Ambert's hand perfectly; they had set everything up for him without even knowing they were. Now, with the evidence turned against them, and only the Witchlings' word, which nobody trusted anyway, Seven knew he would get away with it. He would get away with everything.

The guards took Helio and Dusk in for questioning, and Ambert into the infirmary. It was then that Seven saw with horror that they had already confiscated the chismosas. They would see the footage and it would seal Dusk's fate.

CHAPTER FIFTY-ONE

THE ORACLE AND THE GOLDEN FROG

ONE WEEK HAD PASSED, and the Oracle still could not remember much about the battle in the woods. They had tried to remember, hoping that if they could, they would be able to help prove Seven, Valley, and Thorn right. But every time they tried to recall what happened, they could only see Dusk killing Miss Dewey, Dusk attacking them in the vault, Dusk doing all the things that Ambert had done.

"I believe you when you say Dusk did not do it, but I can't back you up with my own memories," Sybell had said.

With an accusation of this magnitude, the council of Grans, influenced not only by the chismosa's footage but by Ambert as well, had insisted that there needed to be definitive proof to clear Dusk's name.

"They won't even allow the *idea* of using the cuentista spell," Seven told Valley and Thorn.

"The Grans wouldn't want to dabble in a risky spell like that, so I'm not surprised it wouldn't be considered evidence," Valley said.

"So how are we supposed to prove Dusk's innocence?" Thorn asked.

The only witches besides themselves who had experienced Ambert's true nature firsthand were the Oracle, Dusk, Fox, and Miss Dewey. Miss Dewey was . . . gone. The thought of it still made Seven desperate with grief. Fox had been knocked out from an explosion of magic and hadn't actually seen Ambert. Dusk was, of course, currently sitting in the Tombs, the one and only official suspect for Miss Dewey's murder. And the Oracle couldn't remember anything about their fight with Ambert.

Thankfully, Sybell still believed the Witchlings. At least enough to go along with their scheme to reclaim their memories.

The Oracle had sighed when Seven suggested her next idea—touching the Golden Frog.

"Maybe the Golden Frog will be able to reveal the truth to you, or somehow restore what Ambert and Helio took away."

Sybell had shrugged. "I suppose. If you think it might help, I'll try anything."

The magic making the Oracle believe that Dusk had killed Miss Dewey was so strong, so impenetrable, that not even the Gran could get through the haze of it. Now they were standing before the Golden Frog, inside his lagoon in the Hall of Elders.

"What do I do?" Sybell whispered.

"Just touch it," Thorn said. "The frog will do the rest."

"What if it bites me?"

“It won’t,” Valley reassured them, even though she had no way of knowing that. She looked at Thorn and Seven and cringed, and Seven had to fight her urge to laugh.

The Oracle waded into the pond, their robe getting soaked in the glittering water. They looked at the Witchlings. “You owe me a new robe. I can feel fish swimming in there.”

“I’ll make you a brand-new one, to your liking,” Thorn said.

The Oracle nodded. “That’s what I like to hear. All right. Here goes nothing.”

Sybell reached out and touched the slimy skin of the Golden Frog, and closed their eyes. Seven wondered if an Oracle had ever touched the Golden Frog, and hoped they hadn’t just made a colossal mistake.

A light rippled around them, the Oracle opened their eyes, and a golden glow lit their face. Then they began to speak, a chorus of voices, the voices of the Stars, coming from all around them.

“It was the night of the Black Moon Ceremony, one year ago, when the lore began. In the past, little Witchlings sorted as Spares were distrustful of one another, *not* because they were bad or suspicious themselves, but because of how scary and isolating being a Spare was. They had grown up seeing their neighbors in the shadows, not talked to, or loved, or cared for by anyone else, and naturally they began to believe that there was something wrong with them. That Spares were always meant to be Spares. So when they became one themselves, they retreated to the shadows, pushed the world away. Except for you three . . . and it all began with Thorn."

"Me?" Thorn asked softly.

"Thorn never cared about what she was; her only wish was to finally have friends. She had been so lonely after losing her brother. And she found the two best friends she could've hoped for. Right there at the Black Moon Ceremony, she saw you, Seven and Valley, before you were even sorted, and said, *Those witches look like they'd be good friends*. And when you all became Spares, she welcomed it, rather that than the sea of loneliness she'd been drifting in for so very long."

The Witchlings looked at one another with warm smiles. Thorn's face was bright red.

"Then there was Valley. At first, her instinct was to be alone. She didn't trust anyone, after all. But then she felt the warmth of Thorn's friendship, the magic there, and she leaned in just the tiniest bit. And of course, nothing would make her rotten father more upset than to have a Spare as a daughter, so out of spite, she was glad for it."

Valley wiped her eyes, and Seven remembered thinking Valley looked glad to be sorted as a Spare that night. It seemed she had been.

"Finally, you, Seven. You were the most devastated to be a Spare, your heart set on House Hyacinth. But after the initial recoiling, and shock, you furrowed your brow and you invoked the impossible task. Something no witch expected of you, but you are wise beyond your years,

Seven, and most importantly, you are headstrong and determined. Some might even say irritating . . ."

"Hey!" Seven said, and Valley and Thorn snorted.

"But . . . that's only because you are a young girl. If a boy witch were so smart, and unyielding, they would be called charming. They would be called extraordinary. That is what you are, Seven Salazar. And your stubbornness saved you, the three of you. You would do whatever it took to keep your magic, even embrace your Sparedom. Even if that meant breaking what Sparedom meant altogether. And you did. You broke it, but that is the only way to fix a corrupted world. You cannot mend and patch a world that's built on rotten shingles. You must burn it, so that you may build something sound in its place."

Seven wondered if her friends were thinking the same thing she was. That they had burned Ravenskill down, they had turned everything on its head, in order to make it whole again.

"Above all, you mustn't forget that your togetherness is what defeated the evilness. You must never break apart, no matter what. You must always remain Seven, Valley, and Thorn. For your friendship, it is the most powerful magic of all."

CHAPTER FIFTY-TWO

HAPPY BIRTHDAY, SEVEN

THAT NIGHT, Seven's parents threw a surprise birthday party for her. Valley and Thorn came, of course, as did Figgs, Graves, and Poppy. Some of the Spares, Wither and Walnut and even Crimson, all the way from Crones Cliff Manor, also came to her house to celebrate her thirteenth.

Seven wasn't really in the celebrating mood. She was still grieving for Miss Dewey and sick about Dusk being held in the Tombs until his trial, but she was also grateful to be with her friends right now.

"This cake? Divine!" cried Alaric.

"If you keep eating, there will be none left for anyone else," Jonafren huffed.

"Just one more teeny tiny slice won't hurt." Alaric shimmied his ghostly shoulders and floated over to the table to have thirds, or maybe fourths.

Jonafren sighed but followed Alaric's lead, as he always did.

They danced, and ate, Beefy showed off how many witches he could carry at once (four), and the raccoons sat happily on the sofa in brand-new sweaters knitted by Thorn, each with their food-related namesakes stitched beautifully on the front.

"Only because it's your birthday!" Fox had said as she let them in, walking in single file and each holding trash gifts wrapped in ribbon. "Don't get used to it." Seven's mother had winced at the old telecast tapes, banana peels, and broken umbrellas being paraded into their house.

Despite her initial protests, Seven was having a great time. She missed Miss Dewey more than anything, but she knew that if anyone would've wanted Seven to have a wonderful thirteenth birthday, it would be her.

"I got you something," Figgs said, sidling up to Seven as she sat at the bay window in their living room. Fast-paced merengue was playing from her dad's speakers, and everyone was either eating or twirling around the makeshift dance floor. Alaric was doing both.

"Let's see it." Seven smiled as Figgs handed her a flat parcel wrapped in brown paper.

She opened it up to find a painting. A painting of the Strangling Figs.

"Oh," she said, touching the painting lightly with the tips of her fingers. "It's beautiful."

"Yeah? I did it myself. I mean, I'm no expert, but I have always liked to paint," Figgs said, his face red.

"You painted this for me?" Seven asked in awe.

Figgs nodded quickly. "If you don't like it, it's totally okay. You hate it, right? It's fine!"

Seven laughed. "I don't hate it. I the opposite of hate it, actually."

Figgs looked into her eyes, and Seven had to look away, because it was making her feel like flying, and also, her parents were toadstools away.

"I always wanted you to remember . . . that day. I know maybe you thought it was awful because of the wedding and everything after, but it was one of the happiest days of my life so far," Figgs said.

"Really?" Seven smiled.

"Yeah, really. Not every day you get to have your first kiss with a famous witch," Figgs teased.

"Guess not," Seven said with a laugh. "Thank you. It was one of the happiest days of my life so far too."

They stared at each other for a few moments, and Seven wished she could kiss Figgs again.

"The Gran is here!" someone shouted, and Seven and Figgs turned to the window.

Indeed, the Gran was walking down the small path toward Seven's front door, her robe billowing in the cold night.

Talis let her in, immediately trying to give her a plate filled with food, which the Gran politely declined.

"I've only come to bring Seven to her second surprise of the night." The Gran winked.

"A second surprise?" Seven asked, standing up. What

else could she be getting? She already had everything she needed right in this living room.

"All right, all, on to phase two!" Fox announced, opening the door. Everyone had put their cloaks on.

Seven narrowed her eyes, zeroing in on Valley and Thorn in particular. "You were in on this?"

Thorn put her hands up in a show of innocence, and Valley looked smug.

The Gran laughed. "Yes, we've all been conspiring. Now come, walk with me."

They swept out into the night, the Gran and Seven walking ahead as the rest of the party trailed behind.

"How are you feeling now that you're thirteen?" the Gran asked as they walked.

"Weird. Happy but also sad, worried but also excited. Is that normal?"

The Gran nodded knowingly. "It is. It's been a very long time since I was my first thirteen, you know. I turned one hundred and thirteen not long ago but that first time was a special time—confusing, but special. I wanted to give you the good news myself that all the twelve-year-olds from this year's ceremony have been placed in their proper covens. Some in House of Elephants."

"That's good to hear; I'm glad they're all okay. Any news about Dusk?" Seven asked hopefully.

The Gran nodded, a somber look on her face. "I've been to see him. He is in as good of a spirit as anyone could be in his situation."

“And his . . . father,” Seven said, trying to keep rage out of her voice.

“He has retreated, temporarily I believe, to his hometown. Under the guise of grieving, but I do believe he is still planning his run for Chancellor of Magic.” They were walking through town and in the direction of the coven houses.

“Why can’t the Grans’ Council stop him? You believe us, you’re the oldest, they’re supposed to listen to you,” Seven said.

“The council is torn right down the middle, I’m afraid. Some wishing to investigate the incident, some seeing it as a closed case. The Committee for Magical Misdeeds has all but declared Ambert innocent. It is possible he has allies on the inside there, so they cannot be trusted fully, I’m afraid. We do know he is planning a town meeting in a few weeks. Though I do not know the purpose, I am worried. We have one bit of intriguing information—the hex for forgetting was cast on the night Miss Dewey was killed, but it was on a much smaller scale than one that could’ve wiped out the memories of the entire Twelve Towns.”

“Hmmm,” Seven wondered aloud. “The hex for forgetting I witnessed during the Cuentista Spell wiped out the memory of the entire Twelve Towns and required five powerful elders to die and the magic of their younger family members too. Maybe Ambert used Miss Dewey’s death to cast the spell on just the Oracle.”

The Gran breathed in sharply, as if she were surprised.

"That sounds like a very plausible theory. I will work to examine the magic used that night and see if your theory is correct. It would explain his ability to cast such a powerful spell on just one witch."

"And he probably knew Sybell was the only one anyone would believe. No one takes us seriously, no matter how many times we prove ourselves," Seven said bitterly. "He wanted to taunt us."

The Gran nodded. "That may be so. But I have a feeling Ravenskillians and the rest of the Twelve Towns won't be able to ignore just how important you are for long. Now—we have arrived."

They were standing in front of a group of shimmering trees, but Seven could tell they were simply enchantments. Enchantments hiding something big. And by where they were standing, Seven knew all too well what it was.

Seven looked around and realized that somewhere along the way, many more witches had joined her party. There were former Spares and witches she recognized from town or school, healer witches and reporters. One reporter in particular took Seven's breath away.

Tiordan froggin' Whisperbrew was standing right there. They wore a dazzling purple cape, with a matching reporter's cap, a small card tucked in the band around the hat, and a kind smile on their face.

"Seven Salazar, we meet at last," Tiordan said.

"Oh my goats, I'm gonna throw up," Seven whispered.

"I am working on a story about you and was wondering if you'd have time to speak to me later this week."

“Me?! Why?! Yes! Of course, I mean, I’d be honored to speak to you! Is this really happening?” Seven looked around at her family and friends, at the strangers and neighbors she’d grown up around, and they were all smiling at her warmly or laughing at her froggin’ out. She took a deep breath and tried again.

“Tiordan Whisperbrew, you are my idol, I am your biggest fan, and I would be honored to speak to you . . . on the record,” Seven said.

“Fantastic,” Tiordan said. “I’m writing a story about the Elephant House. I think it’ll be important to get down the facts of what happened all those years ago in your own words.”

Seven nodded. “I think it’s important too, but . . . will people believe me? Even if it is the truth.”

“The people who need to hear the truth the most might not listen to it. It’s possible they’ll never see my words or yours, but we still need to say them. We must always shout the truth, so that the lies do not become the only sound,” Tiordan said.

“Wow, you even speak cool,” Seven said, mouth agape.

Tiordan laughed. Seven had made Tiordan laugh!

“I’ve taken up enough of your time. I believe there is quite the surprise for you in store. Happy birthday, Seven Salazar,” Tiordan said.

“You too,” said Seven, cringing and slapping her forehead as she said it.

“Come on, you enormous butt-toad, it’s cold out here,” Valley said, ushering Seven in front of the tree illusion, where the Gran was waiting to speak.

"To commemorate this special night, the night Seven Salazar, the Uncle who is already a thing of legends, turns thirteen, we have an unveiling," the Gran said. "Witches, step forward."

All around them, witches with rainbow amulets stepped forward, holding their necklaces up like Seven, Valley, and Thorn had on the night of their own Black Moon Ceremony.

"You too." The Gran gestured at the Witchlings, and they looked at one another in confusion, before holding up their own swirling amulets.

"None of you had a proper chance to be sorted into your given coven. There are witches as young as twelve here, as old as two hundred and twenty, and all of you have lived out your lives peacefully, kindly, despite the injustice this world has made you endure. But tonight, on this special birthday, we will have a do-over. The Black Moon Ceremony you always should have had. I will seal your covens of three once more, this time under your true name," the Gran proclaimed. "Are you ready?"

A unified yes rippled softly in the night, and the Gran raised her wand as she began to float in the air.

"Knowledge, history, friendship before all . . . House of Elephants!" the Gran cried out, and waved her wand above her head.

All at once, a rainbow light whisked around them, then shot into their amulets, and stopped their wild swirling until the rainbow colors floated serenely in their pendants. At the same time the illusion of trees fell away and before them stood a majestic house, iridescent and shining in every color under the sun when the light of the moon hit it. On the door, which had been polished and refinished, an elephant stood, the words *"An Elephant Never Forgets"* engraved around the perimeter.

"Oh my goats," whispered Thorn.

"I present to you, the official House of Elephants coven house!" the Gran said to wild cheers from the crowd.

The doors to the house flew open and the once-Spares, the once looked-down-upon witches with tattered clothes and hollow futures, took one another's hands, and walked in.

Seven, Valley, and Thorn were last, letting everyone go before them, and when they finally walked over the threshold, to the beautiful, cozy interior decorated in soft, warm colors, Seven turned to Valley and Thorn and smiled.

"Welcome home," she said.

"Welcome home," Valley and Thorn said back.

And together, they prepared to find their brand-new rooms, in the coven house they had always been meant to have.

CHAPTER FIFTY-THREE

THE CHANCELLOR OF MAGIC

WEEKS LATER, there was a town meeting organized by Ambert just as the Gran had said there would be. Seven, Valley, and Thorn were sure to be there in the wings of the stage, watching his every move.

Outside, it was raining, the clouds overhead gray and swollen with the promise of a storm. The cover of the Ravenskill Theater didn't help the day feel any more warm or dry. Umbrellas and muddy boots tracked water and dirt inside the theater, the very place where the missing Spare ordeal had begun earlier in the fall. Ambert was already standing at the podium; rows and rows of his supporters were there, eager and waiting for him to speak. He had in the past few weeks positioned himself as a survivor of a horrible tragedy. A grieving widower, betrayed by his own son. And those who loved him ate up every word. The Witchlings had of course tried to tell the truth, but the more they spread what really happened that day in the woods and Blood Rose Manor, the more his supporters seemed convinced he was telling the truth.

Ambert had gathered the town here under the guise of an important announcement, and the Witchlings weren't going to let him do whatever it was he was planning without a fight.

And they weren't alone.

Though Ambert indeed had many rows of loyal supporters, the rest of the theater was filled with regular, everyday Ravenskillians—those who were suspicious of Ambert and, of course, the Elephant House witches, now decked out in their black robes with shimmering rainbow lining and rainbow amulets to match.

The former Spares looked powerful and confident; they looked formidable because for the first time, they believed they were. Receiving their power from knowledge, the House of Elephants was in the unique position to oversee the rest of the magic world, to help truly bring balance not by being lesser than, but by preserving and recounting the truth. Nobody would be able to cast an unjust spell, or build something harmful to nature or other witches, without the House of Elephants examining the situation and coming to the aid of the less powerful. They were an aid to the Gran and Uncle; they were an advocate for the people and the animals. Or at least, that was meant to be their function. Not everyone in the Twelve Towns recognized this new house, and for now Ravenskill was the only town that had built them their own, rightful coven house. But Elephant House witches existed from Blonkers to Castle Point and every town in between. They were Spares no more.

"Thank you all for coming today. It is a most important day for Ravenskill," Ambert began his speech. "As you know, there has been much turmoil in our great town in the past few years. Unnatural magic that only seems to be growing stronger. Our current leadership has done nothing to stop it—in fact, the Gran has encouraged this troubling display of disregard for our ways and our rules."

Concerned murmurs rippled throughout the crowd.

"They can't believe him, can they?" Thorn asked.

"You'd be surprised what some witches are willing to believe if it means they get to have their way," Valley said.

"And I have evidence that that magic is becoming intolerable! Please." Ambert gestured to the wings, where the Witchlings stood, and Seven's breathing hitched, but it wasn't them he was gesturing to. From behind them a small voice said, "Excuse me. Sorry."

"Mayhem?" Valley asked, but the witch walked right past them, not even looking their way, her cheeks bright red. Trailing her, with a smug look on her face, was none other than Rafflesia Dimblewit.

"Mayhem, please, tell them all what you told us," Ambert said, nudging Mayhem toward the podium.

Mayhem cleared her throat and looked at Seven, Valley, and Thorn with terror in her eyes.

"Sorry," she mouthed.

"Oh no," Seven said. "She's going to spill the beans about the stone hex."

"What do we do?!" Valley asked.

Seven shook her head. "Nothing we can do short of attacking them, but that will only make it look worse. We just have to endure it, for now."

"When I was a stone witch . . . um, from the hexer, it was Seven Salazar that cured me," she said.

Gasps from the audience. How could Seven, Uncle or not, do what the best healers in the Twelve Towns could not?

Unnatural magic.

Forbidden magic.

"Tell them the other part, about the pink-haired one," Rafflesia said haughtily as she stared daggers at the Witchlings.

Mayhem wiped her forehead. "Valley Pepperhorn, she broke free from the inside somehow. I've heard she still has a stone stripe across her heart too. She healed right away, when the rest of us took weeks to recover," Mayhem said.

Now witches were standing, demanding to hear from the Witchlings themselves as Ambert smiled happily, his hands out in a fake attempt to soothe the crowd.

Mayhem was taken offstage on the other side—lucky for her or Valley would've let her have it.

"It is for this, and many, many other instances of incompetence, that I propose a new way of governing . . ." Ambert said.

"What?" Seven spat out angrily.

The crowd hushed to listen.

"I propose we abolish the Grans' Council's reach in

Ravenskill and institute a Chancellor of Magic. One who would rule over Ravenskill at first and then expand his reach to the Twelve Towns. For far too long, we've left the safety of our towns and of our children"—Ambert wiped a tear now, probably trying to remind everyone of his delinquent son Dusk and his golden child Helio—"in the hands of incompetent witches. The Grans are entrenched in the systems of ruling; they've forgotten what the everyday witches, the *real* witches of this town want. I believe I am the only one who can fix these problems, and if you'll give me that chance, I will bring Ravenskill back to prominence. I will restore the Twelve Towns to its former glory so that we are once again the envy of the entire world."

Many witches, too many of them, clapped for him.

"This winter, we will hold a vote. Do we return Ravenskill and the Twelve Towns to the greatness we know they're capable of, or do we fall to the new, corrupted ways that are ensnaring our youth and poisoning our magic? We have the chance to make Ravenskill the powerful town it was always meant to be. Will you seize it?" Ambert asked.

The crowd cheered wildly now, except for the Elephant House witches, who were standing together in solidarity, their faces etched with concern.

Ambert turned to the Witchlings and smiled. And when he did, Seven nearly fell back. Because for the first time, she could see Ambert for what he truly was.

"Are you goats seeing that?" Seven asked Valley and Thorn, but they both gave her confused looks.

“Seeing what?” Valley asked as Seven stared.

Because Ambert did not look like himself. In his place stood a creature with sharp, skinny teeth, black eyes so large Seven could not see the whites of them, and a glowing orb above his head that filled Seven with dread but also, sickeningly, made her want to walk toward him.

That was when she realized, too late, a name prophecy right before her eyes. Lophiifor is Ambert’s family name, but family names can be name prophecies too . . . and Seven could now see Ambert for what he had always been: a predator in disguise, pulling in his victims with a mesmerizing light, just like the anglerfish of the deep sea. Lophiiformes was the scientific classification for unusual, deepwater creatures like the anglerfish. Ambert’s very name had been a clue they missed from the start. He had fooled them. He had fooled them all. And there was nothing she could do to stop him.

But that did not mean she would stop trying.

Seven would never stop trying.

Because monstruos are not afraid, they are feared, and Ambert might be a dangerous creature . . . but so was she.

EPILOGUE

THE NIGHTBEAST CUBS WERE GROWING. In just a few weeks, they had gone from babies to the Witchlings' height. Soon they'd be big enough to ride, if the cubs allowed it. It was time to expand their glade. That would give the cubs and Nightbeast even more space to run, and to help the mother monstruo with something it desperately needed: friends.

"These loud birds will not hurt my babies?" the Nightbeast asked.

"No." Seven smiled. "They're kind."

The "loud birds," as the Nightbeast called them, were the skeleton birds, their bones click-clacking through the air as they flew. Seven had noticed the Nightbeast seemed bored and lonely; the cubs could not speak yet, and the Nightbeast needed other creatures to socialize with. Expanding the glade so that it dipped into the Cursed Forest and allowed certain monstruos to visit them had been difficult but Seven had managed it, and now the skeleton birds and her beloved raccoons could visit the Nightbeast and its cubs. The raccoons alone were enough to keep the cubs entertained for hours at a time, rolling around the glade and giving the Nightbeast a much-needed break.

"These beasts are enormous. Will they eat us?" Scrape asked.

"You are merely bones; what shall I eat?" the Nightbeast scoffed.

This made Scrape and the other birds laugh. Seven had made a good choice.

"Rumors abound that the days without Spares have returned," Scrape said. "Like when I was a baby. Is this your doing, clever witch?"

"In part." Seven smiled as she scratched one of the cubs' heads. Then she perked up, realizing what Scrape had just said. "Wait, you were alive back then?"

"Of course. It was just as I prepared to leave my nest. I could never forget that day. That night, we got word of Spares appearing. It was quite the scandal! Every bird and beast in this forest was talking about it."

Seven's brain raced. Scrape was alive in 1790? If Scrape was really that old, it would mean she might've known the only other witch who could speak to Skeleton birds and monstruos.

"Did you know a witch named Delphinium Larkspur?" Seven asked.

Scrape looked confused. "I . . . do not know. I remember some of those days, of course, but I was a very baby bird. Perhaps my dear mother bird would remember the witch, but her death day has long since passed."

Seven had an idea. "Scrape, have you heard of the cuentista spell?"

Scrape cocked her head, then shook it. "I have not."

"It's a spell that allows a witch to walk through the memories of their ancestors, but I was wondering"—Seven cleared her throat nervously—"if I could walk through your mother bird's memories? To see if I can figure out what happened to a witch I'm trying to find?"

Scrape shook herself, and her bones click-clacked.

"Loud birds," grumbled the Nightbeast.

"I do not see why not," Scrape said.

There were about twenty million reasons why not. For one, the spell was meant to be used on other witches, not monstruos. Second, Seven shouldn't do it alone, but she wasn't sure of the risks to her own safety, so she didn't want to put anyone else in danger too.

Lastly, the memories. It had been painful to lose the one she had last time. What if this time it was worse?

"Well, get on with it. It's almost time for me to sleep again," Scrape said.

"All right," Seven said.

They performed the spell after Seven taught Scrape what to say, and she was transported through a tunnel of shadows and trees, like a nightmare of the Cursed Forest come to life. When she landed in the memory, she was near an unfamiliar place—a small cottage in the Cursed Forest.

She walked around, watching the monstruos slither

and fly, run and stalk, the sounds and the sights all things she was used to. But then . . . she found a witch. The witch walked through the forest, and Seven followed.

"Lousy, silly witches," grumbled the witch. "Don't know their butts from their noses."

Seven followed as the witch stalked ahead, a basket filled with dried flowers in one hand.

"I shall curse them, I shall hex them," the witch spat. "I shall make them a poison soup."

"You shall do nothing of the sort. You will run away as you always do," a skeleton bird called down to the witch.

Both Seven and the old witch looked up.

"And what do you know? You have one baby and think you know it all. Hmph."

"Have you seen my baby, Scrape? She is quite beautiful."

"How can a bone bird be beautiful? Bird brains!" the witch said. She was not old, but she was cranky.

A baby skeleton bird—Scrape—peeked over her nest and cooed sweetly at the witch. Seven's eyes filled with tears to see the ancient bird as a baby.

"What are you searching for?" the mother bird asked.

The witch sighed. "My cottage! I can never remember where I put the door. Those stinking witches from the Five Families are trying to kill me again. I have to get my stuff and get out of here."

The Five Families.

"Just three toadstools to the left," Scrape's mother said, exasperated.

"Bah!" the witch said, but she waved her hand, moving aside a curtain of ivy and revealing a door.

"There you are," she said, smiling, and walked through the door as Seven followed.

Inside, the cottage was filled with herbs and potions and a giant cauldron simmering something green and putrid. Seven walked around carefully, scared of being pulled from the memory too soon. She needed to find this place, if it still existed today.

"I'll best those evil witches yet," the witch grumbled to herself. "I just need to become stronger first and I will. Or my name's not Delphinium Larkspur."

ABOUT THE AUTHOR

Claribel A. Ortega, *New York Times* bestselling author of *Ghost Squad*, the Witchlings series, and *Frizzy*, is a former reporter who writes middle grade and young adult fantasy inspired by her Dominican heritage. When she's not busy turning her obsession with pop culture, magic, and video games into books, she's cohosting her podcast, *Bad Author Book Club*. Claribel has been featured on BuzzFeed, NPR, *Good Morning America*, and *Deadline*.

You can find her on social media at @Claribel Ortega and on her website at claribelortega.com.